Kindred
SPECTERS

Kindred SPECTERS

Death, Mourning, and American Affinity

Christopher Peterson

University of Minnesota Press
Minneapolis • London

Chapter 2 was previously published in *Modern Fiction Studies* 52, no. 3 (fall 2006): 548–69; copyright 2006 The Johns Hopkins University Press; reprinted with permission from The Johns Hopkins University Press. Chapter 3 was previously published in *CR: The New Centennial Review* 4, no. 1 (2004): 227–265; reprinted with permission from Michigan State University Press.

Copyright 2007 by the Regents of the University of Minnesota

All rights reserved. No part of this publication may be reproduced, stored in a retrieval system, or transmitted, in any form or by any means, electronic, mechanical, photocopying, recording, or otherwise, without the prior written permission of the publisher.

Published by the University of Minnesota Press
111 Third Avenue South, Suite 290
Minneapolis, MN 55401-2520
http://www.upress.umn.edu

Library of Congress Cataloging-in-Publication Data

Peterson, Christopher, 1972–
 Kindred specters : death, mourning, and American affinity / Christopher Peterson.
   p. cm.
 Includes bibliographical references and index.
 ISBN: 978-0-8166-4983-9 (hc : alk. paper)
 ISBN-10: 0-8166-4983-9 (hc : alk. paper)
 ISBN: 978-0-8166-4984-6 (pb : alk. paper)
 ISBN-10: 0-8166-4984-7 (pb : alk. paper)
  1. Death in literature.   2. Mourning customs in literature.
 3. Kinship in literature.   I. Title.
   PN56.D4P47   2007
   810.9'3548–dc22   2007014351

Printed in the United States of America on acid-free paper

The University of Minnesota is an equal-opportunity educator and employer.

12 11 10 09 08 07   10 9 8 7 6 5 4 3 2 1

On all sides are ghosts, not of the dead, but of living people.

 —SHERWOOD ANDERSON, *Winesburg, Ohio*

Contents

Acknowledgments
ix

Introduction
1

1. Giving Up the *Geist*
37

2. Beloved's Claim
68

3. The Haunted House of Kinship
97

4. The Kinship of Strangers; or, Beyond Affiliation
135

Notes
157

Index
183

Acknowledgments

For an author who seeks to question the epistemological assumption that allows us to distinguish kin from non-kin, to thank those kin who contributed to the book's completion is problematic, to say the least. What does it mean to acknowledge one's kin in the context of an argument that aims to show how knowledge of others is irremediably compromised by their alterity? How would I know whom to thank? How does recognizing one's collaborators necessarily entail the omission of innumerable others that memory fails to capture? In what follows, I aim to express my gratitude to all those who were kind enough to indulge my turning the conversation to thoughts of ghosts and kinship during the years that I spent researching and writing. If, as I argue in the pages that follow, kinship is always implicated in a violent reduction of the other to the same (kind), I hope that the following acknowledgments commit only the least amount of violence that kinship requires.

This project was generously supported by grants from the Ahmanson Foundation, the Marta Feuchtwanger Trust, and the Josephine De Kármán Fellowship Trust. My parents, John Peterson and Linda Hoffman-Peterson, as well as my siblings, Ann Peterson-Miller, Elizabeth Peterson, and Geoffrey Peterson, all showed much more than the usual amount of interest and support that "blood" relationships are said to require. Numerous friends were also invaluable to my work as well as to my sanity. In particular, I thank Matthew Adler, Bradley Youngston, Cindy Sarver, Christine Coffman, Peter Huk, Mark Hudson, Vinay Swamy, Gary Riley, Diana Anders, Luis Williams, Michelle Peterson, Randy Colvin, Eric Anders, and Robert Byer. I also want to thank those faculty at Northwestern University who inspired me as an undergraduate to pursue the study of literature: Michal Ginsburg, Françoise Lionnet, Jane Winston, and Helen Deustch.

At the University of Southern California I was privileged to be guided by a group of truly extraordinary scholars. Judith Jackson Fossett, Hilary Schor, and Karen Pinkus advised me in the initial stages of my work; Karen warrants special thanks for her long-time friendship and support. Peter Starr lent his keen sense of critical reception, and Ariela Gross provided invaluable historical and legal guidance. The students in the Thematic Option Honors Program at USC who enrolled in my courses "From Spirits to Spooks" (1999) and "Family Fictions" (2000) eagerly read many of the primary texts that form this study and responded with considerable openness to the ideas that I presented. Above all, I thank Peggy Kamuf, who has been the most dedicated advisor and discerning reader I could have wanted. It goes without saying that her influence and provocative insights everywhere haunt the pages that follow.

I was fortunate to participate in Judith Butler's seminar on *Antigone* at the University of California, Berkeley, in the summer of 1999 with an excellent group of students and faculty. Our animated discussions were formative in my thinking about kinship, and I am especially grateful for Judith's continued support. The members of Donald Pease's seminar at the Futures of American Studies Institute, which took place at Dartmouth College in the summer of 2004, responded enthusiastically to a portion of my manuscript that I presented there, and I am especially thankful for Don's guidance in finding the right home for my project.

As a postdoctoral fellow at the University of California, Davis, I was blessed with a cohort of equally patient readers and interlocutors. David Alvarez, Meg Worley, Andrew Strombeck, Tom Hothem, and Anne Zanzucchi read and responded to several chapters from the book and motivated me to complete the project; Tom and Anne deserve special appreciation for their continued friendship, despite their consternation that I do not "believe" in ghosts. I was particularly fortunate at Davis to have had Elizabeth Freeman as my unofficial faculty mentor throughout the revision process. For help in shaping my manuscript into a coherent book, I thank Richard Morrison, Adam Brunner, Rachel Moeller, and Renie Howard at the University of Minnesota Press. I am especially grateful for Michelle Wright and an anonymous reader who generously donated their time to review my manuscript and provided invaluable suggestions for revision. The kindness of strangers indeed.

— Los Angeles, August 2006

Introduction

> The tomb [is] the true house of the family...the
> only place that corresponds to a patriarchal conception
> of the family, where several generations and several
> couples are reunited under the same roof.
>
> —Philippe Ariès, *Essais sur l'histoire de la mort en Occident*

The title sequence of Alan Ball's HBO series about a family-owned funeral home, *Six Feet Under*, opens with a shot of a tree on a deserted hillside. As the camera pulls back, two clasped hands in the foreground of the shot break apart in time with a dissonant piano chord in the soundtrack. The image of the broken hands then dissolves into the hands of a mortician, washing in preparation for embalming. Aligning the icon of "the family tree" with the broken handclasp and the hands of the embalmer, the title sequence suggests a certain temporal adjustment to our conventional understanding of kinship and loss. Mourning does not commence on the occasion of someone's death; rather, mourning conditions the possibility of kinship. Insofar as it denotes a relation to the *same kind*, however, the concept of kinship imagines a certain triumph over mourning, absence, and death by seeking to close the gap between self and other. One gleans something of the phantasm on which kinship is based in the conventional phrase "kindred spirits." To fantasize that someone is our kindred spirit is to imagine that we might bridge the abyss that stands between us. Yet, if the alterity of the other can never be collapsed into the same — if "our" kin are never finally ours — then they are absent from the very beginning.

Mourning, however, is not only implicated in familial or "blood relations." For our relations to others more generally — whether biological or nonbiological — are also haunted by the possibility of loss. As Jacques Derrida argues in *The Politics of Friendship*, relations between and among friends are necessarily and irrevocably shaped by processes of mourning. This nexus of mourning and friendship, for Derrida, is not to be lamented, but rather welcomed as the necessary condition of friendship: "It is thanks to death that friendship can be declared."[1] As Simon Critchley glosses Derrida's assertion: "One is only a friend of that which is going to die."[2] Yet, the impending death of the other is always signaled to me by the unbridgeable alterity that no kinship claim can finally surmount. Hence, even when "our" kin are here, they are not precisely *present*. Given the originary absence of the other, then, how might I respond to a well-meaning friend who implores — no doubt impatient with such seemingly pessimistic talk about mourning and kinship — "But what about living in the present?" How do I explain to my friend that mourning conditions the possibility of his asking the question at all? That his ontological demand paradoxically forecloses our relation to one another? For the imperative to live in the present ultimately negates the relation to the other. If I am always already mourning the "future" loss of my friend, then our relation to one another never exists in any simple present, undivided by absence. And this is not to say that absence is merely destructive, a cruel "fact of life" that always looms large over our most intimate and loving relationships, threatening to rear its ugly head at any moment. From family to friendship and beyond, mourning and loss initiate our relations to others.

The popularity of *Six Feet Under* notwithstanding, American culture tends not to acknowledge the intimate relation among death, mourning, and kinship — no doubt because in the modern West we tend to see the barrier that separates the living and the dead as insurmountable. If we follow historian Philippe Ariès on this subject, however, we see that things were not always so. In contrast to the Middle Ages, in which a certain familiarity with death was displayed, a promiscuous coexistence of the living and the dead, Ariès argues that the rise of modernity witnessed an effacement and interdiction of death. Death was to be put in its proper place, whether "its place" be the newly constructed cemeteries on the outside of the city walls or the hospitals where patients now came to die rather than to get well: "Mourning is thus no longer a necessary period on which society imposes respect. It has become a morbid state that needs to be nurtured, abridged, and erased."³

According to Ariès, the interdiction of mourning is nowhere more vigilant than in the United States, where death is treated almost as an aberration of life. Indeed, the present study focuses on American culture precisely because the American disavowal of death is so vehement. Ariès reads the advent of the mortuary business and the practice of embalming in the United States during the late nineteenth century as a testament to the American denial of mortality. Death could no longer be either too familiar or common, too frightening or painful: "To sell death, one must make it pleasant" (69). This transformation of death into something pleasant — in other words, something that is not death — is symptomatic of the modern segregation of the living and the dead. Following Ariès, Gary Laderman traces the emergence of this peculiarly modern interdiction of death specifically to the postbellum era, which bore witness to the "birth of the death industry."⁴ During the Civil War, a doctor by the name of Thomas Holmes claimed to have embalmed thousands of fallen soldiers. Because most Civil War battles were fought on Southern land, the practice of embalming allowed for the preservation and repatriation of the bodies of fallen Union soldiers. Following the wartime emergence of embalming, Abraham Lincoln became the first U.S. president to have his body embalmed. Lincoln's body, as is well known, was paraded before thousands of mourning citizens on a long, cross-country journey from Washington, D.C. to Springfield, Illinois. As Laderman notes, the parading of Lincoln's body "ensured that embalming — an unacceptable treatment before the war — would change the practice of American deathways" (163). The living could now "look at the face of death and not be confronted by the gruesome details of decomposition and decay" (174). As Jessica Mitford observed in her well-known exposé of the American funeral industry, *The American Way of Death* (1963), the undertaker "put[s] on a well-oiled performance in which the concept of *death* ... play[s] no part whatsoever. ... He and his team ... score an upset victory over death."⁵

While this study accords with the claim that American culture disavows mortality, I do not argue for any simple reversal of this interdiction with an aim toward affirming finitude per se. If death is beyond our experience (as Heidegger among others has observed), if I am ultimately absent from "my" own death, then strictly speaking there is nothing for me to recognize or avow. Yet *dying* is something that I do every day. Indeed, it might be more accurate to say that American culture disavows dying, understood as a process that extends from our birth to our biological demise.[6] Even with such an amended formulation, however, it is not entirely clear whether dying can ever be *fully* affirmed or avowed. That "we live *as if* we were not going to die," as Zygmunt Bauman observes, "is a remarkable achievement," especially given the ease with which we disavow dying on a daily basis.[7] Some degree of disavowal would seem both unavoidable and necessary for our survival. Any effort to prolong one's life, from simply eating well and exercising to taking medications to prevent or treat illness, evidences this disavowal. For Bauman, however, the disavowal of dying often has violent political and social consequences. Noting the wartime imperative "'to limit our casualties,'" for instance, Bauman remarks that "the price of that limiting is multiplying the dead on the other side of the battleline" (34). Drawing from Freud's claim that, "at bottom no one believes in his own death," Bauman argues that death is "*socially managed*" by securing the "immortality" of the few through the mortalization of others (35, his emphasis).[8] The belief in my self-presence, which is also always a belief in my immortality, is thus dialectically conditioned by the nonpresence of others.

Scholars in race and sexuality studies have done much to bring our attention to the ways in which American culture represents racial and sexual minorities as dead — both figuratively and literally. Indeed, this gesture both accompanies and reinforces the larger cultural dissimulation of mortality by making racial and sexual others stand in for the death that haunts every life. The history of American slavery tells a familiar story of how American consciousness disavows and projects mortality onto its "others." Orlando Patterson has described the institution of slavery in terms of a process of kinship delegitimation that constructs slaves as "socially dead."[9] For Patterson, slavery — across its various historical forms — emerges as a substitute for death, a forced bargain by which the slave retains his/her life only to enter into the liminal existence of the socially dead. As a substitution for death, slavery does not "absolve or erase the prospect of death," for the specter of material death looms over the slave's existence as an irreducible remainder (5). This primary stage in the construction of the socially dead person is followed by what Patterson refers to as the slave's "natal alienation," his/her alienation from all rights or claims of birth: in short, a severing of all genealogical ties and claims both to the slave's living blood relatives, and to his/her remote ancestors and future descendants. Although Patterson does not approach the problem of social death through a psychoanalytic vocabulary of disavowal and projection, one might say that the presumptive ontology of slave-owning, legally recognized kinship, was dependent on a deontologization of slave kinship that worked to deny the death that each life bears within itself.

Building on Patterson's argument, Toni Morrison observes in *Playing in the Dark* that, "for a people who made much of their 'newness' — their potential, freedom, and innocence — it is striking how dour, how troubled, how frightened and haunted our early and founding literature truly is."[10] For Morrison, African-American slaves came to shoulder the burden of the darkness (both moral and racial) against which America defined itself. The shadow of a racialized blackness did not so much threaten the ostensible "newness" of American life as it conditioned the latter's appearance as new and free. Hence "freedom," she writes, "has no meaning...without the specter of enslavement" (56). Echoing Morrison, Russ Castronovo asserts in *Necro Citizenship* that nineteenth-century American politics constructed the citizen in relation to a morbid fascination with ghosts, séances, spirit rappings, and mesmerism. Taking his point of departure from Patrick Henry's infamous assertion, "give me liberty or give me death," Castronovo explores how admission into the domain of citizenship required a certain depoliticization and pacification of the subject: "The afterlife emancipates souls from passionate debates, everyday engagements, and earthly affairs that animate the political field."[11] From Lincoln's rumored dabbling in spiritualism, to attempts by mediums to contact the departed souls of famous Americans, to a senator's introduction of a petition in 1854 asking Congress to investigate communications with the "other side" — so numerous are Castronovo's examples of what he calls "spectral politics" that we would have a difficult time contesting his diagnosis that nineteenth-century American political discourse worked to produce politically and historically dead citizens. That these citizens were constructed in tandem with the production of large slave populations — noncitizens who were urged by slavery proponents and abolitionists alike to believe that emancipation existed in a promised afterlife — would lend still more credence to the argument that nineteenth-century America propagated a dematerialized politics.

One wonders, however, how Castronovo's argument sits in relation to Ariès's contention that American life tends toward an interdiction of death, and if Castronovo's rejection of necropolitics, moreover, is not finally symptomatic of this very disavowal. Castronovo maintains that, "for cultures that fear death...necrophilia promotes fascination with and helps tame an unknowable terror" (5). American necrophilia, according to Castronovo, responds to an overwhelming fear and denial of death. Castronovo thus aims to turn us away from such preoccupation with ghosts, spirits, and the afterlife toward "specific forms of corporeality," such as the laboring body, the slave body, and the mesmerized body, in order to avoid "reinscrib[ing] patterns of abstraction" (17). Yet, this move away from general to specific forms of embodiment still retains the notion of "the body," and therefore of a self-contained, self-present entity. If nineteenth-century politics required that the citizen be disembodied and dematerialized, it does not follow that a move toward embodiment remedies such a spiritualized politics. Although Castronovo cautions that recourse to the body "does not automatically guarantee resistance," the overall tenor of his project pathologizes the spectral (18). Indeed, one has the sense that Castronovo would like to untether politics from death altogether — as if political life is not always haunted by finitude. Reversing the terms of political necrophilia, he offers something like a political necrophobia that sees every intrusion of the spectral as synonymous with depoliticization. If nineteenth-century spiritualism infused American political life with a familiar set of distinctions between spirit/matter, soul/body, that says nothing about how these binaries might be displaced rather than merely reversed.

A binaristic approach to the subject of mortality is also legible in Sharon Holland's *Raising the Dead*, which asserts that "bringing back the dead (or saving the living from the shadow of death) is the ultimate queer act."[12] Drawing from the activist slogan "silence = death" from the early years of the AIDS epidemic, and extending this activist imperative to address the social death of sexual and racial minorities more generally, Holland observes that the deaths of queer and racial subjects serve "to ward off a nation's collective dread of the inevitable" (38). Yet, as in Castronovo's critique of necropolitics, this imperative to "raise the dead" reverses rather than displaces the logic through which dominant, white, heterosexual culture disavows and projects mortality onto racial and sexual minorities. While we must address the particular effects that social death has on racial and sexual minorities, this social reality must also be thought in relation to a more generalizable principle of mourning. For the "shadow of death" haunts all lives, not just queer ones. The "ultimate queer act," pace Holland, would be to deconstruct rather than reinscribe the binary between life and death, to resist the racist and heterosexist disavowal of finitude.

The Betrayal of Presence

That Americanist literary criticism on the subject of mortality remains implicated in the larger cultural disavowal of dying suggests that we ought to reassess our critical energies, particularly as these powers are enlisted to address how American political ideology produces the "death" of racial and sexual others. Indeed, I would argue that such criticism remains invested — despite all claims to the contrary — in an American exceptionalist project.[13] American exceptionalism names, in part, a fetishization of novelty and futurity that initially defined America against an ostensibly decaying and moribund Europe. As David Noble has argued, the doctrine of exceptionalism excluded America from "the human experience of birth, death, and rebirth" by figuring Europe in terms of time and America in terms of timeless space.[14] If, as George Berkeley put it, America is "time's noblest offspring," history gives birth to its final progeny in order that the latter might escape time altogether. America thus becomes eternally present while "Europe breeds in her decay."[15] If the "new world" *qua* new must deny mortality, then reanimating the excluded from within the terms of a dialectical reversal *re*news rather than dismantles the American exceptionalist project.

Challenging the ideology of American exceptionalism is particularly crucial for a post–9/11 politics that aims to resist the transformation of American exposure to injury and death into a newly reconsolidated sense of innocence and immortality. As Donald Pease has argued, 9/11 transformed "virgin land" into "ground zero," effecting an ideological shift from a "secured innocent nation to a wounded, insecure emergency state."[16] Drawing from the work of Giorgio Agamben, Pease describes the emergency state as a nation that — by exempting itself from its own democratic rules of free speech, due process, and above all, the rules of war — marks a division between those whom the state protects from injury and those whom the state is free to injure and kill with impunity (13). The reduction of the Arab other to that which cannot be killed because it is already dead works to cover over the wound that ground zero opens up under the surface of virgin land. The emergency state (or what Agamben calls the "state of exception") thus also names a nation that attempts to except itself from the universal condition of mortality. As Bauman notes, "if mortality and transience are the *norm* among humans, durability may be attained only as an *exception*" (67, his emphasis).

To displace the dialectic of immortality/mortality requires the introduction of a third term, the specter, which cannot be reduced to either spirit or body. Derrida characterizes the specter as being "*of the spirit*," appearing as "its phantom double."[17] As the ghost of spirit, the specter is neither present nor absent, neither immortal nor mortal. Spectrality thus corresponds to the logic of the *revenant*, that is, to a "body" that can never fully return to itself as a living presence. Irreducible to the construction of racial and sexual others as abject or socially dead, then, spectrality names the condition of being-toward-death to which no-body is immune.[18]

From the social death of slavery, to the imagined threat of contamination and devolution that miscegenation posed in postbellum America and beyond, to contemporary anxieties that the birth of gay marriage portends the death of heterosexual marriage (and perhaps civilization itself) — this study explores how non-normative forms of kinship come to bear the burden of the death that nevertheless haunts all social bonds. As critics of the *Defense of Marriage Act* (1996) have asked: why now, for the first time in the history of the United States should the constitution be amended to define marriage as a relation between a man and a woman? Although one could answer that at no point in the history of the United States has heterosexual marriage felt itself to be so dangerously threatened, it is also true that *The Defense of Marriage Act* only makes retroactively explicit the abiding cultural logic that converts the norm of mortality into an exception that must be borne by sexual minorities. The "presence" of heterosexual marriage, in other words, has always been defined over and against the "absence" of homosexual marriage, which means that heterosexual marriage has been defending itself against a perceived homosexual menace long before 1996. Indeed, one might describe this dialectical relation in terms of a Hegelian "struggle to the death" in which heterosexuality can claim victory only by killing off its homosexual counterpart once and for all. The gay and lesbian activist demand for social and legal recognition of same-sex relationships, moreover, is largely motivated by a desire to make present what has been historically absent. If to engage in kinship relations that are socially and legally recognized is to secure for oneself the status of being socially alive, then to be without kin, or to engage in sexual and social relations that are unrecognized or unrecognizable as kinship within established norms, is to live among the ranks of the socially dead.

The political question then becomes: how does one resist the reduction of one's existence to the liminal status of social death? In *Antigone's Claim: Kinship Between Life and Death,* Judith Butler provides a familiar answer to this question in a discussion that considers how the transgressions of Sophocles' eponymous heroine deprive her of the "ontological certainty" reserved for those who fall within the norms of kinship (78). Situating Antigone's ontological deprivation in the realm of contemporary politics, Butler argues that the socially dead "remain on the far side of being, as what does not quite qualify as that which is and can be."[19] In another context, Butler describes her work, in part, as an effort to "endow ontology to precisely that which has been systematically deprived of the privilege of ontology."[20] For Butler, social death correlates directly to a form of ontological deprivation. Although Butler seeks to displace kinship from the biological model in order to imagine a vast array of social arrangements, this reorganization of kinship remains no less ontological. Critiquing the abjection of the socially dead, Butler fails to question the ontological certainty of the "socially alive." What makes the ontology of the socially alive any more secure than that of the socially dead? Are not the socially alive themselves specters? While the conflation of social life with a presumptive heterosexual ontology may indeed condition the production of the socially dead, that says nothing of how the fiction of the former might itself be exposed and stripped of its ontological conceit. That the kinship relations of the so-called socially alive are also negotiated "between life and death" is a possibility that eludes Butler's reading of *Antigone,* and has important implications for her effort to rethink kinship beyond the structure of the normative family. For if the assumption of self-presence begins by disavowing the death that haunts any life, then the production of the socially dead describes the process by which the *hauntological* condition of the socially alive is disavowed and projected onto those who transgress the norms of kinship.

I borrow the term "hauntology" from Derrida, whose coinage in *Specters of Marx* means to displace the binary opposition between presence and absence, being and nonbeing, life and death. Hauntology is thus another name for the spectrality that conditions all life. No kinship relations — even those of the socially alive — can claim immunity from the spectral. And this is neither to say that we are all socially dead in one form or another, nor to affirm the spectrality of kinship as an alibi for not addressing the alienation of slaves and other abject populations. What Patterson calls social death or what Butler (following Kristeva) understands as social abjection is *not* synonymous with what I am calling spectrality.[21] For the latter is implicated in — but not fully reducible to — the social effects of racism, sexism, and homophobia that engender a field of unlivable, abject beings. The abjection and social death of racial and sexual others is initiated by the white, male, heterosexual's denial of his own being-toward-death. While this spectrality is a generalizable condition of all "beings," this is not to say that its effects homogenize the social field: the social deaths of slaves, racial minorities, women, and queers are the effects of incommensurate — yet often intersecting — sociohistorical forces. To be socially dead, then, is in some sense to be *doubly ghosted:* for an African-American, this may mean that one's lived experience is one of being both a specter (in the generalizable sense) *and* a spook (to invoke the familiar racist trope of utter disembodiment). The presumptive ontology of whiteness is thus purchased precisely through the construction of the racial other as spook.[22]

While "being" black can mean that one is dematerialized, however, it can also mean, paradoxically, that one is burdened with a body that is figured within dominant racist discourses as menacing and violent. In Richard Wright's *Native Son,* for instance, Bigger finds himself in the bedroom of an inebriated and sleeping Mary Dalton, protected from discovery only by the blind eyes of her mother who stands by the bedroom door, "a white blur... silent, ghostlike."[23] Although whiteness has become ghostly in this dialectical reversal, Bigger's corporeality fails to exonerate him of the threat that he supposedly is to white womanhood. Indeed, Bigger stands petrified, "afraid to move for fear of bumping into something in the dark and *betraying his presence*" (97, my emphasis). The entire scene hinges on this "betrayal," which connotes, on the one hand, Bigger's inadvertent revelation of his presence, and on the other, the recuperation of this presence according to the cultural stereotype of the sexually violent black male. Bigger is betrayed *by* his own presence, or rather by the racist construction of that presence as a threat. Bigger's "agency" in Mary's murder is circumscribed by his effort to guard against becoming the violent presence that the murder only shows him to be. He murders Mary, who is beginning to stir from her slumber, so that she will not reveal his presence to the blind, white eyes of Mrs. Dalton, eyes that, in their very blindness, can only see the black male body as a threatening presence.

Wright's account of Bigger's betrayed presence prefigures the famous opening passage in Ellison's *The Invisible Man* where the narrator remarks upon what it is like to be "bumped against by those of poor vision," that is, by those who can see the black male only as a "spook" or a "phantom."[24] Angered by the blindness of white eyes, the narrator begins to "bump people back" (4). Rather than demonstrating that he is a "man of substance," however, his violent, bodily confrontation with a white man in the street only seems to affirm his ghostliness (3):

> In my outrage I got out my knife and prepared to slit his throat, right there beneath the lamplight in the deserted street, holding him in the collar with one hand, and opening the knife with my teeth — when it occurred to me that the man had not *seen* me, actually; that he, as far as he knew, was in the midst of a walking nightmare! And I stopped the blade, slicing the air as I pushed him away, letting him fall back to the street.... He lay there, moaning on the asphalt; a man almost killed by a phantom. (4, his emphasis)

Whereas Bigger's violence makes him menacingly present, almost overly corporeal, the invisible man's violence fails to materialize his body. But if Bigger becomes the "man of substance" that the invisible man endeavors to be, he does so only to experience the betrayal of that corporealization. When the invisible man asserts that he is "not a spook like those who haunted Edgar Allan Poe," this rejection of the racist stereotype demands to be read other than as a move from the incorporeal to the corporeal (3). That he is not a "spook" would seem irrefutable. But this refusal of pure disembodiment does not preclude the possibility of his spectralization. Spectrality, as I use the term, is inclusive of the material while not being reducible to corporeality. As the narrator informs us, "I did not become alive until I discovered my invisibility," which suggests a move from *spook* to *specter* that displaces the racist construction of the black male as both all and no body, as both menacingly present yet irrevocably absent (7).

In promoting a move from spook to specter (rather than from spook to body), this study contends that political and theoretical responses to the social death of racial and sexual others too often sustain the ontological presumptions through which the binary between social life and social death emerges. From Butler's effort to endow the socially dead with ontology, to Castronovo's substitution of necrophobia for necrophilia, to Holland's raising of the dead, these political moves rely on a logic of dialectical reversal whereby the excluded are imagined as coming to inhabit the ontological field. But if the ontological emerges through the suppression of the hauntological, then reanimating the socially dead through a logic of reversal only preserves the ontological differentiation that recognizes some lives as present and others as "dead."

What I am calling *redoubled ghostliness* situates racial and sexual minorities in intimate contact with death. This heightened proximity to mortality is not only social, moreover, but material. As Karla Holloway observes in *Passed On: African-American Mourning Stories,* black Americans historically have had a "particular vulnerability to an untimely death," from lynching to suicides, from police violence to disease.[25] Echoing Holloway, Abdul JanMohamed argues that African Americans are "death-bound-subject[s]... formed, from infancy on, by the imminent and ubiquitous threat of death."[26] Tracing the emergence of this subject in Richard Wright's fiction, JanMohamed argues that slaves, and by extension, "emancipated" black Americans, live under a constantly commuted death sentence. Drawing from Heidegger's account of death in *Being and Time,* JanMohamed notes that, "if natural death marks the termination of life and, thereby, retroactively defines the entirety of life, then this is even more so the case for the slave because he faces the imminent presence of death on a mundane basis" (284). JanMohamed is certainly right that Heidegger's account of death does not provide a detailed account of death's unequal social and historical distribution. Yet, in "correcting" this elision, JanMohamed *reduces* death to its political deployment. He writes:

> The existential description of death tends to be radically agnostic about the source or agency of death.... For the slave, death is not an eventuality that somehow "comes" or "arrives" in the natural course of events... but rather something deliberately brought and imposed on him by another, by the master. (15)

The problem with this formulation, however, is that it figures death as originally exterior to the slave, coming to inhabit him only via the master's monopolistic violence. As Bauman astutely observes with regard to the modern interdiction of mortality, "we do not hear of people dying of mortality. They die only of individual *causes*, they die *because* there *was an individual cause* (138, his emphasis). Hence, we ought to say that the slave's availability to death is first conditioned by his "having" a body, which means that death is *both* what "comes" or "arrives" and is what the master wields as a form of coercive control.[27] If finitude were "always embodied in the agency of the master," then death would name a condition unique to the slave as such (294). Indeed, by insisting on a radical disjunction between the death that haunts all life and the historical particularity of the immanent death to which African Americans are uniquely bound, JanMohamed reinscribes the exceptionalist logic through which the master evades death by projecting it onto the slave. In short, JanMohamed's analysis *overparticularizes* death, thereby reproducing the "state of exception" that he seeks to avoid. According to this logic, the master presides over the slave's life and death all the while exempting himself from the death that he deploys.[28] While JanMohamed contends that the slave, unlike the master, "has always already been condemned to death *in the present*," this presumes that the master's ontology is not *also* always already put into question by the spectrality that disturbs each and every present (282). Death is not a "final punctuation mark that retroactively defines" the "syntax" of one's life (298). On the contrary, death stretches along the syntax of each and every life according to incommensurate social and political grammars.

To speak of the redoubled ghostliness of racial and sexual minorities, then, is not to subsume the particularity of social death under a universal being-toward-death that effaces political and social distinctions. Unlike what has often been said of death, spectrality is *not* the great equalizer. However, one cannot fully separate the particularity of social death from the generality of each subject's being-toward-death, as if finitude were reducible to its political distribution, or for that matter, to its *external* imposition. This does not mean that we should turn our attention away from the particular political and material losses exacted by the history of racism and heterosexism in America. Indeed, the readings of literary texts by Chesnutt, Morrison, and Faulkner offered in subsequent chapters bear witness to this violence while working to rethink the law's erasure of minority kinship in relation to the absence that founds all social relations. Before turning to those literary readings, however, the remainder of this chapter aims to elaborate further how kinship is implicated in a dialectical negation that "precedes" any legal effacement of particular kinship relations.

Kinship with the Dead

That conventional conceptions of kinship are profoundly ontological certainly does not mean that either traditional kinship systems or scholarship on the subject eschew death and mourning altogether. For instance, when Creon begins his edict forbidding Antigone's burial of Polyneices by voicing a "kinship with the dead," he announces a proximity to death that haunts all affective bonds. Notwithstanding his assertion that no one "shall...honor [Polyneices] with a grave and none shall mourn" him, Creon betrays his implication in the very mourning that his proclamation ostensibly denies.[29] Indeed, in his *The Ancient City* (1917), Fustel de Coulanges — who, along with Morgan, Durkheim, and others, counts among kinship's key "inventors" — traced a certain "cult of the dead" back to ancient Greece and Rome:

> This religion of the dead would seem to be the oldest that existed in this race of men. Before conceiving and adoring Indra or Zeus, man loved the dead; he was afraid of them, and he addressed his prayers to them. It seems that religious sentiment began with this. It was perhaps in regarding the dead that man had for the first time the idea of the supernatural and a hope beyond what he saw. The dead were the first mystery; it put man on the path to other mysteries. It raised his thoughts from the visible to the invisible, from the transient to the eternal, from the human to the divine.[30]

While later, especially Christian, understandings of death would take the soul to be both immortal and separable from the finite body, for the ancient Greco-Romans the soul remained and continued to live with the body: "The rites of the sepulture clearly show that when one put a body in the tomb, one believed at the same time to be placing something living in it" (8). Ancient burial rituals involved bringing wine and food to the grave for the dead to consume. Some Roman tombs, according to Fustel, even contained kitchens especially for this purpose.

This *necrophilia* that Fustel describes, however, is to be distinguished from the *spectrophilia* that inaugurates kinship. Whereas the former describes exclusively a love for those who are *already* dead, the latter encompasses as well our relation to those who *will die*. As Fustel demonstrates, the notion that one's kin include not only those who are presently living, but also those who are dead is certainly not foreign to traditional (particularly premodern) understandings of kinship. To suggest, however, that one's kin are never *fully* present, that the other is lost from the very beginning, is to make tremble the entire ontological basis of kinship. Rather than understand one's relation to one's kin in terms of possession — as when one claims the other as *my* son, *my* daughter, or *my* friend — one would have to confront the irreducible alterity of one's kin, a resistance to *being ours* that marks one's kin as originarily absent. Such a formulation of kinship-as-mourning might find leverage in what Simon Critchley, enabled by Derrida's reading of *Antigone* in *Glas*, calls an "ethics of the singular."[31] He continues:

> Such an ethics would not be based upon the recognition of the other, which is always self-recognition, but would begin with the *expropriation of the self in the face of the other's approach*. Ethics would begin with the recognition that the other is not an object of cognition or comprehension, but precisely that which exceeds my grasp and powers.... In mourning, the self is consumed by the pain of the other's death and is possessed by the alterity of that which it cannot possess: the absence of the beloved. Might not the death of the beloved, of love itself, and the work of mourning be the basis for a non-Christian and non-philosophical ethicality and friendship?

The ethics that Critchley outlines here is something other than a Hegelian dialectic of mutual recognition, one that inevitably cancels the other in and through the return to the self. To understand the other as always already absent is to refuse the closed circuit of dialectical recognition that absorbs and contains all otherness. Our relation to others would be anterior to the ontological violence of a self-presence that always appropriates the other to itself. As Emmanuel Levinas would have it:

"The relation with the other person is not an ontology. This bond with the other... is not reducible to the representation of the other, but to its invocation."[32] For Levinas, the invocation of the other precedes ontology.

The conventional notion of kinship as a bond of love or affection tends to disavow the violent, dialectical absorption of otherness inherent to the concept of kinship. If the phantasm of kinship allows us to imagine that we might bridge the gulf between ourselves and others, then were its ideals to be fulfilled, kinship would efface the other entirely: if the other were the same — if the other were "my" kin — then the relation to the other would be no relation at all. That the term "kin" poses a relation to others of the *same kind* means that, even when displaced from the biological, kinship retains the threat of reducing the other to the same. In the most literal sense, the term kin denotes an erasure of difference: *you are my kin* means we are the same, we are of the same kind. That is, any relation to an other — biological or nonbiological — remains haunted by kinship and its posing of the same against difference. The language of kinship, moreover, permits us to make a distinction between kin and non-kin, between blood relations and nonblood relations, between friend and stranger, and so on. But what guarantees the coherence and stability of such distinctions? How can I claim that *this* other is my kin, while *that* other is not? What makes some others the same (kin) and some others other (non-kin)?

One might approach this question through the aphorism that Derrida works to untangle in *The Gift of Death:* "Tout autre est tout autre" (Every other is absolutely other/every other is [the same as] every other).[33] For Derrida, any ethics that professes to begin with the other cannot claim immunity to the violence of the same. Although Derrida does not explicitly address the language of kinship (either in English or in French), if we follow the implications of his argument into the domain of kinship, ethics could not oppose itself to kinship on the grounds that the latter denotes a relation to the same. There would, in fact, be nothing that rigorously separates ethics from kinship if the relation to the other, as Derrida observes in his reading of Levinas in "Violence and Metaphysics," is not a relation to some "absolute" other, but rather, to an other who is other than me, and who can remain other only by being posed in relation to me, and therefore to the same.[34]

Although one cannot get away from kinship's posing of sameness against nonsameness, kinship cannot simply be abandoned in the name of ethics. But neither can we simply cast aside an ethics based on alterity because it fails to reveal otherness in some pure, "absolute" form. On the contrary, I continue to use the terms *kinship* and *ethics* in order to problematize them in and through their cross-contamination. If the duplicity of "kinship" is that it poses a relation to others through the language of sameness, the duplicity of Levinasian ethics is that it imagines the possibility of an absolute other that can only be posed in relation to me, to the same, and by extension, to kinship. Indeed, Levinas's own reliance on the language of kinship betrays his effort to affirm the other as "*tout autre.*" In *Otherwise Than Being,* he writes that the relation to the other constitutes a "relation of kinship *(parenté)* outside all biology.... It is not because the neighbor would be recognized as belonging to the same genus as me that he concerns me. He is precisely *other.*"[35] This movement outside biology, however, remains fully within the vocabulary of the same. *Parenté* stems from the Latin *parere,* meaning "to bring forth or produce." The English "parity" comes from the same Latin verb, and denotes both the state of being the same or equal and the condition of having borne children. As with the English term kinship, *parenté* connotes a relation to the same that is at odds with Levinas's invocation of an absolute other. While Levinas claims that my neighbor concerns me not because he belongs to the same genus, but rather, because he is other, this "kinship beyond all biology" cannot finally move outside the logic of sameness. The point here is not to imagine how we might succeed in affirming this absolute other where Levinas failed to do so, but rather, to recognize this very failure as the site on which to build another ethics, an ethics otherwise than (purely) other.[36]

To speak of the duplicity of kinship or the duplicity of ethics runs counter to many of our most deeply felt beliefs. We are not accustomed to thinking about kinship or ethics as inherently violent. Indeed, the opposition between kinship and violence conditions most analyses on kinship, from Patterson's work on social death to more recent scholarship on queer kinship. Queer activism and scholarship, moreover, frequently invoke the legacy of American slavery by comparing the former proscription on interracial sex and marriage with the current legal ban on gay marriage. The politics of this analogy are problematic, to say the least. In chapter 3, I turn to the analogy within the context of a discussion of Faulkner's *Absalom, Absalom!* in order to ask what it means — politically, legally, and ethically — to affirm a certain kinship between racial and sexual minorities with regard to the delegitimation of their respective intimate relations. To what extent is the miscegenation analogy invested in a violent reduction of the (racial) other to the "same" of queer political struggles? If, on the other hand, no ethical relation is devoid of violence, then can we imagine a relation between the struggles of racial and sexual minorities that would *not* be implicated in analogy? Whereas this study aims to remain critical of the analogy, queer activists tend to invoke it as fact. The analogy allows activists to assign historical precedence to the current exclusion of gays and lesbians, and to imagine the latter's final overcoming in legalized same-sex marriage. Whatever the merits of the analogy, I cite it here in order to demonstrate a longstanding critique inherent in the political struggles of racial and sexual minorities that identifies violence only with the *exclusion* of certain forms of kinship from social, legal, and state recognition.

The activist demand for gay marriage must be read, in part, as a desire to reanimate the socially dead, to ontologize the social and sexual lives of those who claim relations that deviate from the norms of heterosexual kinship. According to the logic of many political activists, if gays and lesbians are the ghost in the heterosexual machine, then gay marriage would make their relations recognizable, intelligible, and above all present. Yet, how does the desire to participate in a sphere of kinship predicated on one's social death preserve the very ontological conceit that conditions one's social death in the first place? How does the ontologization of gay kinship reverse rather than deconstruct the opposition between being and nonbeing, presence and absence, life and death, consequently reproducing within queer sociality the same political/ontological differentiation between the socially alive (monogamously married queers) and the socially dead (unmarried, nonmonogamous queers)? If a presumptive heterosexual ontology is purchased through the deontologization of queers, then legal recognition of gay marriage only promises to shore up the border between the legitimate and the illegitimate, between the living and the dead.

In contrast to the dominant trends in queer activism, an important body of scholarship has evolved at the intersection of queer, race, and critical legal studies to address the violence that would necessarily attend the *inclusion* of queers in state-sanctioned marriage. Informed by a Foucauldian suspicion of state regulation and power, scholars such as Judith Butler, Michael Warner, Katharine Franke, and Elizabeth Freeman have called our attention to the violence that always accompanies legal and state recognition. Addressing how "contemporary civil rights struggles" have inherited the battles won and lost by and on behalf of African Americans in the Reconstruction era, Franke, for instance, interrogates the tendency within rights-based discourses to ignore the regulatory power of those institutions in which minorities seek inclusion.[37] She shows that slave couples who were "married" under slavery and/or continued to cohabitate after emancipation were often automatically married in the legal sense — or forced to get married — by newly enacted state statutes. Although seemingly liberating, these laws also worked to regulate the intimate relations of former slaves by prosecuting those who thwarted the law for fornication and adultery. With a nod to contemporary debates around gay marriage, Franke isolates the political goal of marriage as one example of a discourse that "fixes as victory participation" in a state institution while remaining blind to its coercive function (253). Freeman's work on representations of the wedding ceremony in American Literature and culture also follows in a Foucauldian vein by disaggregating the wedding from state-sanctioned marriage in order to ask what belonging and intimacy mean outside the purview of the state.[38] Asking us to consider if "there is a productive non-equivalence between the institution of marriage and the ritual that supposedly represents and guarantees it," Freeman offers various literary and cultural examples in which weddings do not necessarily lead to state-sanctioned couplehood (xv).

These critiques of state power are welcome rebuttals to the political naïveté of some recent activism. Yet, to separate weddings and other rituals of kinship from the state is still not to address the violence that haunts all kinship relations. The violence of kinship, after all, is not reducible to state power, and is therefore not reducible either to the exclusion or inclusion of the socially dead. By identifying violence only with state regulation and discipline, both sides of the gay marriage debate retain an idealized conception of kinship. For even as it displaces kinship from the state, family, reproduction and so forth, queer theory continues to rely on the belief that kinship might supercede alterity. This triumph over alterity, moreover, is implicated in an ontological conception of kinship whereby the other is understood to be both present and "mine." While David Schneider argues in *A Critique of the Study of Kinship* that the fundamental assumption underlying all kinship studies is that "blood is thicker than water," we might indeed ask if, in its more dominant presumption, kinship is understood as a relation between and among those who are *presently living*.[39] As I argue in chapter 4, despite the tireless efforts of queer scholars to displace kinship from biology, the extension of kinship beyond the biological fails to amend the ontological presumptions that sustain the concept of kinship.

From Melancholia to Originary Mourning

To understand kinship as a process of mourning without any proper beginning or end requires a revision of the Freudian paradigm of mourning, a model that pathologizes any deviation from the supposedly finite process of mourning. Indeed, the very division between "healthy" (finite mourning) and "unhealthy" (interminable mourning) works to efface the originary alterity and absence of the other: first, by assuming that the other becomes lost *only* on the occasion of his/her physical absence; and second, by supposing that this loss might be overcome through the substitution of a new love object. For Freud, "the work of mourning is completed [and] the ego becomes free and uninhibited again" after "reality-testing" shows that "the loved object no longer exists."[40] The melancholic, however, is unable to displace his libidinal investment in the lost object onto a new one, which results in an incorporation of the object into the ego. The melancholic thus refuses the act of substitution that would put an end to mourning.

It remains unclear, however, how this substitution can be separated from the work of mourning that it ostensibly terminates. Indeed, in *The Ego and the Id* (1923), Freud remarks that "the character of the ego is a precipitate of abandoned object-cathexes and that it contains the history of those object-choices."[41] Although Freud writes that, in melancholia, "the shadow of the object [falls] upon the ego," it might be said that this "shadow" haunts all egos, despite their having substituted a "new" object for the lost one. That is why Derrida insists that mourning is "interminable, without possible normality, without reliable limit" (*Specters* 160). If melancholia is in some sense the precondition of mourning — in that both modes of grief must struggle with an attachment to a lost love object — the substitution of a new object for the old one does not mean that in mourning the loss has been overcome. "It is the end of mourning that we would be able to dream," Derrida remarks. "But this end is the process normally completed by mourning. How to affirm another end?"⁴² Derrida goes on to imagine a "beyond of the principle of mourning," only to confirm that this "beyond of mourning can always be put in the service of the work of mourning" (101). This mourning of "successful" mourning can no longer "sound a death knell that is its own (its *knell*) without breakage or debris" (100, his emphasis). Indeed, the notion that loss can be overcome through substitution relies on a dialectic of self-recognition in which the "presence" of the other is enlisted as the "guarantee" and "proof" of one's self-presence. The Freudian model of mourning thus involves a fetishization of the other that assumes that the other is or was at one time "mine." This logic of possession, however, is itself melancholic insofar as it effaces the alterity of the love object, and thus disavows the originary loss of the other.

In this sense, melancholia might be understood as a synonym for what Derrida has often called "the metaphysics of presence." Notwithstanding the ethics of the singular that says "*this* Other and no other Other," the dialectic of presence requires a certain obliteration of the other, one that recognizes the other as "present" if only to negate its presence through one's own coming into being, one's own self-presence. To understand one's self-presence in terms of an originary mourning, however, would be to eschew the priority granted to *being* over the other, to affirm a pre-ontological responsibility to the other, an openness to alterity that does not begin with the self. The "I" that says "I am mourning (someone or something)" might be read, then, less transitively than reflexively, insofar as the "I" that announces its self-presence is always already mourning its own death.

Recent scholarship in race and sexuality studies has revisited the Freudian distinction between mourning and melancholia in order to counter Freud's pathologization of melancholia. Despite (or rather because of) their efforts to reclaim melancholia for politics, however, these analyses remain implicated in a quintessentially American disavowal of dying. As David Eng and David Kazanjian remark in their editorial introduction to *Loss: The Politics of Mourning*,

> we find in Freud's conception of melancholia's persistent struggle with its lost objects not simply a "grasping" and "holding" on to a fixed notion of the past but rather a continuous engagement with loss and its remains. This engagement generates sites for memory and history, for the rewriting of the past as well as the

reimagining of the future. While mourning abandons lost objects by laying their histories to rest, melancholia's continued and open relation to the past finally allows us to gain new perspectives on and new understandings of loss.[43]

With this assessment of the enabling powers of melancholia, Eng and Kazanjian repeat what has now become a familiar call to engage with the political possibilities of loss and mourning. Addressing the enduring legacies of racism, Anne Cheng argues that "American racial politics demands an alternative formulation whereby the desired goal may not be to 'work through' or 'get over' something but rather to negotiate between mourning and melancholia in a more complicated, even continuous way."[44] Like Eng and Kazanjian, Cheng advocates a politics that would depathologize melancholia. The problem, however, with such calls to affirm a melancholic politics is that these analyses tend to "forget" that melancholia is predicated on a refusal of absence and loss. As Cheng herself puts it: "The melancholic must deny loss as loss in order to sustain the fiction of possession" (9). The depathologization of melancholia focuses on the divergent processes through which mourning and melancholia *resolve*, or in the latter case, do *not* resolve. Because Freud distinguishes between mourning and melancholia by asserting the latter's interminability, the move toward melancholia would at first seem like an attractive alternative to the premature closure of Freudian mourning. Yet, the crucial difference between mourning and melancholia lies less in how each process ends (or does not) than in how each "begins": melancholia commences by disavowing the other's absence. This refusal of absence and loss means that melancholia always already terminates the process of mourning: for the melancholic, mourning is over before it begins.[45]

Cheng, Eng, and Kajanjian thus champion melancholia for its political potential to address the ongoing effects of racism and other social injustices. Focusing entirely on the resolution of grief, however, these analyses are implicated in a melancholia of presence that fails to recognize the originary loss that founds all social relations. The scholarly reclamation of melancholia thus tends to reduce the problem of loss to the effects of racism, heterosexism, war, genocide, and other forms of violence and injustice. As I argued with regard to JanMohamed's portrayal of the slave's heightened proximity to death, we must avoid overparticularizing the unequal political labor of spectrality. While there are crucial reasons to address the grief that attends the lived experiences of racial and sexual minorities, mourning is irreducible to racial and sexual politics. As Alexander García Düttmann observes in a Heideggerian-inflected reading of AIDS, the knowledge that one will likely die of a terminal illness does not change the fact that "one could die at any moment" of causes completely unrelated to the virus (24). In this sense, the particularity of being-toward-death that attends HIV infection — as well as the disproportionate access to treatment that maps this trajectory — must also be thought in relation to the everyday ubiquity of loss and mourning to which no one is immune. While there is no denying the uneven allocation of loss, it cannot be fully collapsed onto the political. Always at work in the ordinary, mundane events of social life, mourning not only has no end; it also has no origin.

From Spirit to Specter

Nowhere is the disavowal of absence and alterity that conditions kinship more apparent than in its reproductive form, in which the father immortalizes himself in the body of the child. The dialectic of normative reproduction, to put it in Hegelian terms, "cancels" both the maternal and filial bodies in and through the return of the father's seed to itself. This dialectical structure is thus first and foremost a relation to the other's body. As Jean-Luc Nancy remarks in *Corpus*, "*An other is a body* because only *a body is an other.*"[46] Nancy goes on to suggest that — given the ob-jection, the expropriation, of one's own, proper body — "'other,' 'others' are not even the right words, but only bodies.... It is the world of bodies" (30). In this sense, the expropriation of one's body in the body (of the)/other, is present, as it were, in any kinship relation — reproductive or nonreproductive, biological or nonbiological — that nevertheless predicates itself on the presence of one body to another. The body is implicated in kinship insofar as the latter weds itself to the ontological, to the presence of one body to another, a presence that depends on a conception of bodies as being either finite or immortal.

The dialectic between finite and immortal body is exemplified by the Christian construction of the divine family in which, as Derrida reminds us in *Glas*, "the infinite father gives himself, by... self-insemination... a finite son who... dies as the finite son, lets himself be buried, clasped in bandages he will soon undo for the infinite son to be reborn."[47] Derrida goes on to remark that the human family is not merely modeled on its divine counterpart, but is indissoluble from it:

> The human family is not something other than the divine family. Man's relation of father-to-son is not something other than God's father-to-son relation. Since these two relations are not distinguishable, above all not opposed, one cannot feign to see in the one the figure or metaphor of the other. One would not know how to compare one to the other, to feign knowing what can be one term of the comparison before the other. One cannot know, outside of Christianity, what is the relation of a father to his son. (76)

As in the divine family, the human family names a spiritual relation between father and son, a relation in which the mother, like Mary, is figured as a temporary detour through materiality, one that enables and conditions the return of the father/spirit to itself. This oscillation engenders the sublation of spirit/matter, of father and mother, a synthesis that is achieved in the reproduction of the father in the child. As Hegel writes in the section "The True Spirit: The Ethical Order," from the *Phenomenology of Spirit*: "This relationship [between husband and wife]...has its actual existence not in itself but in the child — an 'other,' whose coming into existence is the relationship."[48] Here Hegel's characteristic use of the copula does not merely describe but, indeed, performs the linking of subject to predicate whose implied reference is husband and wife: the copula copulates.[49]

While Hegel's *Geist* should not be conflated with the Father-Spirit of Christianity, a similar dialectical logic obtains in the latter's movement out from itself, its incarnation in the son of God. The immortality of God-Father-Spirit is conditioned by his becoming finite, his becoming mortal, and his eventual death and resurrection. Although Hegel does not align husband and wife at either end of the spirit/matter polarity, his designation of the child as the sublation of husband and wife rehearses the circular movement of the spirit's return to itself that we see in the divine family. For Hegel, the child *is* the relationship because the former is "that in which the relationship itself gradually passes away" (273). Or as Derrida writes in *Glas* regarding Hegel's family: "They guard there [in the child's becoming] their own disappearance, regard their child as their own death" (151). The child is at once the sign of their mortality and its refusal. Regarding their disappearance, they retard it, appropriate it; they maintain in the monumental presence of their seed — in the name — the living sign that they are dead, not that *they are dead*, but that *dead they are*, which is another thing. Ideality is death, certainly, but to be dead — that is the whole question of dissemination — is that *to be* dead or to be *dead*? This very slight difference of stress, conceptually imperceptible, the inner fragility of each attribute produces this oscillation between the presence of being as death and the death of being as presence. (151)

This "death of being as presence" signals a mode of being other than the ontological one, a shift from *being* dead to being *dead*. But this other manner of being, this "hauntology," is disavowed by the parents, and especially by the father, who seek to retard and appropriate death, to maintain the "presence of their seed," that is, to secure their own immortality: "One's own proper death, when contemplated in one's child, is the death that one denies, the death that *is*, that is to say denied. When one says 'death is,' one says 'death is denied'" (151). The reproduction of the father in the child posits a death that *is*, a death that is denied because it is posited. The positing of death marks the return of ontology at the moment of finitude, a return that recovers (from) all loss, all absence. That is why Derrida identifies this positing of death with the Hegelian *Aufhebung:* cancellation, preservation, supercession: "The *Aufhebung* is the amortization of death" (151).[50]

One might approach the Derridean distinction between *being* dead and being *dead* through Edgar Allan Poe's *The Facts in the Case of M. Valdemar,* in which the eponymous subject of an experiment in postmortem mesmerism responds to P ——'s question, "Do you still sleep," several minutes after the doctors have pronounced him dead, declaring: "Yes! — no; — I *have been* sleeping — and now — now — I *am dead.'"*[51] Poe writes neither "I *am* dead" or "I am *dead*," but "I *am dead,* emphasizing at once both the presence of "being" and the absence of "nonbeing." The italics thus extend the undecidability of the "Yes! — no" that begins Valdemar's sentence: "Yes I am sleeping, or rather, no I *have been* sleeping, and *now* I am dead." This "now — now," repeated twice, and thus insisting on the speaker's presence to himself, is nonetheless in contradiction with what he *is* now, which is *dead.* This passage appears as an epigraph to Derrida's *Speech and Phenomena,* in which Valdemar's catachrestic assertion of being dead is invoked to illustrate a point about the nature of language: "My death is structurally necessary to the pronouncing of the *I*.... The utterance 'I am living' is accompanied by my being-dead and its possibility requires the possibility that I be dead; and conversely. This is not an extraordinary story by Poe here, but the ordinary story of language."[52] For Derrida, the constative "I am" only makes sense if it can be repeated above and beyond the absence of the speaker. Hence, the repeatability of any speech act requires the possibility of my "future" absence. The "I" can emerge only on account of this prosopopeic voice, of this voice that speaks from beyond the grave, and so says what it cannot properly say. The "I" announces itself as present, but it also presents that presence as dead, leaving the living, breathing, speaking "I" haunted by that death which it, properly speaking, cannot be. M. Valdemar's presence is shown to be always already haunted by absence. In this sense, "I am *dead*" might be taken as uncovering the suppressed or disavowed death that inhabits any constative that begins "I am." As Derrida puts it: "I *am* thus originally means *I am mortal*" (60).

What follows after Valdemar's announcement is a prolonged mesmeric-induced sleep, a sleep that delays the coming of death. Upon attempting to wake him, Valdemar screams: "For God's sake! — quick! — quick! — put me to sleep — or, quick! — waken me! — quick! — I *say to you that I am dead*!'" (58, his emphasis). Put me to sleep or wake me up, implores Valdemar. Caught in a liminal space between sleep and death, Valdemar begs for a resolution to this undecidability. Finally, he gets his wish:

> As I rapidly made the mesmeric passes, amid ejaculations of "dead! dead!" absolutely *bursting* from the tongue and not from the lips of the sufferer, his whole frame at once — within the space of a single minute, or even less, shrunk — crumbled, absolutely *rotted* away beneath my hands. Upon the bed, before that whole company, there lay a nearly liquid mass of loathsome — of detestable putridity. (59, his emphasis)

Valdemar's speech occasions a perversion of the performative utterance that, according to J. L. Austin, brings into being what it names.[53] Here the utterance performs Valdemar's demise, brings his death into being, which is to say that it brings him into nonbeing. Against the ontological conceit of Austin's performative utterance, Valdemar's explosive speech performs a certain implosion of the body, depriving the reader of *both* the return to the body *as* living presence and its transformation into spirit. Refusing to give us either body or spirit, Poe leaves us with something like a specter, the remains that are left behind after the deconstruction of the body/spirit duality.⁵⁴

That what operates under the signifier of "the family" in Western cultures is implicated in the either/or of spirit/body seems to be confirmed if one consults the anthropological literature on kinship. In *A Critique of the Study of Kinship*, Schneider shows that nineteenth-century thinkers — from Lewis Henry Morgan to Emile Durkheim — were preoccupied with whether or not kinship had a biological, material basis. In his voluminous *Systems of Consanguinity and the Affinity of the Human family*, Morgan claimed that

> The family relationships are as ancient as the *family*. They exist in virtue of the law of derivation, which is expressed by the perpetuation of the species through the marriage relation. A system of consanguinity, which is founded upon a community of blood, is but the formal expression and recognition of these relationships.⁵⁵

While Morgan identified consanguinity as synonymous with the family, Durkheim, in one of his many contributions to *L'Année Sociologique*, suggested that "one has the right to wonder if, by itself and in a general way, kinship is not an essentially religious thing, of which consanguinity may be the ordinary condition, secondary but not essential."⁵⁶ This religiosity by which all kinship is rendered "artificial" is further reflected, as Marc Shell notes, in the "emphasis placed on male procreation by the Christian religious and legal traditions," which evince a "fearful uncertainty about paternity."⁵⁷ He continues: "To call any child some man's son or daughter — or any particular man someone's father — is a fiction insofar as all paternity is inevitably indeterminable" (5).⁵⁸

Yet, the unknowability of paternity — or indeed, of kinship more generally — is not the result of our inability to "prove" consanguinity beyond any scientific doubt. As Shell notes, "whether there is an unequivocal blood or DNA test to detect lineage or parentage and whether true parentage is other than consanguineous remain unsettled questions ("Children" 196). Although he implies here that kinship is not reducible to blood relations, Shell also seems to suggest that scientific advances might someday allow for absolute, unequivocal determination of kinship. Despite his overarching thesis that kinship is a fiction, then, Shell imagines the possibility that these "unsettled questions" might some day be resolved, that kinship might someday forsake its figurative status for its final literalization. That Shell ultimately reinstitutes the biological model of kinship is confirmed by his assertion that conjoined twins "present the only case where literal (consanguineous) kinship is undeniably known" (196). But even if two people are physically joined, that does not "prove" that they are kin — unless, that is, kinship is reducible to biology. Posing conjoined twins as the exception to the rule, Shell fails to recognize that the unknowability of kinship is not due to an unreliable science, but to the alterity of the other. We can never determine who constitutes our kin precisely because they remain irreducibly other. In other words, we cannot prove or verify that conjoined twins are kin because — despite their physical connection — they are no more fully identical than two complete strangers are fully different. As with all *other* others, the alterity of conjoined twins persists notwithstanding their corporeal bond.

In a manner that recalls Shell's argument, Schneider also challenges the assumption of consanguinity only to end up anchoring kinship once again in the material. Identifying in the anthropological literature on kinship a consistent tautology whereby the very effort to free kinship from biological referents only seems to reaffirm the material basis that it wants to displace, Schneider concludes his chapter on "The History of Some Definitions of Kinship" with a curious analogy: "To do this [to free kinship from reproduction] would have been as much as to take all the sense of the supernatural out of the idea of religion. Robbed of its grounding in biology, kinship is nothing; robbed of its grounding in the supernatural, religion is everyday life" (112). While it remains unclear whether Schneider seeks to prescribe such an analogy or if he intends it merely as a description of the conventional view of kinship, the analogy would seem to appeal to the following logic: whereas religion depends on that which transcends the material and the corporeal (the soul, the afterlife, the spirit, etc.) — kinship is ostensibly grounded in all that religion appears to scorn. Schneider's analogy is significant for two reasons: (1) it metonymically links kinship with the supernatural, of which religion has been robbed. Kinship risks becoming kin to the supernatural: it becomes, in other words, something spectral and ghostly; (2) the appearance of religion as the second term in the analogy speaks to the duplicity inherent in normative kinship (by which we mean "the family") in which the material is both negated and preserved. What does it mean to claim that ungrounding kinship from the biological or the material transforms it into "nothing" if kinship names a spiritual relation between father and son on the one hand, and a material one between mother and child on the other? Has not kinship always been about the father/spirit, with the consequence that matter/*mater* emerges only on the condition of its erasure, that is, of its absence?[59] How might we read in Schneider's claim a certain disavowal of the patriarchal, Christian model of kinship in which the spiritual relation between father and son always supercedes the materiality of the mother/child relation? It would make no sense, then, to talk of ungrounding kinship from the material if the material is that which kinship ultimately seeks to cancel and suppress. The very question — "is there a material basis for kinship?" — denies or forgets the supplanting of father/spirit for mother/matter that obtains in both the divine family and its various Western incarnations. To articulate a move from what we might call the "spirit of kinship" to something like its specter is to free kinship from the reproduction of the father/spirit in and for itself. Interrogating the assumptions of kinship studies from a transhistorical perspective, then, Schneider shows not so much that kinship has always been wedded to the trope of blood, to biology, materiality, and so on, as it has been yoked to the thought of presence — to a dialectical oscillation between spirit and matter that forecloses the possibility of the specter.

Schneider's *American Kinship: A Cultural Account* further illuminates this dialectic.[60] According to his research, the symbolic system of American kinship corresponds to a crude dialectical model:

> As a symbol of unity, or oneness, love is the union of flesh, of opposites, male and female, man and woman. The unity of opposites is not only affirmed in the embrace, but also in the outcome of that union, the unity of blood, the child. For the child brings together and unifies in one person the different biogenetic substances of both parents. (39)

Schneider goes on to remark that "love is what American kinship is all about" (40). While his research does not suggest that Americans explicitly subscribe to the model of the divine family in which father/spirit supplants mother/matter, this dialectical structure cannot but refer, tacitly at least, to the Christian model of the family. For Schneider, "all of the significant symbols of American kinship are contained within the figure of sexual intercourse" because it is through sexual intercourse that the union of opposites is realized (40). Schneider makes it clear that "sexual intercourse" is itself a "symbol," the latter of which he defines as "something which stands for or represents something else to which it is not intrinsically related" (31). This understanding of kinship in terms of a symbolic system in which only an arbitrary relation holds between signifier and signified forms the basis of Schneider's analysis of American kinship. What is curious about this system of symbols, however, is that it is understood to be independent of how Americans say, think, and do kinship:

> This book is *not* to be understood as an account of what Americans *say* when they talk about kinship and family, although it is based on what Americans say. It is *not* about what Americans *think*, as a rational, conscious, cognitive process, about kinship and family, although it is based in no small part on what Americans say they think about kinship and family. This book should *not* be construed as a *description* of roles and relationships which Americans can be observed actually to undertake in their day-to-day life, although it is based on what Americans say they do and on what they have been observed to do. This book is about symbols, the symbols which are American kinship. (18, his emphasis)

Not reducible to speech, thought, or even performance, American kinship is a purely symbolic system that need not correspond to any given "reality." Among the examples that Schneider offers of different symbolic systems or "cultural units," as he sometimes calls them, are "a person, place, thing, feeling, state of affairs, sense of foreboding, fantasy, hallucination, hope, or idea" (2). Even if kinship is nothing more than a hallucination or a fantasy, Schneider insists, it exists as a symbol.

To illustrate his claim that a cultural unit need not refer to any "object elsewhere in the real world," Schneider asks us to consider the "cultural construct" of the ghost and the dead man:

> The ghost of a dead man and the dead man are two cultural constructs or cultural units. Both exist in the real world as cultural constructs, culturally defined and differentiated entities. But a good deal of empirical testing has shown that at a quite different level of reality the ghost does not exist at all, though there may or may not be a dead man at a given time and place, and under given conditions. Yet at the level of their cultural definition there is no question about their existence, nor is either one any more or less real than the other. (2)

What is striking about Schneider's example of the ghost is that it is introduced in a completely arbitrary manner, as if it has no relation to the cultural construct of kinship whose status as symbol the ghost is nonetheless intended to illustrate. How are we to understand the appearance of this ghost here in the opening pages of a text that purports to tell us something about American kinship as a symbolic system? It is as if the dialectical, spiritual kinship that will later come to reveal itself *as* spirit emerges first as a certain ghost of spirit. Or as Derrida remarks in *Specters of Marx,* "the first spiritualization also, and already, produces some specter" (203). Would it be going too far, then, to suggest that the specter is anticipated in the spirit of kinship, that the spirit of kinship is always haunted by this "second" ghost, the specter that remains, that cannot be assimilated into identity, to unity and oneness? This "second" ghost will have already been the "first" ghost, the specter that resists totalization.

The dead return later in Schneider's study as a "problem," one that emerges on account of some informants' uncertainty as to whether they should include the deceased on their list of relatives (70). Remarking on the tendency on the part of informants to wonder whether the dead constitute a relative, Schneider writes:

> Death terminates a relationship but does not undo or erase what is and was a fact. A dead person remains person enough to be located on a genealogy; person enough to be counted as an ascendant or descendant; person enough to be remembered if there is some reason to do so. Marriage is '... until death do us part.' The *person* was and is; the *relationship* is no longer. (71, his emphasis)

While Schneider's account gives oblique reference here to mourning by noting the status that remembrance achieves for the dead person *as* "person enough to be counted," his claim that "the person was and is," but "the relationship is no longer" disavows the haunting effect that the very question — "Do you want me to list the dead ones too?" — brings into play. Given that the informants recognize their relationship to the dead, how can that relation be said no longer to exist? Does not the reflection on one's relation to the dead betray a failure to establish that relationship as terminated, as fully mourned and forgotten? Moreover, the suggestion that the dead person both *was* and *is* constitutes the dead person as present both in some past present and in the *present*

present — against the possibility that a dead person is a relative because a relative is always, in some sense, a dead person.

Given the 1968 publication date of Schneider's study of American kinship, one might question whether it speaks to more contemporary conceptions of family, reproduction, and so forth. Judging from recent political and legal debate, however, the dialectical understanding of kinship is alive and well. Following from Augustine's understanding of marital communion as an instrumental good in the service of procreation, classicist John Finnis, a so-called theorist of "new natural law," recently argued against gay civil rights and marriage in *Romer v. Evans*, insisting that "the union of the reproductive organs of husband and wife really unites them biologically.... The spouses are indeed one reality."[61] The sexual acts of homosexuals, on the other hand, "cannot make them a biological... unit. So their sexual acts cannot do what they hope and imagine" (1066). Yet it is clear from Finnis's own language that this union that two men or two women are said to imagine is simply a projection of what Finnis fantasizes heterosexual reproduction as accomplishing, revealing more what he fantasizes homosexuals to be fantasizing about than how they might view the purpose of their sexual acts. While we might be tempted to dismiss Finnis's argument as the ranting of an aberrant homophobe, the publication of his argument in the context of recent legal debates, particularly the testimony that he (as well as other leading classicists and philosophers, including Martha Nussbaum, who critiqued his position) gave in *Romer v. Evans*, requires that we take notice of the frequency with which this claim is made. Consistent with the obvious hyperbole of Finnis's claim that sexual reproduction "really unites" men and women biologically, the most recent version of this claim has emerged in the federal Defense of Marriage Act (and its various incarnations at the state level), which asserts that marriage must only consist of a relation "between one man and one woman." The dialectical spirit lives on indeed.

American kinship, then, corresponds to a certain "metaphysics of presence" in which the other must be assumed, consumed, and assimilated into a structure of identity that suppresses difference. To spectralize kinship, then, is to advocate a Derridean economy of *différance* that resists the assimilation of the other. *Différance* displaces kinship's logic of identity through a spatiotemporal deferral of any dialectical union of opposites.[62] As another name for *différance*, spectrality thus eschews the amortization of death inherent in the patriarchal conception of kinship, in which the father's presence is secured through the negation of the maternal and filial bodies.

This disavowal of death, moreover, is one of the defining characteristic of Hegel's dialectic insofar as it always manages to recover from its failures. As Butler remarks with regard to Spirit: "There is little time for grief in the *Phenomenology* because renewal is so close at hand."[63] Butler's reading of Spirit's death/resurrection figures Spirit as disavowing finitude, a disavowal that is conditioned by the *Aufhebung* of the body — that is, the cancellation, preservation, and supercession of the corporeal. No doubt Hegel's most well-known illustration of the movement of the *Aufhebung* remains his chapter on "Lordship and Bondage." Although Hegel's analysis of the master/slave relation does not address corporeality in any direct way, Butler has worked to revise the master/slave dialectic precisely in terms of this negated corporeality. Butler's rewriting of the master/slave relation in terms of the body, moreover, describes an ambivalent scene of corporeal exchange and suppression that resonates with what we have been calling the *Aufhebung* of kinship. In the context of the master/slave dialectic, the body, Butler maintains, emerges as that which the master must disavow and project onto the slave. The slave in this sense is/becomes the body of the master in and through this disavowal.

To the extent that they are both implicated in a certain negation/preservation of the body, then, kinship and slavery are intimately connected. This is not to suggest that all forms of kinship are tantamount to slavery, only that they both involve a relation between one spectral body and another, a "kindred possession," to invoke Saidiya Hartman's words, of one body in and by another.[64] Understood in terms of such kindred possession, the economy of slavery is not as distinct from the economy of kinship as we might imagine and want it to be. To the extent that it fabricates self-presence through the cancellation and preservation of the other, normative kinship substantiates an obliteration of the other/body that is not fully distinguishable from the dialectical logic of slavery.

This interimplication of slavery and kinship, as I noted above, is denied by analyses that oppose slavery and kinship, such as Patterson's *Slavery and Social Death*. Echoing Patterson, Hortense Spillers has argued famously that kinship "loses meaning" with the advent of slavery, "*since it can be invaded at any given and arbitrary moment by the property relations.*"[65] Kinship, however, does not become "invaded" by property relations, as if the latter were merely external to the former. The assumption that property relations contaminate an otherwise nonviolent and nonappropriative kinship depends on an idealized conception of kinship — one that is belied from both a theoretical and a historical perspective on American slavery. Historian Dylan Penningroth's *The Claims of Kinfolk* uncovers a wealth of evidence showing that American slaves developed a complex informal economy of property ownership that — while not legal recognized — was customarily recognized by other slaves as well as slave masters.[66] Claiming property, Penningroth goes on to argue, was intimately linked to claiming kin. Kinship was articulated *not* in opposition to property, but rather in and through claims of possession and ownership. What counted as kinship for slaves, moreover, extended well beyond biology and blood relations to include friends and neighbors. Penningroth's account of slave property ownership and its role in organizing kin relations among slaves implicitly challenges the definition of slavery as connoting the absence of kin. Classifying as socially alive only those kinship relations recognized by the law or only those relations that correspond to the patriarchal, biological family, Patterson excludes those non-normative, extralegal relations that nevertheless counted as kinship for enslaved Americans. In this sense, Patterson's analysis does not merely describe an existing binary between the socially dead and the socially alive but, rather, participates in the production of this very division.

Although Penningroth focuses on how the claims of *material* property were linked to the claims of kinship, he does not pursue the ethical dimensions of this linkage. The claims that black Americans made on their kin both during and after slavery suggest something of the chiasmatic relation that obtains between kinship and slavery more generally. To claim my kin as *mine* is to invoke an ideology of possession and ownership that is not finally opposed to slavery. In chapter 2, I read Toni Morrison's *Beloved* against theoretical and historical accounts of ethics, kinship, and violence in order to ask what it means to claim one's kin as property. While kinship and slavery are not fully identical, they are nonetheless implicated in corresponding forms of corporeal possession and subjection.

If claiming the other as one's own disavows the other's alterity and absence, then how might kinship be rearticulated beyond such an economy of presence? Moreover, how does the invocation of the body as presence, of a body that is either finite or immortal, disallow the possibility of a spectral form of kinship — an alternative idiom of kinship that would displace the dialectical model? One might approach this question in relation to what Nancy identifies as one of the prevailing truisms of Western culture: Christ's pronouncement, "this is my body." With regard to the bread, Jesus says not only, "this is my body," but "this is my body, given to you. Eat this in remembrance of me." The giving over of Jesus's body for consumption by his disciples performs the sublation of the finite and the infinite, the transfiguration of the finite body into infinite spirit. This proffering of one's body enables the return of the father/spirit to itself, and inaugurates the paradigm of Christian kinship: the relation between God-the-father and his children. This gift of the body, however, this offering up of the body for consumption, belies the indexical force of the "this" as well as the propriety of the "my." If the finite body can be given to others for consumption and assimilation, then that body can no longer be understood as one's own. Nancy's claim that *this is my body* is "an impossible appropriation," that the relation to one's body is never proper, suggests that the appropriation of the other/body is finally impossible as well (29). The relation to one's own body is always improper, which means that it is not finally distinguishable from the relation to the other's body *as* other and not me/mine. The body is always other to itself, and the fiction that occasions the belief that "this is my body" — far from disallowing the appropriation of the other/body — is the enabling possibility of this very appropriation that it denies. The possession of the other emerges as a possible impossibility only as a consequence of the belief in my own self-possession. For only on account of the conceit that this is my body can the body of the other be imagined as becoming mine through appropriation. To articulate an ethical relation to the other/body that affirms the other's alterity requires that one *first* affirm one's improper relation to one's own body, one's otherness to oneself.

While Nancy's suggestion that "body" is synonymous with "other" has important implications with regard to an analysis of kinship, it also begins to account for the logic that subtends various historical forms of human slavery. Remarking on the apparent contradiction in Western forms of slavery in which slavery bears an intimate relationship to the idea of freedom, Patterson observes that "Plato and Aristotle and the great Roman jurists were not wrong in recognizing the necessary correlation between their love of their own freedom and its denial to others" (ix). Indeed, there is nothing "peculiar" about the peculiar institution if the affirmation of one's freedom, one's self-possession, does not contradict but rather conditions the enslavement of others. As I aim to show in my reading of Charles Chesnutt's *The Conjure Woman* in chapter 1, resistance to appropriation is possible only by avowing the originary dispossession of one's body. Indeed, this impropriety of one's proper body asks us to rethink the notion of appropriation altogether. If *my* body is not finally my own, indeed, if I can no longer say with certainty that this is my body, what forms of resistance are available to counter what we name "expropriation"? How, in particular, can the socially dead slave be reanimated if there can be no final coming into possession of one's body?

1

Giving Up the *Geist*

> Metaphysics always returns...and *Geist* is the
> most fatal figure of this *revenance*.
>
> —Jacques Derrida, *Of Spirit: Heidegger and the Question*

If "kinship" involves a dialectical reduction of the other to the same, then it is not altogether opposed to slavery.[1] Kinship, in other words, must be understood not only in terms of love and affection, but also in terms of violence. Contemporary analyses of slavery, however, tend to oppose kinship and slavery. Orlando Patterson's seminal work on "social death" is exemplary of this line of thinking.[2] For Patterson, slavery destroys slave kinship structures, even as it works to justify itself by reintegrating slaves into its own domestic economy. Alienated from all rights or claims of birth, slaves are severed from all genealogical ties to their living blood relatives, and to their ancestors and descendants. For Patterson, then, to oppose kinship to slavery is both to contest the negation of slave kinship relations, and to expose the discourse of paternalism that justifies the institution's existence. For "the proslavery argument... justified slavery as part of a household system, on a continuum with marriage and childhood."[3] This "moral economy of dependency" involved a "concept of dependent rights and reciprocal duties" in which slaves were believed to exert as much control over their masters as the latter exercised over their dependents (874, 878). The propagandist notion of "a good, painless, or benign slavery," moreover, was played out in the construction of the slave as childlike and therefore in need of guidance and protection.[4]

While Patterson recognizes that the discourse of paternalism effaces the rigid opposition between kinship (understood as *positive* affect) and appropriation, this erasure is read as intrinsic to the institution of slavery rather than as a generalizable condition of our relations to others. One of the unintended consequences of Patterson's rigid determination of kinship against slavery is that it idealizes the former, chiefly by rendering it immune to violence. While the kinship-slavery opposition purposes to critique the negation of slave kinship, then, it also serves to protect the domain of kinship from interrogation. If, as Judith Butler has argued, the master exploits the body of the slave by making him in some sense *be* the master's body, such corporeal inhabiting is not far removed from the model of the divine family that we considered in the Introduction, in which the father/spirit incarnates himself in the body of the finite son if only to negate that body in and through its transfiguration into spirit.[5] While the violence of the father/son relation has often been remarked (and I will explore its ramifications through a reading of Faulkner's *Absalom, Absalom!* in chapter 3), the negativity of the mother/child relation has received less attention, in large part because that relation is conventionally understood to be devoid of violence. Indeed, its negativity emerges only through what has historically been read as a shocking affront to kinship, such as Euripides' *Medea*, or more recently, Morrison's *Beloved*. I will turn to this latter text in chapter 2 in order to trouble the apparent binary between the mother's claim on her daughter and the master's claim on his property. In what follows, however, I explore how the violence of appropriation inherent in any relation to alterity also implies an originary dispossession and mourning of "my" body as mine.

Claiming that the master projects *his* body onto the slave, Butler implies that the master's body is his prior to its disavowal. This belief in possessive individualism, however, constitutes one of the prevailing assumptions in the West. As René Descartes asks in the *First Meditation*, "how can I deny that these hands and this body here belong to me, if not perhaps by comparing myself to the insane?"[6] While Descartes is not explicitly concerned with the problem of autonomy that his question nonetheless raises, such an interrogation is crucial to an investigation of the cultural truism, "this is my body," either as it appears in the Christian tradition, in various political responses to slavery, or as it emerges in the dialectical model of kinship. Descartes's question seeks to interrogate not only the autonomy of his body but also that of his hands. He thus directs us to those bodily appendages that are involved in manual labor. Speaking specifically of labor, John Locke remarks in an often-cited passage from his *Second Treatise of Government*: "Every man has a *Property* in his own *Person*, This no Body has any right to but himself. The *Labour* of his Body, and the *Work* of his Hands, we may say, are properly his."[7] Yet, this doctrine of possessive individualism must come to terms with the paradox that "freedom," as Toni Morrison puts it, "did not emerge in a vacuum. Nothing highlighted freedom — if it did not in fact create it — like slavery."[8] The doctrine of possessive individualism, in other words, presupposes slavery. For the appropriation of the other can emerge only on the condition that one's "proper" relation to one's self has already been "established." The possession of the other is first occasioned by the conceit that this body is *my* body. But if the other's body is understood to be alienable, how can I assume that my body is exempt from this corporeal estrangement?

Slavery predicates itself on the fiction that the body of the other might be instrumentalized as an extension of the master's body. In this way, slavery involves a reduction of difference to identity whereby the other/body is/becomes the body of the master. As Jean Luc Nancy has argued, however, if "my" body is always other, then it makes little sense to talk about "*the* body of the other," for such language implies that there *is* a body prior to its coming into relation with other bodies, a body that is autonomous prior to any act of appropriation. For Nancy, "*an other is a body* because only *a body is an other*."[9] "My" body is always implicated in the body of the other, and conversely. Strictly speaking, slavery (or kinship for that matter) ought not to be construed as a relation of *one* body to another, a relation in which the property of "my body" is suspended in and through its expropriation. For "the [one] body" is always already thrown into relation with other bodies, which means that we can never speak of "the body" in the singular. The ethical abrogation of slavery lies not in the transformation of the body of the slave into the body of the master, but rather, in the violence that reduces the *différance* between and within bodies to the *idea* of "the one." Slavery exploits the appropriability of all bodies insofar as the other/body is understood to transmogrify fully into the body of the master without remainder. The terms by which we understand the master's disavowal of "his" body must thus be revised beyond the logic of possession implicit in Butler's claim that the master's body is his prior to its disavowal and projection onto the slave. For what is disavowed here is not so much his body but the fiction of bodily possession that conditions the possibility of the master's disavowal. Only on account of the conceit that his body is his own does that body become available for its denial.

Nancy's claim of a fundamental corporeal dispossession offers a means of challenging the conventional opposition between autonomy and subjection. In the *Economic and Philosophic Manuscripts of 1844*, for instance, Karl Marx claims that capitalist labor "estranges man's own body from him."[10] This account of estranged labor thus prefigures the distinction between use-value and exchange-value that Marx will make in the first volume of *Capital*. For Marx, the production of commodities as so many exchange-values confers upon the worker his own exchangeability. While Nancy maintains that the body is always already estranged from itself, this does not mean that all bodies are estranged in the same way, or to the same degree. Nancy's claim, however, might be enlisted to address the limitations of an account of alienated labor that proceeds from the premise that the laboring body is *not* in some sense already different from itself. An account of alienated labor ought not to begin with an uninterrogated distinction between use-value and exchange-value. For if all bodies are in some sense estranged from themselves, then the difference between the nonalienated laborer and the alienated one, or the nonslave and the slave, does *not* mark a stable distinction between the "species being" and the worker *as* exchange-value — the former understood as a living, universal, and free being (75). Rather, the difference between free and unfree labor would be the difference between two forms of exchange-value.

While resistance to bodily appropriation would seem to require a non-exchangeable, nonsurrogate, fully autonomous body, what would it mean if exchangeability marks the body as available not only to expropriation, but to resistance and agency as well? The ambiguities involved in the distinction between free and unfree labor are well known. In Reconstruction America, blacks were subjected to forced contract labor, often on the very plantations where they had formally been slaves, both by the infamous Black Codes and the strict rules of conduct mandated by the Freedmen's Bureau. The Mississippi Black Code of 1865, for instance, required that "every freedman, free negro and mulatto shall... have a lawful home or employment, and shall have written evidence thereof."[11] The Mississippi law also adopted language that prohibited vagrancy and made it illegal to entice a free person away from "his or her master or mistress." As one contemporary observer put it: "People assume that the negro will not labor, except on compulsion.... They acknowledge the overthrow of the special servitude of man to man, but seek through these codes to establish the general servitude of man to the commonwealth."[12] As Saidiya Hartman reminds us, the rhetoric of compulsion and accountability attendant to the construction of the "free subject" makes it difficult to distinguish freedom from slavery:

> The joyfully bent back of the laborer conjures up a repertoire of familiar images that traverse the divide between slavery and freedom. If this figure encodes freedom, then it does so by making it difficult, if not impossible, to distinguish the subjection of slavery from the satisfied self-interest of the free laborer.[13]

While she notes that the construction of the liberal subject "effectively yielded modern forms of bonded labor," Hartman reads the nexus of freedom and subjection primarily in terms of the specific political forces that reproduced the servitude of black Americans in the postbellum era (120). No doubt the construction of "the joyfully bent back of the laborer" served to justify the continued exploitation of black labor. But if the fiction of the liberal subject conditions rather than disallows enslavement, then we cannot so easily separate out the historical conditions of forced free labor from the generalizable condition of constrained freedom.

While the historical record demonstrates that liberty and enslavement were intertwined both before *and after* emancipation, the violence of appropriation is not fully reducible to forced labor. Certainly Hartman is right to insist that the "disappointments of freedom constantly reiterated in slave testimony," far from evincing a "longing for slavery," demonstrate a "longing for an as yet realized freedom, the nonevent of emancipation, and the reversals of slavery and freedom" (139). That Hartman participates in this longing for freedom is made clear when she describes her project as constituting, in part, "an examination of eclipsed possibility and another lament of failed reconstruction" (126). But can the failure of Reconstruction finally be reduced to historical forces? If freedom and servitude are bound to one another, such that the rhetoric of the liberal subject only produces the enslavement it means to refuse, then how are we to await the final "reversals of slavery and freedom"? While there is no denying the existence of coerced labor throughout the postbellum era and beyond, to critique this exploitation does not require a return to an autonomous subject, immune to alterity.

Historians of American slavery are no doubt acutely aware that progress, as Eric Foner puts it, does not unfold along a "straight line toward ever greater liberty and human dignity."[14] Like Hartman, however, Foner reads this failure of the progressive narrative *only* as a result of political and social inequality. Remarking on the conflicting definitions of freedom in the postbellum era, Foner asserts that "the concrete historical reality of emancipation posed freedom as a historical and substantive issue, rather than a philosophical or metaphorical one" (454). Yet, given the undeniable nexus of philosophical, political, and historical conceptions of freedom and slavery from the Enlightenment through Reconstruction and beyond, history does not so easily trump political theory. Insofar as Enlightenment political ideologies of absolute freedom required rather than prohibited the enslavement of others, pure freedom does not lie on the other side of an as-yet-to-be-crossed historical frontier. As Wendy Brown puts it, "freedom neither overcomes nor eludes power."[15] Addressing the "full measure of power's range and appearances," we come to understand freedom as "that which is never achieved" (25).

Hartman's ultimate acquiescence to the fiction of the liberal subject is rather unanticipated, given her claim that slave resistance is too often excluded from the "proper locus of politics" because it fails "when measured against traditional notions of...the unencumbered self, the citizen, the self-possessed individual, and the volitional and autonomous subject" (61). Focusing on the "inadvertent, contingent, and submerged forms of contestation" performed by slaves, Hartman would appear to understand autonomy as that sphere of politics from which slaves are excluded *as such*, but that nonetheless would become available to free individuals on the occasion of their "true" emancipation (62). But if the "everyday practices of the enslaved occur in default of the political," and if the subjection of the free laborer is not simply reducible to those historical forces that circumscribed the former slave's freedom, then resistance emerges at the site of a laboring body that — whether enslaved or emancipated — never fully escapes appropriation.

Goophering the Black Body

Charles Chesnutt's *The Conjure Woman* is particularly ripe for an exploration of such questions as slave resistance, autonomy, and the paradoxes of "free labor."[16] Published in 1899, yet set in the Reconstruction-era South, Chesnutt's stories are told in dialect by a former slave named Julius, who becomes the hired hand of John, a carpet-bagging opportunist who arrives in the South with his sickly wife Annie. Julius is introduced in "The Goophered Grapevine," the first story collected in the *Conjure Woman*, which explains how John buys an abandoned plantation "for a mere song," despite Julius's warnings that the land is "goophered," that is, bewitched by a conjure woman (31). At the close of "The Goophered Grapevine," John discovers that Julius has been living on the property for many years and "had derived a respectable revenue from the product of the neglected grapevines" (43). John thus determines that the story of the bewitched grapevine was meant to dissuade him from buying the land. This is just the first of many occasions upon which Julius's conjure tales are dismissed as mere fiction precisely because they appear to conceal hidden motivations on the part of Julius. Julius's stories of slaves transformed into trees and slave masters magically turned into slaves cannot possibly be true, according to John's logic, because they always reveal Julius to be a trickster who tells stories to get what he wants — the vineyard in "The Goophered Grapevine" or a place of worship in "Po' Sandy," to name two examples.

Although Robert Bone suggests that "Julius is a kind of conjurer, who works his roots and plies his magic through the art of storytelling," if we understand the relation between John and Julius as mirroring in a postbellum context the antebellum dialectic of master and slave, then it should come as no surprise that the relation between the two would replicate a series of dialectical reversals in which the question of who is conjuring and who is being conjured, or who is the trickster and who is being tricked, is repeatedly staged and renegotiated.[17] Moreover, by staging the telling of the tales in terms of an act of solicitation from John, the would-be plantation owner, to Julius the would-be slave, Chesnutt reveals how John's ostensible disbelief of the conjure tales folds over onto belief. If, notwithstanding the official discourse of plantation life, the slave master not only "believes" in ghosts, but actively produces ghosts in the formless form of the socially dead slave body, then the master/slave dialectic that obtains between John and Julius reproduces the phantasmatic climate of antebellum plantation life in which conjuring — by which I mean both that of the master and that of the slave — centers on questions of belief, epistemology, and power.[18]

John's appeal to reason as an antidote to Julius's seemingly irrational stories is worth pausing to consider, if only because it is so oddly unreasonable. For we might indeed ask why John seeks recourse to empirical evidence in order to dismiss Julius's tales as fiction. That John needs to discover an explanation behind the conjure tales other than the one that Julius supplies (i.e., that it is simply witchcraft) suggests that John not only believes in the tales on some level, but that this belief betrays a curiously literal reading of the tales themselves, one that seems completely unattuned to both their ironic and allegorical significance. John's duplicity runs something like this: on the one hand, he seems to interpret the tales as the quaint musings of an ignorant and superstitious former slave; on the other, he suggests that Julius knows full well what he is trying to accomplish by telling these stories, and thus, that he is well aware that they are fiction. But if Julius knows that the stories are fiction, and uses them accordingly to dupe John and his wife Annie, then why does John repeatedly explain away the tales by uncovering Julius's hidden motivations? There would be no need to anxiously reassert the fictitious status of the stories if John was finally secure in his belief, as it were, that he does not believe.

The question of belief is complicated by the dialectic between Julius-as-storyteller and John-as-solicitor of those stories insofar as we read the act of solicitation itself as an act of conjuring. In this sense, John's empiricist doubt recalls that of Descartes, who compares the hallucinations of those who believe they are kings with those who question the "mineness" of the body, only to deny his implication in the production of these very fantasies. As Butler puts it, Descartes "conjures such possibilities precisely at the moment in which he also renounces such possibilities as mad, raising the question whether there is a difference between the kind of conjuring that is a constitutive part of the meditative method and those hallucinations that the method is supposed to refute."[19] This collapse between empiricist doubt and conjuration is revealed in "Sis' Becky's Pickaninny," in which John instructs Julius that his "people will never rise in the world until they throw off these childish superstitions and learn to live by the light of reason and common sense" (83). The tale concludes, however, with John's discovery of Julius's lucky rabbit's foot tucked in the pocket of his sickly wife's dress (83). Given that his wife's condition has taken a turn for the better, John pauses to consider if the rabbit's foot has anything to do with his wife's recovery. John's ambivalent relation to conjuring is further unveiled in the tale directly following "The Gray Wolf's Ha'nt," where, at the request of his wife, John reads aloud the following passage of the book he is reading:

> The difficulty of dealing with transformations so many-sided as those which all existences have undergone, or are undergoing, is such as to make a complete and deductive interpretation almost hopeless. So to grasp the total process of redistribution of matter and motion as to see simultaneously its necessary results in their actual interdependence is scarcely possible. (94)

Despite the caricatured philosophical language, we are to conclude that John is seeking out possible explanations for the transmogrifications that Julius's conjure tales suggest. While John's wife calls the philosophical passage nonsense (a designation that echoes her response to Julius's tale of "The Conjurer's Revenge"), John appears to be beginning to wonder about the possibility that conjuring is not merely a superstition.

The relationship that obtains in the frame story between John the proprietor and Julius the hired hand would appear to underscore black servitude and white mastery even as it shows John to be rather dull to how Julius often exceeds his role as would-be slave. As the narrator of the frame story, John informs us at the beginning of "Mars Jeems's Nightmare" that Julius was "very useful when we moved into our new residence" (55). Detailing Julius's uncanny familiarity with their property, John remarks that Julius's "attitude" toward it

> might be called predial rather than proprietary. He had been accustomed, until long after middle life, to look upon himself as the property of another. When this relation was no longer possible ... he had been unable to break off entirely the mental habits of a lifetime, but had attached himself to the old plantation, of which he seemed to consider himself an appurtenance. (55)

Just as Mars Jeems — who in a later tale is conjured into a slave — cannot be broken in by slavery, Julius, according to John, cannot be broken from it. He is "attached" to the plantation in much the same way as Henry, who is turned into a grapevine in "The Goophered Grapevine," or Sandy, whom the conjure woman turns into a tree in "Po' Sandy." Moreover, this figuration of Julius as an appurtenance of the plantation, an appendage of the land, mirrors the means by which the slave functions as an extension of the master's body, a tool or prosthesis through which the will of the master is exercised. Just as the slave's laboring body is positioned as being in some sense closer to things material than that of the master, John's description of Julius figures the latter as being closer in proximity to the land, indeed, as being so "close to nature" that he becomes a naturalized extension of it (55). To the extent that he exploits Julius for his peculiar affinity with the land, John effectively naturalizes black servitude.

What is most striking about John's understanding of Julius's "attachment" to the plantation, however, is how John gets it both so right and so wrong. Never mind that, historically speaking, a proprietary attitude toward their former plantations was exactly what many newly emancipated slaves vociferously asserted. Perhaps the most well-known proprietary claim made by former slaves involved the South Carolina Sea Islands, where fleeing white inhabitants left behind ten thousand slaves, who remained on the plantations and raised food for their own subsistence. Later, General Sherman ordered that the Islands and a portion of the Carolina coast be set aside for former slaves. He promised forty acres and the assistance of mules, all of which were eventually revoked when the lands were returned to pardoned southerners.[20] That John can only disavow Julius's proprietary claim is made clear by his initial recognition that Julius "derived a respectable revenue" from the vineyard (43). John's dismissal of Julius's proprietary attitude thus reinscribes Julius's servitude.

John is thus not entirely wrong is his assertion that Julius is attached to the plantation. Yet, Julius is "attached" in a manner that allows him to resist the relation of identity between master/slave that reduces the slave to a mere extension of the master's body. Throughout the *Conjure Woman*, Julius works to resignify this attachment such that his double status as object *and* potential subject of property is insistently renegotiated. His prosthetic relation to John thus traverses the opposition between free and unfree labor. While John's resistance to seeing Julius as anything but servile would seem to lend credence to the historical claim that compulsory "free" labor in the form of forced labor contracts, and the promise and inevitable denial of land to former slaves (among other egregious acts), can ultimately account for the failure of Reconstruction, this argument assumes that slavery and freedom are ultimately opposed. That labor is never entirely free registers one explanation for why the work of Reconstruction remains necessarily unfinished. To claim that the work of Reconstruction is interminable, however, is not to consent to servitude. On the contrary, to measure the "success" of Reconstruction by the achievement of absolute, unfettered freedom conflates the historical reinscription of black servitude with the principle of constrained freedom. In a paradoxical sense, the possibility of Reconstruction lies precisely in its remaining unfinished and "unreconstructed."

In this regard, when Foner asserts that we have not yet "come to terms with the implications of emancipation and the political and social agenda of Reconstruction," this familiar lament of failed Reconstruction — though an accurate diagnosis of the continuing legacy of racism and social inequality — also denies the interminability of the work of mourning that, as Derrida insists, "is not one kind of work among other possible kinds."[21] For Derrida, the work of mourning lacks any metalanguage by which we might distinguish it from other forms of work. *All* work is mourning in the sense that a machine (or body) works "at such and such an energy level" until death (143). Mourning names the force or energy that propels all labor. Work *works* on the principle of mourning. If, as we saw in the Introduction, "I am" always implies that "I am mortal," then my body is always already laboring toward its death.[22] Moreover, the relation of appropriation that opens between myself and others presages my "future" absence by effecting a certain loss of corporeal autonomy and freedom. That "my" body is never fully mine means that I am in some sense absent to myself from the very beginning. Thus, when Hartman suggests that the unfinished work of Reconstruction lies in the future emancipation of a "burdened subject no longer enslaved, but not yet free," this reassertion of the liberal subject also registers a disavowal of mourning, of the corporeal self-dispossession that conditions any relation to alterity (206).

This originary mourning of "my" body is allegorized by Maupassant's short story *En Mer*, which tells of a young sailor who loses his arm in a fishing-boat accident only to discover that he is unable to let go of the arm. Although his older brother instructs him to cast the amputated limb into the sea, Javel refuses, examines the arm sadly, and gives it to his fellow sailors who pass it among themselves. They finally decide to preserve the arm in a barrel of ice marked with a cross. When the sailor returns home, his wife and children repeat the gesture of examining the arm, passing it among themselves, before placing it in a tiny coffin. The tale thus concludes with the final interment of the detached arm. If Javel refuses to let go of his arm, however, that refusal is marked from the beginning by an originary otherness of his body that the amputation only literalizes. We might read the retention of the arm and its circulation among the community of sailors as dramatizing the failure of mourning. Yet their fascination with the lost appendage betrays the possibility that their bodies, their hands, and their arms are already in some sense other. Indeed, only by becoming physically other does Javel's arm become available to grasp as his own. As Javel asserts to his older brother: "It belongs to me, does it not, since it is my arm."[23] The arm becomes "his" at the very moment when he holds it in his remaining hand as something other. Its phantasmatic return to him in the present is allegorized by the linguistic chain that links the present, the now, to the *main-tenant:* literally "holding in hand." To hold on to one's lost appendage is to fantasize the convergence of the present with one's body, *la main* with the *maintenant*, notwithstanding any temporal discontinuity between the two.

The finite character of "my" body is thus anticipated in the becoming other of this body. This originary loss and absence of "my" body in its coming to inhabit the other — its coming to live in and as the other — marks that body from the beginning as available to the possibility of its death. As Anne Cheng notes in her reading of Maupassant's novella, the gangrenous arm (which she reminds us was synonymous with "mortification" prior to the invention of antibiotics) "literalizes an embrace of the morbid."[24] Contesting the Freudian paradigm of "successful mourning," Cheng argues that "the story tells of young Javel's success in *not* abandoning his arm" (98, her emphasis). She goes on to propose that the circulation of the mortified arm among Javel's ship mates and family asks us to consider "how a community might be constituted and imagined through a kind of *enlivening morbidity*" (99). To claim, however, that Javel is "successful" in his failure to mourn is still to assume that the arm is *his* prior to its physical loss. That mourning is unsuccessful is confirmed not so much by the retention of the arm as by its return as absent, as always already detached and lost. Mourning, in other words, is not occasioned by the physical loss of one's body, or part of one's body, or (to return to the subject of slavery) by the loss of one's corporeal autonomy; rather, mourning signals an originary loss inherent to all bodies. And this constitutive loss is no less true for the slave master, whose "social life" is produced through the disavowal and projection of his mortality onto the slave. The master's refusal to labor, then, must also be read as a denial of how *all* bodies work (on mourning). If all work is a sign of mortality, then one who does not labor does not die. Indeed, the master's corporeal denial occasions his phantasmatic transformation into "spirit," a universal subject immune to the body's mortality.

Resistance emerges in *The Conjure Woman* from within the terms of a spectral corporeality, one in which the exchangeability of the body occasions both its appropriation — *as* difference reduced to identity — and the contestation of that very reduction. This refusal of identity, this spatiotemporal deferral of the slave body's final transformation into the body of the master, resists the restricted economy of the master/slave relation.[25] According to Butler's rewriting of Hegel in terms of the body, the master/slave dialectic institutes a coerced exchange in which the master forces the slave to be his body for him, "but be it in such a way that the lord forgets or disavows his own activity in producing the bondsman" (35). Butler further notes that "this forgetting involves a clever trick" in which the master commands the slave: "You be my body for me, but do not let me know that the body you are is my body." Butler's use of the term "trick" to designate this transmogrification of the slave's body into the body of the master echoes Robert Bone's suggestion that "slavery is itself an act of conjuration," indeed, a "magic trick" of sorts by which the master takes possession of the slave's body, forces the slave to labor for him, and thus, in some sense, forces the slave to be the laboring body that the master refuses to be (89). Slavery thus performs a certain transmogrification of the slave's body. Whether into a mule, a tree, a grapevine or a ghost, such transformations invite us to read slavery as a "form of witchcraft in which one man takes possession of the body of another and uses it for his own purposes" (Bone 92).

Butler's rewriting of the master/slave dialectic, however, invokes a certain spectralization of the body only to conjure it away by remaining fully within the terms of Hegel's restricted economy. Insofar as the master takes possession of body of the slave and demands that the latter "be" his body, the slave would appear to become possessed by the master's body. Giving up his body to the slave, the master himself becomes a kind of ghost. But to the extent that the master reanimates his body by suppressing that of the slave, the master reassumes his bodily life through that suppression. Butler notes that "if the suppression of the body is itself an instrumental move of and by the body, then *the body* is inadvertently preserved in and by the instrument of its suppression" (57, my emphasis). That is to say that the body suppresses the body. From within the fiction of this restricted economy, the master's disavowed body returns as his own body, whereas the materiality of the slave's body remains bound to the terms of a contract that requires that he forfeit all claims to his bodily life. The return of the body to the master is conditioned by the fiction of bodily possession whereby the master paradoxically preserves his corporeality through the very movement of negation. Although both the body of the master and that of the slave are in some sense preserved, the terms of this preservation are not reciprocal: the master's body is fantasized as returning to itself, whereas the slave's body is dematerialized precisely as a consequence of this return.

To the extent that the chapter on "Lordship and Bondage" in Hegel's *Phenomenology* describes for us a dialectical reversal whereby the slave in some sense "becomes" the master, such becoming is always provisional, indeed, circumscribed by a set of inversions through which the slave as such is never fully materialized, but only made to move back and forth in that liminal space between embodiment and disembodiment. In this sense, the restricted economy of the master/slave dialectic determines that the body of the slave always matters either too much or too little, that the slave is figured as both all and no body. To claim that the materialization of the slave is provisional, then, is not to naturalize the servitude of the slave; for the very naturalization of servitude thwarts any attempt to reanimate the socially dead from within the terms of the master/slave dialectic. Such reanimation requires a displacement of the dialectic, not a temporary reversal within its own logic. Butler's insertion of the body into Hegel's dialectic of Spirit can only show us how a restricted economy proceeds by way of negating or affirming the body in an endless circuit of dematerialization and rematerialization. To what extent does this preservation of the body prevent us from imagining new life forms that exceed the boundaries of the corporeal? How might we move beyond the polarization of body versus spirit toward the alternative life form of the specter?

Chesnutt's tales of "The Goophered Grapevine," "Mars Jeems's Nightmare," and "Po' Sandy" all foreground the provisionality of such an internal dialectical reversal. Indeed, they explore both the potential and limitation of the slaves' attempts to intervene in the master's refusal to recognize slave kinship relations. In Julius's stories, that is, conjurers are most often called upon to resist the master's violent negation of bonds between slaves. Conjure emerges, then, as a means by which slaves might counter their social death. Chesnutt's fictional tales thus reflect the historical role that conjure played in plantation life as a mode of resistance to the master's domination.[26] Such acts of intervention range from turning a slave into a tree to prevent him from being torn away from his wife ("Po' Sandy") to temporarily turning a master into a slave because he refuses to allow his slaves to marry ("Mars Jeems's Nightmare").

While conjure is most often employed by slaves, in "The Goophered Grapevine" Mars Dugal McAdoo calls on the resources of a conjure woman named Aunt Peggy to prevent his slaves from eating grapes off his vines. Aunt Peggy "goophers" the vines so that "w'at eat dem grapes 'ud be sho to die inside'n twel' mont's" (37). Unaware of Aunt Peggy's conjure, Henry, a stray slave from the next plantation, stumbles across the vineyard and eats some of McAdoo's grapes. Because he is ignorant of the goopher, however, Aunt Peggy takes pity on Henry and gives him a potion to stave off the effects of the conjure until the following spring. At that time, Aunt Peggy instructs Henry to apply sap from the vines to his bald head every year so that the goopher will continue to have no effect on him. Henry follows her advice, only to discover that grapes have begun to grow out of the top of his head. Indistinguishable from the crop that he grows and harvests, Henry becomes inextricably tied to the seasonal changes in the vines; when the vines are bare, Henry becomes just as bald as he was before, and when the vines begin to bear fruit the following spring, grapes shoot out of his head once again. Ever the opportunist, Mars McAdoo sees how spry Henry acts every spring and decides that he would make more money off him if he sold him for fifteen-hundred dollars and bought him back for five-hundred in the fall when Henry, like the vines that he has become, begins to whither away. The next year, however, a

"Yankee" convinces McAdoo that he can make the vines bear twice as many grapes if he follows his techniques. But when the Yankee cuts too close to the vines, the grapes, and thus Henry, wither away and die.

For Robert Bone, the allegory of "The Goophered Grapevine" lies in its

> lesson in the economics of slavery. The slaves were in fact worth more in the spring, with the growing season still to come; in the fall prices declined, for an owner was responsible for supporting his slaves through the unproductive winter season. These fluctuations in price underscore the slave's status as *commodity*, his helpless dependence on the impersonal forces of the market. (85)

Indeed, the metonymic relation that obtains between Henry and the grapevines affirms Marx's claim that the commodity represents the congelation of labor. Given this metonymic relation between labor and commodity, whatever becomes of the commodity becomes of the labor that produced it. If the commodity becomes an exchange-value and is thus abstracted of its use-value, so too does the worker whose labor is embodied in the commodity. In "The Goophered Grapevine," the fluctuations in the value of the grapes produce an attendant effect on Henry's body. His body withers away every fall only to resurrect itself every spring. Henry's annual "return from the dead" asks to be read within the terms of the restricted economy of slavery, which can only negate and preserve the body of the slave in an endless cycle of death and resurrection. This economy ultimately leads to a negation of Henry's body from which he can never recover. What remains of Henry? Nothing, that is, from within the terms of this economy that "exhaust[s] itself to appropriate every negativity."[27] Mars Dugal gets the vineyard up and running within a year's time and thus the economy of slavery is restored. If there is some trace of Henry, some remainder, we might look for it in the figure of Julius who, by telling Henry's story, produces a discursive excess that cannot be assimilated into the economic system of slavery. Henry *remains* in the figure of Julius, of an ostensibly "free-laborer" who is "attached" to the plantation, but in a prosthetic manner irreducible to the insidious means by which Henry becomes identical with it. Denying Julius's proprietary claim to the vineyard, however, John attempts to reinsert Julius into the economy of (un)free labor by employing the latter as his coachman. Julius may not succeed in maintaining the vineyard as his own, but he does win other, smaller victories by telling his stories. "Mars Jeems's Nightmare," Julius's story about the devastating consequences of a slave master's excessive violence, convinces Annie to allow Julius's grandson Tom, who John thinks is lazy and careless, to continue in their employment. And in "Po' Sandy," Julius's tale of the haunted timber scares Annie away from having the schoolhouse torn down in order to use the wood in the construction of a new kitchen. Julius thus secures a venue in which his church can hold its meetings. These admittedly nonheroic victories nonetheless accomplish for Julius the articulation of a prosthetic relation between John and himself whereby the presumption that Julius is *merely* an extension of the land, or of John's own body, is repeatedly contested.

While "The Goophered Grapevine" shows the devastating effects of the restricted economy of slavery, which allows for nothing to escape its reduction of the other to the same, "Mars Jeems's Nightmare" explores both the potential and limitation of slave conjuring as a form of resistance. "Mars Jeems's Nightmare" tells the story of a slave master who, refusing to allow his slaves to marry, sells one of his female slaves (unnamed in the tale) to another plantation far away from her lover, Solomon. Solomon then turns to Aunt Peggy and asks her to conjure Mars Jeems. Aunt Peggy puts together a "goopher mixtry" and tells Solomon to ask the cook at the "big house" to put it in "Mars Jeems's soup de fus cloudy day she hab okra soup fer dinnah" (60). The next day Mars Jeems leaves the plantation to take care of some business, leaving the overseer in charge. Soon after, Mars Dunkin McSwayne shows up at the plantation with a "stray nigger," and asks the overseer, Mars Johnson, to break him in. Resistant to Johnson's attempts to break him in, the slave is sent back to Mars Dunkin McSwayne who decides to sell the would-be slave down the river. Before the slave can be sold, however, Aunt Peggy intervenes once again with her goopher mixtry. She tells Solomon to go find the slave and feed him a "sweet'n 'tater" while he is sleeping. The next day, Solomon runs into a poor, raggedy dressed white man who, on closer inspection, turns out to be Mars Jeems. Although Mars Jeems tells Solomon that he had a horrible nightmare and that a man robbed him and swapped his clothes, at the end of the tale we find out that the nightmare to which he refers was in fact the effect of Aunt Peggy's goopher that turned him into the resistant slave that Mars Johnson almost sent down the river.

If Mars Jeems's brief stint as a slave bespeaks the provisionality of the Hegelian dialectical reversal, then it also works to naturalize black servitude. Indeed, Jeems's lingering whiteness prevents him from being broken in by slavery: "He didn' mix' wid ner talk much ter res' er de niggers, en couldn' 'pear ter git it th'oo his min' dat he wuz a slabe en had ter wuk an min' de w'ite folks, spite er de fac' dat Ole Nick gun 'im a lesson eve'y day" (62). Mars Jeems's resistance to becoming a slave recalls the concluding dialogue between Delano and Don Benito in Melville's "Benito Cereno" in which "again and again it was repeated how hard it had been to enact the part forced on the Spaniard by Babo."[28] The overall moral of Chesnutt's story would appear to be that, despite such temporary reversals, the master is still the master and the slave is still a slave.

Although Mars Jeems's life as a slave is short lived, indeed, only a "nightmare" from which he eventually awakes, the conclusion of the tale would have us believe that Aunt Peggy's goopher was at least successful both in making him a kinder, gentler master, and in countering his refusal to allow his slaves to marry. Indeed, Mars Jeems sends for Solomon's "junesey," and the "niggers... tuk ter sweethea'tin en juneseyin' en singin' en dancin', en eight er ten couples got married" (68). And yet, any social transformation that Mars Jeems's nightmare might have engendered is immediately undercut by this stock plantation-tradition image of the "happy darkies." The very improbability of such a transformation in Mars Jeems obscures the violence of his earlier refusal to recognize kinship relations among his slaves, making such an easy reanimation of the socially dead — like Aunt Peggy's "sweet'n' 'tater" — difficult to swallow.

The transformation of the slave back into Mars Jeems by the means of a goophered "sweet'n' 'tater" is particularly interesting in terms of how Aunt Peggy's conjuring both resists the master's act of conjuring that produces the socially dead slave body and yet finds itself in some sense mirroring its racist imaginary. After instructing Solomon to find the slave and make him eat the "sweet'n' 'tater," Aunt Peggy sprinkles him with a mixture that makes him invisible to the white "patteroles." Although the white "patteroles" cannot see Solomon, Aunt Peggy's goopher allows him to see in the dark: "De nigger couldn' see 'im, ob co'se, en he couldn' 'a' seed de nigger in de da'k, ef it hadn' be'n fer de stuff Aun' Peggy gun 'im ter rub on 'is eyes" (64). While the slave ostensibly cannot see Solomon in the dark because he lacks Aunt Peggy's power of conjure, we might also read the slave's/Mars Jeems's inability to see Solomon in terms of the familiar racist trope of the "spook," a cognate of the Dutch term whose English usage can be traced to 1801.[29] Although the racial connotations of the term appear not to have emerged until the mid-twentieth century, this more contemporary usage articulates a ghostliness already implicit in the institution of slavery. If the slave cannot see Solomon, perhaps that is because he is, after all, still seeing through Mars Jeems's white, racist vision, eyes that see blacks as either all or no body — as either "body" or "spook."

Although Aunt Peggy's goopher makes Solomon invisible, and in that way appears at first to conform to the slave master's conjuration that both negates and preserves black bodies, his invisibility is intended to work as a mode of resistance by which he can stealthily goopher the slave, and thus, change him back into the new-and-improved slave master. But this final goopher that Aunt Peggy works on Mars Jeems performs the recuperative gesture by which he reassumes his bodily life as slave master. The restoration of the master/slave dialectic is thus made possible once Aunt Peggy's conjuring begins to shadow the racist imaginary of the master's own acts of conjuration. As competing modes of phantasmatic power, then, the masters' and the slaves' acts of conjuration are not necessarily opposed in Chesnutt's tales. That is, despite the final image of the "happy darkies" that the tale would have us read as signaling the restoration of slave kinship relations, it is less the body of the slave than that of the master that gets reanimated. Given the well-known politics surrounding the publishing of Chesnutt's tales — that is, the fact that Chesnutt (who was light skinned) could and effectively did pass as white when his publishers withheld his racial identity from the public — we might well pause to consider how Chesnutt's tales might be read as in part a product of a white imagination.[30] Conjure risks, in Chesnutt's hands, being assimilated to the insidious institution that goophers the black body into slavery. And yet, to the extent that Chesnutt's stories of transmogrification expose the final transformation of the black body into a mule, a tree, a grapevine, or a ghost as nothing less than a ruse, his tales are not finally reducible to the projection of a white imaginary. Indeed, while "Mars Jeems's Nightmare" allegorizes the provisionality of the master/slave reversal, the tales as a whole also reveal the failure of the institution of slavery to fully transmogrify the black body. Chesnutt's tales betray the institution's own acts of conjuration that insistently negate and preserve black bodies.

Sentient Specters

This failure to transform fully the black body into the laboring body that the master refuses to be is allegorized in Chesnutt's "Po' Sandy," a conjure tale about an eponymous slave who is shuttled back and forth between different plantations, until finally his "junesey," Tenie, turns him into a tree so that he will not have to move anymore. Tenie then promises to turn the two of them into foxes so they can escape the plantation, but before she can accomplish the transformation, Sandy is chopped down. After Sandy's body is made into timber, his master uses the timber to construct a new kitchen. Upon discovering that his new kitchen is haunted, the slave master takes the kitchen apart and uses the timber to build a schoolhouse. The frame story picks up at this point when John's wife Annie asks him to build her a new kitchen. Deciding to tear down the old schoolhouse, John takes the lumber to the sawmill, at which point Julius tells John Sandy's story.

The violent act of cutting down the tree sets in motion a complex series of transformations in which the materiality of Sandy's body is repeatedly negotiated. Such transformations of Sandy's body follow from Tenie's initial conjuration of Sandy into a tree. In this sense, the transmogrifications of Sandy subsequently performed by his master ask to be read as themselves acts of conjuring, transformations that violently recuperate Tenie's original intention to employ conjure as a means of resistance to Mars Marrabo's negation of slave kinship relations. Sandy thus does not escape slavery as he and Tenie had planned, but becomes a material part of the plantation. Indissoluble from the materiality of Mars Marrabo's plantation kitchen, however, Sandy manages in some sense to reverse the proprietary terms of the master/slave relation. Although Mars Marrabo appears to achieve the ultimate means by which he can possess his slave, he is less in possession of Sandy than he is possessed by him.

When Sandy haunts his master's kitchen, he performs an act of resistance to the slave master's conjuration that resonates with what Teresa Goddu aptly refers to as "haunting back."[31] For Goddu, such haunting back involves a rematerialization of the "ghosts of America's racial history." Dematerialized by slavery, and by extension, those sometimes "sensationalist" aspects of Gothic accounts of slavery, slaves such as Stowe's Cassy in *Uncle Tom's Cabin,* according to Goddu, manage to resist the terms by which the Gothic "dematerializes" history. These supposedly dematerializing effects of the Gothic would thus appear to mirror the institution of slavery that dematerializes slaves and thereby produces them as figures of ghostliness. Goddu's argument that the Gothic tends to dematerialize history assumes, however, that the problem with both the Gothic and the institution of slavery lies only in their respective tendencies toward dematerialization, when, as we have seen, slavery does not simply negate or dematerialize the bodies of slaves, but also preserves them, if only so they can be reassimilated back into its restricted economy. In short, Goddu "forgets" that slaves are always constructed as both all and no body, which means that recourse to their materialization is far less insurrectionary than it might seem. Sandy's "haunting back," on the contrary, charts less a move from dematerialization to rematerialization than a spectralization that is unsettling precisely because it marks a return "not to the living body," but to "*a prosthetic body, a ghost of spirit.*"[32] Becoming a ghost, Sandy reconfigures the terms by which Mars Marrabo renders him "socially dead." That is, Sandy's "haunting back" effectively resignifies the trope of social death, such that his ghostliness transforms itself from an effect of the master's conjuration to an act of revenge and terrorization of the master and his family.

Sandy's spectral resistance thus involves what Derrida understands as a "paradoxical incorporation" that refuses any return to the body *as* presence: "For there is no ghost, there is never any becoming-specter of the spirit without at least an appearance of flesh" (*Specters,* 202). In this sense, spectrality names a surplus of materiality that is not reducible to a "body." If Sandy manages to terrorize his master's family from beyond the grave, such "haunting back" suggests that Sandy is never fully transformed into Mars Marrado's property, indeed, that there is a surplus of Sandy irreducible to the violent, re(de)materializing effects of slavery. Although Sandy's body is transformed into the timber with which his master constructs his new kitchen, the materiality of his body persists even after it has become wood. Sandy's body does not become "wooden" in the sense of being without feeling, insentient.

On the contrary, the wood moans and groans as "the circular saw... eat[s] its way through the log," and the plantation family hears groaning noises coming from the timber after it has been used to construct the kitchen (45). Still capable of feeling pain, the wood has failed to become strictly timber. Indeed, the material traces of Sandy's body cannot fully be erased either after Tenie turns him into a tree and Sandy endures the painful pecks of a woodpecker, or when he receives scars after one of Mars Marrabo's slaves taps the tree for turpentine, or even later when he is finally cut down and made into the master's kitchen. This wood that still feels pain continues to bear the material traces of the slave master's violence.

In this way, the transmogrification of Sandy's body into wood resignifies the trope of "woodenness" or "thingliness" beyond the slave master's disavowal of black pain, even as this transformation allegorizes the denial of black sentience that effectively provides an alibi for the master's violence. The replaceability and interchangeability of the tree, the timber, and Sandy would appear to underscore what Hartman refers to as the "fungibility" of the slave body — that is, the function of the black body as a commodity, a "dispossessed body" that is "the surrogate for the master's body since it guarantees his disembodied universality and acts as the sign of his power and dominion" (21). Hartman's notion of slave fungibility echoes Butler's claim that the master/slave relation involves the substitution of the slave's body for that of the master. Transformed into the disavowed body of the master, the slave is temporarily materialized. Yet, while being the body of the master would appear to materialize the slave body, if only by proxy, the "materiality of suffering regularly eludes (re)cognition by virtue" of the slave body's replaceability (21).

That Sandy-as-wood remains sentient despite his uncontainability raises the question of whether the affirmation of the slave as a sentient being requires the assertion of the slave's corporeality. Consider that as an exemplary ingredient, wood can compose many things. But its participation in the construction of things does not "contain" wood in the same way that we might conventionally think of the body as a container, as in both the Platonic and Christian conception of the body as the container of the soul. In this way, Sandy's return as wood recalls the Greek *hyle,* which signifies both wood — or more specifically, timber — and more generally the category of matter. Sandy's ghostly return in and as wood figures his materiality — by virtue of its participation in the infinitely transformable material of wood — as that which cannot be contained by a body. While Hartman's argument about slave fungibility recalls Marx's claim that exchange-value is synonymous with alienation and expropriation, Sandy's capacity to feel pain despite his exchangeability — despite his having no body in the proper sense — asks us to reconsider the conventional materialist claim that understands exchange-value only in terms of estrangement. Does being an exchange-value necessarily entail alienation and expropriation? As we see in the case of Sandy, the exchangeability of the laboring body can lead both to a violent appropriation and a powerful resistance. Only on the condition of his exchangeability does Sandy amass the phantasmatic agency to haunt back, to resist his social death. Only as a specter can Sandy resist the terms by which the master/slave dialectic figures him as either all or no body. For if the "thingliness" of the slave is produced by maintaining a rigid distinction between the material and the immaterial, then when does the materialist insistence on the corporeality of the laboring body reproduce, despite its aims to the contrary, the logic that reduces the slave to the status of mere thing?[33]

As Orlando Patterson reminds us, the Roman doctrine of absolute property affirmed that only material things could be objects of property, a determination that in turn conditioned the designation of the slave as thing. Marx's distinction between use-value and exchange-value in the opening pages of *Capital* is exemplary of how the rigid determination of the material over and against the immaterial reasserts itself even as Marx begins to uncover the phantasmatic quality of the commodity. Although he goes to great lengths to show how the laborer is a "corporeal, living, real, sensuous" being, his effort to affirm the materiality of labor inadvertently mimes the strict demarcation between the corporeal and the incorporeal that affirms the slave's thingliness.[34] Marx's formulation whereby what is done to the commodity is also necessarily done to the laborer who produces it sets up a kind of chiasmatic relation between labor and commodity, one in which the abstraction of use-value is understood as strangely acting upon the one who produced the object. If exchange-value "represents human labour in the abstract," to abstract the use-value of a thing — to turn it into ghostly nothing — is effectively to turn the laborer into a kind of ghost (*Capital*, 310).

Critiquing the alienation that attends the production of commodities, Marx gives the example of a coat and ten yards of linen, in which the value of the former is set at twice that of the latter. If the value of the coat is double that of the linen, then twenty yards of linen would equal one coat: "So far as they are values, the coat and the linen are things of a like substance, objective expressions of essentially identical labor" (*Capital*, 310). But tailoring and weaving, as Marx immediately points out, are different kinds of labor. As Marx sees it, the transformation of these use-values into exchange-values erases the qualitative differences in their respective labor. As exchange-values, the coat and the linen become "mere homogeneous congelations of undifferentiated labor" (*Capital*, 311). To erase the differences between the labor that is embodied in different objects is to dematerialize commodities. It is this "coarse materiality" that Marx wants to save from idealist abstractions of exchange-value, in which "not an atom of matter enters into [their] composition" (*Capital*, 313). How are we to understand this chiasmatic relation that Marx theorizes between the commodity and labor alongside his other claim that both the substance of each use-value and the labor expended in the production of each object are fundamentally different? That is, insofar as the abstraction of the commodity abstracts the labor embodied in the commodity by extension, the substantive integrity of labor and commodity is called into question. Although Marx argues that the becoming exchange-value of the commodity dematerializes both the thing and the labor that produced it — finally estranging the laborer's body from himself — if the commodity, labor, and the laboring body are related in this phantasmatic way, then they become — within the terms of Marx's own argument — fundamentally ghostly things. It is precisely this ghostliness, pace Marx, that always already haunts the use-value of the commodity.

In the opening lines of *Capital*, Marx writes that "to discover the various uses of things is the work of history" (303). It is this thingliness that Marx wants to affirm in the commodity. If the commodity and the laborer haunt one another within the terms of their chiasmatic relation, then the exorcism of exchange-value is crucial to the affirmation of the laborer as a corporeal being. But given this phantasmatic relationship that obtains between the laboring body and the commodity, together with the consequential blurring of the demarcation between use-value and exchange-value, can we any longer seek recourse to the materiality of the commodity in order to affirm the laborer as a living, corporeal being? And does not Marx's insistence that the use-value is "not a thing of air," that it is a "material thing," finally construe the laboring body as thingly by extension (*Capital*, 303)?[35] For this is a body that materializes in relation to the production of the commodity *as* use-value and dematerializes in relation to the becoming ghostly of the commodity as exchange-value. If the laboring body *is* whatever becomes of the commodity, then it follows that Marx's own affirmation of the object's "thingliness" inadvertently confers a certain thingly status to the laboring body. Moreover, Marx's claim that the dematerialization of the laboring body follows *only* on the occasion of the abstraction of the commodity denies the chiasmatic relation that he theorizes between the commodity and labor by reasserting the material integrity that the chiasmus calls into question.

Marx's well-known example of a certain wooden table in this same passage from *Capital* recalls the magical conjurations of Sandy, and in a manner that inadvertently deconstructs the strict opposition between use-value and exchange-value. Despite its transformation into a table, the wood out of which the table is constructed, according to Marx, continues to be wood, "a common, every-day thing, wood" (320). But once it "steps forth as a commodity, it changes into something transcendent. It not only stands with its feet on the ground, but, in relation to all other commodities, it stands on its head, and evolves out of its wooden brain grotesque ideas, far more wonderful than 'table-turning' ever was" (320). In the German, there is no explicit reference to "table turning" or conjuring (although the Moore/Aveling translation cited here captures the reference to nineteenth-century spiritualism that is only implied by Marx's figure of the dancing table). The phrase that their translation renders here as "far more wonderful than 'table-turning' ever was" is given in the original as "viel wunderlicher, als wenn er aus freien Stücken zu tanzen begänne" [more wonderful than if it had begun to dance of its own free will].[36] The phrase *aus freien Stücken* — literally, "out of free pieces" — suggests that the coming together of the table is conditioned by a certain imprisoning effect, one that contains a more disparate, "free" materiality. These "free pieces" recall Sandy's materiality, which becomes scattered and dispersed by virtue of its uncontainability. If "aus freien Stücken" suggests that the table dances because it comes together from disparate parts, the translation of Marx's dancing table as "table turning" associates the commodity with a ghostliness that Marx very much wants to exorcise. For Marx, the becoming commodity of the thing is conditioned by a certain conjuring trick that transmogrifies the ordinary, everyday materiality of the thing into a ghost. And yet, as Derrida remarks of this passage in *Specters of Marx:*

> the said use-value of the said ordinary sensuous thing, simple *hyle*, the wood of the wooden table that Marx supposes has not yet begun to "dance" ... must indeed have been promised to iterability, to substitution, to exchange, to value, and taken the first step, however small, toward an idealization that permits one to identify it as the same throughout all possible repetitions.... If it is *not, presently,* use-value, and even if it is not *actually present,* it affects *in advance* the use-value of the wooden table. (254, 255, his emphasis)

Against Marx's effort to know the precise moment that the ghost arrives, Derrida maintains that it is always already there, and that Marx's effort to mark such a moment is itself an act of exorcism. Just as the ghostly return of Sandy as something other than a body calls into question the strict distinction between use-value and exchange-value in terms of the supposed alienation that inheres in the latter, the materiality of the table is never only and simply "wood," that is, if Marx means by this material ingredient something uncontaminated by the temporality of its subsequent idealizations. Like Sandy, the table is a specter prior to becoming a specter as such.

Kindred Possession

The denial of slave sentience was routinely made by insisting that Africans lacked any developed sense of consciousness. As Hegel asserts in a well-known passage from *The Philosophy of History,* "in negro life ... consciousness has not yet attained to any substantial objective existence.... We must lay aside all thought of reverence and morality — all that we call feeling — if we would rightly comprehend him."[37] Because they have no conception of any "higher Being," moreover, Africans possess "no knowledge of the immortality of the soul" (95). In this sense, Tom's steadfast belief in *Uncle Tom's Cabin* that he will be saved in the afterlife works to contest the notion that blacks are incapable of moral or religious reflection: "His bible seemed to him all of this life that remained, as well as the promise of a future one."[38] Tom's accession to Christianity, however, does little to challenge the ideology of the body-as-container that produces the slave as both all and no body. If the denial of slave consciousness makes the slave into nothing but an inert and insentient body, the belief in an afterworld utterly denies the slave's corporeality, and thus, the reality of slave pain: hence, Tom's assertion that Legree "an't done me no real harm, — only opened the gate of the kingdom of heaven for me" (591).[39]

Sandy's return, on the other hand, marks less a preservation of "the body" as a vessel of containment than a remaindering that exceeds the imprisoning effects of the body. The return of this uncontainable, spectral body deconstructs the Socratic notion of the body as container, a "prison" of the soul.[40] In colloquial English, to "give up the ghost" means not merely to die, but to release the immortal spirit or soul from its bodily container. In conventional usage, then, the trope of giving up the ghost is enabled by a certain idealism — Platonic, Christian, or Hegelian — that opposes absence and presence. To consider bodies as originarily spectral, however, is to understand their ghostliness as inhabiting a temporality otherwise than the linear progression of life *then* death.

In this way, Sandy's dismemberment recalls the preface to the *Phenomenology*, in which Hegel writes: "The life of Spirit is not the life that shrinks from death and keeps itself untouched by devastation, but rather the life that endures it and maintains itself in it. It wins its truth only when, *in utter dismemberment*, it finds itself" (19, my emphasis). We have remarked how Spirit always finds itself within the reflexivity of Hegel's dialectic. This return of Spirit to itself involves a "tarrying with the negative" that is but the precondition of Spirit's conversion into being (19). Miller's translation of the German *Zerrissenheit* as "dismemberment," moreover, suggests an odd corporealization of Spirit. For how exactly can a spirit become dismembered? *Zerrissenheit* can also be translated as "tearing" or "shredding," yet this shift away from the corporeality that "dismemberment" implies still leaves us with a certain materialization of Spirit. But if Spirit returns to itself by virtue of its dismemberment, Sandy's dismemberment affords no return to a body. Whereas negativity remains a resource for Spirit's return, Sandy's return leaves us with only the remains. These are the remains that

Tenie wants to ontologize, to make present, if only so she can explain to Sandy that she did not leave him "ter be chop' down en sawed up" (51).

While Sandy's body cannot be "reconstructed" into a containable whole, it manages to subvert those ideologies of containment that characterized antebellum slavery. His initial request of Tenie that she transform him into something immobile like a "tree, er a stump, er a rock, er sump'n w'at could stay on the plantation fer a w'ile" is profoundly ironic, given the mechanisms of control that worked to keep slaves in their place: spatially, hierarchically, and temporally (47). Slaves were prohibited from traveling without a pass, a regulation that emancipation saw thrown away almost instantly when blacks fled the plantations. Although whites often interpreted black mobility in the postbellum era as aimless wandering, Hartman notes that, for a population that had never seen freedom, "locomotion was definitive of personal liberty" (151). The question of containment versus mobility would reach all the way to the Supreme Court by 1896 in *Plessy v. Ferguson,* in which the debate over "separate but equal" would involve an effort to impede the migration of a man of one-eighth black blood to the other side of the color line, a prohibition of movement that marked, albeit in a different register, the central constitutional question of providing separate accommodations on locomotives for whites and blacks. As I will argue in chapter 3, the one-eighth rule worked to contain blackness, no matter how indiscernible, by anchoring itself in the conventional figure of the body-as-prison. The containment of the slave, however, is also legible temporally in the production of the slave as a "genealogical isolate," as Patterson puts it, severed both from his ancestors and his descendants (5). In this sense, Sandy *as* slave, "lives" only in the present. But his "presence," as it were, is one that bears no relation to the past or to the future. Sandy's "life" is a dead presence. The call to make the socially dead present thus misses how the socially dead are nothing but present, immobilized in time. Contesting the spatiotemporal containment of slavery, Sandy persists in the materiality of the plantation in such a way that his immobilization — both temporal *and* spatial — is refused. Recall that he is first transformed into the kitchen, then the schoolhouse, and finally almost becomes a kitchen again if it were not for Annie who, persuaded by Julius's story, allows Julius to hold church meetings in the schoolhouse. Sandy's exchangeability is thus double-edged: it confirms his status as commodity at the same time that it allegorizes an uncontainability that allows him to exceed his immobilization.[41]

Sandy's haunting, moreover, betrays what Hartman refers to as the "inadvertent, contingent, and submerged forms of contestation" that characterize slave resistance in the antebellum era (62). While Sandy's agency elucidates the "nonautonomy of the field of action," it does so at the price of being excluded from the "proper locus" of the political (61). This exclusion has the consequence, Hartman maintains, of recognizing only those practices of resistance that measure up against conventional notions of autonomy and agency. If, however, "the everyday practices of the enslaved occur... in the absence of the rights of man or the assurances of the self-possessed individual," then the barring of such contingent contestation effectively limits the recognition of slave resistance only to "heroic action and oppositional consciousness" (62).[41] As I remarked earlier, Hartman contests the assimilation of resistance to the paradigm of the autonomous self only to reinscribe it when she asks us to imagine the possibility of a slave body that is unimplicated in the body of the master — in short, a fundamentally nonprosthetic body that is fully separate from that of the master. In this sense, Hartman's insistence on *absolute* difference emerges as something like the corollary to Butler's logic of identity. If Butler inadvertently reduces the *différance* between and within bodies to the same, Hartman refuses this reduction only to reproduce a binary relation between master and slave.

Hartman's reinscription of the master/slave binary is particularly legible in her critique of white empathy. She maintains that empathy "is double-edged, for in making the other's suffering one's own, this suffering is occluded by the other's obliteration" (19). Hartman rightly argues that the substitution of oneself for the other involves a dialectics of "mutual recognition" that consumes and ultimately destroys the other. Discussing John Rankin's fantasy of his own enslavement, she writes: "Rankin begins to feel for himself rather than for those whom his exercise in imagination presumably is designed to reach" (19). But what finally determines the difference between feeling for oneself and feeling for the other? How can empathy proceed without some sort of incorporation that calls into question the difference between my body and the other's body? While Hartman suggests that it is Rankin's function as "proxy" that obliterates the other for whom he is trying to feel pain, how are we to imagine a relation between bodies in which "the body" of the other is not already different to itself both in terms of its noncontemporaneity with itself and in its coming into relation with the other/body? Hartman remarks that

> Empathic identification is complicated further by the fact that it cannot be extricated from the economy of chattel slavery *with which it is at odds,* for this projection of one's feeling upon or into the object of property and the phantasmatic slipping into captivity, while it is distinct from the pleasures of self-augmentation yielded by the ownership of the captive body and the expectations fostered therein, is nonetheless entangled with this economy and identification facilitated by a *kindred possession* or occupation of the captive body, albeit on a different register. (21, my emphasis)

Both empathy and slavery involve a "phantasmatic slipping" of one body into another. It is precisely this "kindred possession" that Hartman argues might ultimately be superceded, either as it appears in empathic identification or in the economy of slavery itself. Hartman appears to understand this kindred possession as obtaining only within the restricted economy of slavery that obliterates the other, against the possibility that this spectral inhabiting of one body in another is generalizable.

What is perhaps most striking about Hartman's argument is how the obliteration of slave sentience is assimilated both to the "hyperembodiedness" of the slave and to the "spectral character of suffering," the "ghostly presence of pain" (20). Caught between wanting to materialize black pain on the one hand, and refusing the "thingliness" of the slave on the other, Hartman's effort to articulate black sentience finds itself in much the same predicament as that of Wright's Bigger Thomas or Ellison's Invisible Man, both of whom understand that — within the terms of the racist imaginary — "body" and "spook" respectively are the only modes of being available to them. A consideration of bodies as always already spectral, however, would allow us to challenge the argument that equates the ghostliness of the commodity with estrangement and alienation, and thus enable us to envision alternative ways that the slave might be reanimated. Does the reanimation of the socially dead require their corporealization? Might "haunting back" rather necessitate a transformation from "spook" — that racist trope of pure disembodiment — to "specter," understood as neither spirit nor body, but as a surplus that comes up against the Hegelian sublation of master (body/spirit) versus slave (body/spook)?

One cannot think social death apart from the spectrality that estranges one's body from itself without reproducing liberal notions of autonomy, self-possession, and ultimately self-presence that preserve one's body through the obliteration of the other/body. The chiasmatic relation between bodies is not only the condition of slavery. For *my* body is always in some sense inhabited by the body of the other, and conversely. This inhabiting of one body in another, however, does not mean that the other is fully or finally incorporable. The other/body remains as an *un*incorporable, *un*assimilable ghost whose singularity exceeds my grasp and comprehension.

2

Beloved's Claim

> Slavery is cannibalism, not that of eating, but of selling human flesh and blood; one cuts the man up for food, and the other sells him for money.
>
>
> —John Jolliffe before Commissioner Pendery, *Garner Fugitive Slave Case*, 1856

> The moral question is thus not, nor has it ever been: should one eat or not eat...but since once must eat in any case...how for goodness sake should one eat well?
>
>
> —Jacques Derrida, "Eating Well"

What does it mean to claim one's children as property? When Sethe declares in Toni Morrison's *Beloved*, "she my daughter. She mine," what is the difference between *her* claim and the slave master's?[1] That is, how can we understand the relation between a maternal claim and a property claim other than in terms of simple opposition and contestation? And what of Beloved's claim, the claim of a ghost who reaches across time and space, trespassing the borders that separate the living and the dead? In the closing pages of the novel, Morrison writes: "Although she has claim, she is not claimed" (274). The grammar that allows one to *have* claim figures the claim as itself claimed. One not only claims one's due — whether what is due constitutes a slave master's abstract right to property or, in the case of Beloved, recognition and address (or perhaps redress) — but one claims one's claim. Prior to *what*

I claim, the claim itself must be mine. The *mineness* of the claim ensures that the claim always returns to me, as if to compensate in advance for the possibility of not having one's demand answered, indeed, for not getting what one claims. The mineness of the claim, then, describes the compensatory fantasy by which dispossession ceases to be dispossession, where absence and loss are always recuperated.

Dispossession, of course, is not only entangled with loss and mourning, but with the activities of exclusion and abjection as well. Indeed, Beloved's demand for recognition finds itself in tension with the will of a community that seeks to exorcise her, to "disremember" her. The women quit their claim on Beloved: they dismiss, release, or otherwise absolve themselves of it. For Morrison, disremembering names a process of incorporation by which the "chewing laughter swallow[s] [the other] all away" (274). To disremember is thus to *dismember*, indeed, to cut the other up into incorporable, digestible pieces. Yet, if we take the spectral other in only to disclaim or dispossess ourselves of it, what does it mean to say that a *ghost* has claim, that it claims us with an urgency prior to any claim that we might make on it? What is this strange sense of possession that emerges anterior to our claim, as if we do not so much possess our kin — as the vocabulary that permits one to say *my* daughter or *my* mother suggests — as we are possessed by them?

Certainly the conventional language of kinship does not suppose that one possesses one's children in the same way that a slave master owns his slaves. Kinship is not identical to slavery. Yet, as I noted in chapter 1, the conventional opposition of slavery and kinship tends to idealize the latter by insulating it from property relations. In her widely influential essay, "Mama's Baby, Papa's Maybe," Hortense Spillers claims that "kinship loses meaning" at the hands of slavery, "*since it can be invaded at any given and arbitrary moment by the property relations.*"[2] Like Patterson, Spillers preserves kinship as the sphere of positive affect, bloodlines, love, and connectedness. Although she shifts the terms of kinship away from the patrilineal focus of Patterson's theory of social death toward an exploration of the captive mother's relation to her offspring, Spillers does little to challenge the primacy of what David Schneider has called the "idiom of kinship," that is, the notion that blood ties constitute the privileged domain of social belonging.[3] Kinship becomes the foil to the violent negativity of the master/slave dialectic, notwithstanding the possibility that kinship, both paternal *and* maternal, might be implicated in that very negativity. While it may be true that kinship has the potential to undermine the institution of slavery insofar as the recognition of slave kinship would affirm that one's offspring "'belong' to a mother and a father" (75) and not to the slave master, what are we to make of this displacement of one set of property relations for another? Although the property relations that obtain between parent and offspring and those between master and slave are certainly not equivalent, they are both property relations nonetheless. As legal scholar Barbara Bennett Woodhouse observes, "our culture makes assumptions about children deeply analogous to those it adopts in thinking about property."[4] Indeed, parental "rights" have historically been upheld under the rubric of the Fourteenth Amendment's guarantee of liberty. This ironic appeal to the constitutional protection of freedom to assert a property claim in one's children recalls the ideology of slavery whereby Southerners insisted on their "right" to own slaves. Although children are not considered property in a strictly legal sense (parents do not have the exclusive right to possess, use, transfer, or sell their children), the proximity of property and kinship claims requires that we resist the tendency to oppose slavery and kinship absolutely.

Challenging the kin/property opposition, historian Dylan Penningroth's *The Claims of Kinfolk* overturns the longstanding assumption that slaves were always objects rather than subjects of property. Penningroth details how American slaves made extralegal claims on material property that were customarily recognized not only by other slaves but by masters as well. Despite the absence of written documentation of ownership, former slaves were often successful in receiving compensation from the Southern Claims Commission for property that had been foraged by Union armies during the Civil War.[5] Both during and after slavery, moreover, black Americans articulated their kinship relations in and through property claims: "Part of property's value for slaves, apart from its capacity to be used or consumed, lay in the social relationships it embodied, ready to be called into action.... By bequeathing property, slaves over and over again defined not only *what* belonged to them but also *who*" (91). While Penningroth warns that we should not assume from the existence of such an informal economy of property ownership that slaves were not oppressed, his analysis opens the door for a consideration of the ethical implications of defining kinship through property. What does the intersection of property and kinship suggest about the violence of kinship? To what extent is the violence of appropriation not only a question of corporeal enslavement but of any relation to an other?

According to ethical philosopher Emmanuel Levinas, violence emerges in any dialectical relation in which the other is narcissistically reduced to the same. Against the entire Western philosophical tradition and its thought of being, Levinas locates ethics, and therefore the other, prior to ontology. For Levinas, "I" am always called *to* the other, to whom I am held hostage by an "unlimited responsibility," a responsibility that extends to the point of substituting myself for the other. Ontology promotes a dialectical relation to others that seeks to appropriate and come into possession of the other, and thus ultimately effaces the other's alterity. Echoing Sethe's claim, Beloved declares possession of Sethe in a way that would appear to fall squarely within this philosophy of the same: "I am Beloved and she [Sethe] is mine" (210). Indeed, what is perhaps most striking about Beloved's language is that it transforms the object of love — the beloved — into a subject that might claim to possess others: "I" am Sethe's or Denver's beloved, but also, I *am* Beloved. The reflexivity of her claim thus works to secure a certain self-presence that is in considerable tension with Beloved's spectral condition.

Despite its apparent possessiveness and ontological certainty, however, Beloved's claim does exhibit elements of a Levinasian ethics. For those whom she haunts are possessed by her prior to any acceptance of responsibility or obligation. Her claim is therefore consistent with Levinas's notion that ethics does not commence with a conscious decision, but with a responsibility anterior to my liberty, a "passivity more passive than all passivity."[6] Perhaps it is no accident, then, that the novel begins with an address — 124 — which is both a street address, and therefore the address *of* the ghost, and a call to address ourselves *to* the ghost: "124 was spiteful. Full of baby's venom" (3). The ghost comes first. From the beginning, we are held hostage to its demands, to its jealous desire to be loved. Commenting on the opening of her novel, Morrison remarks: "I wanted the sudden feeling of being snatched up and thrown into that house, precisely the way they [slaves] were."[7] We are thus urged to understand our reading in terms of being somehow enslaved to the other/ghost, and in a manner that recalls Levinas's notion that we have a responsibility to the other that precedes our freedom.

Levinas's claim, as it were, is undoubtedly rather hyperbolic in its affirmation of exteriority, of an absolute other that cannot be reduced to an object of my comprehension. For Levinas, the other *always* come first, as if the violence of ontology can only be countered through a language that marks a decisive rupture with that tradition: "Ontology as first philosophy is a philosophy of power."[8] Yet, if only a radical reversal of the primacy of being can affirm a nonegological relation to the other, such a claim tends to imagine the other as absolutely outside the same, notwithstanding the notion that appropriation might be both inevitable yet finally impossible.

It is precisely this originary violence that Derrida takes to be the condition of ethics. Despite Levinas's claim that the ethical relation to the other is a relation *without* relation, that is, a relation in which the other is absolutely other, and not other *than* me, Derrida observes in "Violence and Metaphysics" that "I" am also always the other of the other, which means that the same (the self) is always "other." Given that I am the other's other, the relation to alterity is conditioned by a certain violence that cannot but relate the other to me. For if I were to have no relation to the other, then alterity would be utterly effaced. In order that the other remain other, then, I must still relate that other to me, which means that alterity will always be haunted by the threat of trespass and violence. This "transcendental origin, as irreducible violence of the relation to the other, is at the same time non-violence since it opens the relation to the other."[9] In short, violence is necessary for ethics.

Derrida's interest in "Violence and Metaphysics" is to highlight those textual moments in which Levinas's tendency to oppose ethics to ontology inadvertently effaces the other. Despite Levinas's claim that ontology is solipsistic, his ethics of the other cannot help but be imagined in relation to the same. It is not that Derrida offers a vision of alterity that meets the Levinasian demand for an absolute other; rather, Derrida shows not only that such a demand can never be answered, but that the effort to realize it runs counter to ethics. If, for Levinas, the other is absolutely other, then for Derrida the other is *irreducibly other*, meaning that the other can never be fully reduced either to pure sameness or to pure otherness.

I want to suggest that something akin to this conflict between sameness and difference is played out in *Beloved*, insofar as it moves between a logic of solipsism and possession on the one hand, and an ethics of singularity on the other. 124 marks a site of violence: of Sethe's infanticidal act and of an angry baby ghost, but also of the originary violence that haunts any ethical relation to the other. This violence recalls the biblical story of Abraham and Isaac that Derrida reads in *The Gift of Death*. Abraham's sacrifice of Isaac to God (as absolutely other) requires that Abraham betray all others. "One cannot be responsible at once before the other and before the others, before the others of the other."[10] Derrida then generalizes that, as in Abraham's duty to God, every ethical obligation to an other necessitates that one be irresponsible with regard to all others. In language that resonates with Sethe's infanticidal act, Derrida remarks: "I offer a gift of death, I betray, I don't need to raise my knife over my son on Mount Moriah for that. Day and night, at every instant, on all the Mount Moriahs of this world, I am doing that, raising my knife over what I love and must love, over those to whom I owe absolute fidelity" (98). For Derrida, violence is not so much an aberration of kinship as it is the necessary condition of our fidelity to others.

As in the biblical sacrifice of Isaac, 124 marks a site where "pure ethics" and "pure violence" converge. Remarking on the contradiction inherent in such formulations, Derrida notes that "pure non-violence, non-relation of the same to the other (in the sense that Levinas understands it) is pure violence. Only a face can stop violence because only a face can first provoke it" (*L'Écriture,* 218). The so-called pure ethical relation to the other, the relation without relation in which the other emerges as pure exteriority, is pure violence. I am always cannibalizing the other, taking the other in, if only to find that the other finally resists any effort to incorporate it fully. Far from constituting an "ethical miscarriage," as Penelope Deutscher describes the view from the position (not hers) of pure-ethics, the incorporation of the other is both necessary yet not finally possible: something of the other remains beyond our grasp, which means that the incorporation of the other that conditions kinship always fails.[11] Yet this failure to incorporate the other, this failure to mourn fully, is also the sign of a certain respect for the alterity of the other.

One of the fundamental questions that *Beloved* raises is whether there can ever be a *pure* ethical relation to the other, that is, whether Sethe's maternal claim on Beloved might not in some way repeat the master's (paternal) violence that it seeks to prevent. While it is somewhat commonplace to speak of paternal violence — whether the subject is slavery or the Christian tradition of paternal self-reproduction through which the father/spirit preserves his immortality through the death/negation of the son — the normative vision of maternity tends to elevate the mother/child relation to an idealized field of ethical action. Given this idealization of motherhood, infanticide is most often read either as an unintelligible aberration from normative kinship, or as an act of pure love, in which case it is thought to be completely *intelligible*. In his *Modern Medea*, Steven Weisenburger observes that the infanticide committed by Margaret Garner, the historical figure on whom Morrison loosely based her character of Sethe, was "used in support of the most poisonous racist theory, or it was a tableau of the most divine mother love."[12] That infanticide could quickly be assimilated into the ripened image of slave animality is confirmed by Paul D's reaction to Sethe's revelation: "You got two feet, Sethe, not four" (165). Yet infanticide also could and was appropriated by the abolitionist movement to show the tragic ends to which slavery always led. As the headline from the Cincinnati *Gazette* of January 29, 1856, summarized it: "A Slave mother murders her child rather than see it returned to slavery."[13] Or as an anonymous poem put it in response to the events in Cincinnati: "The very love she bears her child/Has nerved her arm to deal the fatal blow" (Weisenburger, 246). Mary Livermore's poem, "The Slave Tragedy at Cincinnati," also affirms this sentiment: "Well I know no stronger yearning than a mother's love can be — ... Ay, my hand could ope the casket, and thy precious soul set free:/Better for thee death and Heaven than a life of slavery!"[14] These reactions represent more or less an interpretative consensus regarding Margaret Garner's act, and slave infanticide more generally, insofar as they read infanticide as an act of pure, motherly love.

The critical reception of *Beloved*, moreover, has done little to challenge the normative conception of motherly love. When Slavoj Žižek, for instance, argues that Sethe "kills her children *out of her very fidelity to them*," he exorcises maternal love of any specter of violence.[15] Sethe may indeed strike at herself with her act of infanticide, as Žižek maintains, but she also *makes a claim* on her child that returns that child *to her*. The murder *as claim* thus returns Beloved to Sethe in advance of this daughter's spectral return. In a similar vein, Homi Bhabha asserts that Sethe "regain[s] through the presence of the child, the property of her own person. This knowledge comes as a kind of self-love that is also the love of the 'other.'"[16] Bhabha then goes on to equate Sethe's act with "an ethical love in the Levinasian sense," attributing to Levinas a notion of self-love anathema to his philosophy as well as discounting the violence evinced by Sethe's act. As Yung-Hsing Wu observes, the critical reception of *Beloved* has tended to assume that "love is all that interpretation needs because it can comprehend the infanticide and render it understandable."[17] This uninterrogated concept of love understands Sethe's act only as an *effect* of the invasion of property relations into the domain of kinship rather than as a testament to the violence of love as such.[18]

The reflexivity of Sethe's act — which is both a striking at oneself, a negation of self, as well as a preservation of self — requires an interrogation of conventional notions of love and fidelity, especially as they pertain to motherhood. As Elizabeth Fox-Genovese observes, "all cultures have valued motherhood, but nineteenth-century bourgeois culture raised it to unprecedented heights of sentimentality."[19] Along with this sentimentality came the obligation to exclude violence from the normative view of motherhood, or in the case of Margaret Garner, to absorb the violence of her act into preconceived images of motherly love. Weisenburger argues that contemporary responses to Margaret Garner's child-murder most often missed her "absolute singularity" and

> persisted in seeing Margaret as a figure they already knew.... Far more imaginary than she ever was real... the infanticidal slave mother had by January 1856 become a potent icon signifying everything unnatural and unholy about the "peculiar institution." It was almost as if the icon had always awaited and demanded a Margaret Garner. (247)

The assimilation of Margaret to the already saturated image of the "good mother" subsumed slave infanticide under the cult of motherhood. Weisenburger also notes that the more recent "discovery" of Sudden Infant Death Syndrome (SIDS) and its higher prevalence among slave populations (largely due to poor diet and hygiene) casts doubt on the long-held belief that infanticide was widely practiced by slave mothers.[20] This revelation lends credence to the notion that the "imaginary" infanticidal slave mother fed the abolitionist cause by reinforcing the bourgeois image of motherhood.

With *Beloved*, Toni Morrison undoubtedly contributes to this imaginary construction of the infanticidal slave mother. As is well known, Morrison was inspired to write her novel after having come across an 1856 newspaper article detailing the basic facts of the murder. Morrison claims she did not do any more research into Margaret's life beyond reading the article because she "wanted to invent her life."[21] Although Morrison gives only passing attention to the historical details surrounding the case, she clearly grasps the larger political and legal implications involved — namely, the conflict between the Fugitive Slave Law of 1850 and the abolitionist effort to have Margaret tried for murder.[22] Since we know that Sethe does jail time for the murder, we can assume that the abolitionists won out over the supporters of the Fugitive Slave Law in Morrison's version. As Weisenburger shows, however, Margaret Garner's fate was far less happy. Despite the fact that the case marked the longest fugitive slave trial in American history — an astonishing four weeks — Margaret was finally remanded to slavery.[23]

Morrison thus imagines a triumph over the Fugitive Slave Law that should caution readers against the almost unanimous characterization of *Beloved* as a novel of historical recovery rather than of historical invention.[24] As Weisenburger reports, John Jolliffe, who argued the Garner case on behalf of the defendants, won only one fugitive slave case out of the eleven that he argued during the 1850s, a fact that further marks Sethe's story as anomalous (100). Morrison's effort to envisage what might have happened had Margaret *not* been returned to slavery suggests that *Beloved* conjures up a certain abolitionist spirit of divine motherly love. Indeed, Sethe tries to convince Beloved throughout much of the novel that "what she had done was right because it came from true love" (251). Sethe seeks to make her actions intelligible to Beloved and to the larger community that has made the former into a pariah, indeed, into a sign of abjection and unintelligibility. To consider her act of infanticide as either wholly unintelligible or fully intelligible, however, does little to trouble the normative equation of maternity with ethical nonviolence. While the conception of infanticide as an unintelligible aberration leaves the sphere of normative, white maternity untouched by negativity, so too does its assimilation to ethical love, insofar as it quickly cancels out any trace of violence. For racist ideologues, slave infanticide is further proof of an animality inherent in black motherhood: a propensity to violence from which white motherhood is exempt. For abolitionists, slave infanticide emerges both as proof of slavery's evils and of a mother's love for her children in the face of an institution that disregards slave kinship. If racist ideologues fail to comprehend slave infanticide because normative (white) maternity precludes the possibility of violence, abolitionists can claim to understand it fully only by disavowing the violence that is both the condition and limit of ethical action.

How do we begin to consider Sethe's act in such a way that it remains neither unintelligible nor fully intelligible? If to read is to make intelligible, and thus in some sense to own or possess what one reads (as in the colloquial expression, "what did you *get* from reading...?"), then reading will always reveal its own violence. We must begin, then, by avowing this violence as the condition of our reading. Beloved is no more *ours* than she is Sethe's. Yet, from the celebration of *Beloved* as a novel that bears witness to aspects of slave life "too horrible and too dangerous to recall," and that therefore allows readers to reclaim and come into possession of facts omitted from "official" histories, to Oprah Winfrey's purchase of the film rights to the novel, to the more recent claim made by an Ohio writer, Joanne Caputo, who believes that she is the child whom Margaret Garner murdered in 1856, now reincarnated — the reception of Morrison's novel and of Garner's child-murder is the history of this proprietorial violence.[25] This is not to say that one does violence to a text in the same way that one exercises violence over another person. Yet the asymmetry between interpretative violence and violence committed against another does not mean that there is no relation between these two registers. If there is a violence of reading, it lies in the reduction of the text, this *other* other, to the self: hence, Winfrey's rather narcissistic insistence that she not only own the rights to the film adaptation of *Beloved*, but star in it as well, that she might say, with Sethe, "Beloved, she my daughter. She mine."[26] A nonpossessive relation to the other, however, is what Sethe is given to learn when Beloved, her "best thing," evaporates and becomes "just weather" (275). While 124 Bluestone Road is quite literally haunted by the language of possession, "nonsensical" speech from which Stamp Paid can make out only the word "mine," it also thematizes a certain dispossession as the condition of kinship: I am always kin with someone who is going to die, and who is therefore never "mine" (172). Finitude defines kinship *as* alterity. *Our* kin are always in some sense Beloved from the start, marked by a loss and dispossession that is also the possibility of our kinship.

The following reflections seek to uncover the nexus of violence and ethics that the critical reception of *Beloved* has more or less failed to address. In connection with this critical oversight, I ask how the idealization of maternal love that *Beloved* constructs is redoubled by the novel's omission of miscegenation from the infanticidal scene. Although Margaret Garner was by all available accounts a mulatta, *Beloved* excludes the possibility of mixed-blood from Sethe's lineage. Rarely has the critical reception of *Beloved* made mention of this exclusion of miscegenation. One notable exception is Barbara Christian's "Beloved, She's Ours," where she observes how Morrison "eliminates" the "rationale" that Sethe may have been "striking out at the master/rapist" in order to resist "perpetuating the system of slavery through breeding" (41, 42). Christian goes on to note the ubiquity of miscegenation in the novel, but does not pursue the implications of its omission from Sethe's bloodline, that is, how its exclusion perpetuates the idealization of motherly love. Given that this idealization of maternity tends to ignore how "love," as Christian herself remarks, "can seek to own," it is striking that she does not connect the omission of miscegenation to Sethe's "thick love."[27] For this exclusion, I argue, further overdetermines the novel's often idealized conception of maternal love.

Sethe's Gift of Death

That infanticide hyperbolizes a violence inherent to kinship is suggested by Sethe's explanation for the murder: "If I hadn't killed her she would have died and that is something I could not bear to happen to her. When I explain it she'll understand, because she already understands everything already" (200). Sethe kills Beloved so that no one else might kill her. Although seemingly contradictory, Sethe's actions make sense as a form of resistance against the slave master's claim. To kill her own daughter is to claim that daughter as her own over and above the master's claim.

Killing thus becomes equated with claiming. But if to kill is to claim as one's own, then the reverse is also true: the claim of possession is always violent. As Fox-Genovese puts it, Sethe cuts her daughter's throat "to ensure that she could be a daughter — that Sethe could be a mother" (*Unspeakable*, 108). The terms of kinship are thus born of violence, which means that the violence of Sethe's claim is not opposed to the explanation that she gives Paul D: that she had to put her children "where they'd be safe" (164). Although Paul D is shocked by Sethe's talk "about safety with a handsaw," this seeming incongruity between love and violence is conditioned by the normative equation of motherhood and ethical purity (164). For Sethe's handsaw is not so much an expression of either aberrant violence or of pure motherly love as it is a reminder of the nonpure ethical relation that is motherhood. As Paul D ruminates: "More important than what Sethe had done was what she claimed" (165). *What* Sethe claims signifies not only her daughter, but also what she claims for her act of infanticide: namely, that it is an act of pure love. To Sethe's notion of pure love, Paul D counters that her love is "too thick" (164). Echoing the familiar trope that "blood is thicker than water," Paul D's characterization of Sethe's too-thick love figures that love as excessive, and implicitly connects this excessiveness to violence. Read next to the conventional configuration of blood and kinship whereby the "thickness" of blood relations marks them as superior to nonblood relations, Paul D's notion of a love that is too thick challenges the elevation of the blood relation to a higher ethical plane. Although Paul D goes on to link Sethe's claim to animality, and therefore seems to reinforce the racist doctrine of slave savagery, this seemingly aberrant animality also names the disavowed violence that haunts any relation between self and other. The black slave thus comes to embody the animality that normative whiteness must deny: "The screaming baboon lived under their own skin; the red gums were their own" (199). When Sethe responds to Paul D that "thin love ain't love at all," she reaffirms the equation of thick love with the blood relation, at the same time that she suggests that love — by virtue of its thickness — not only carries the threat of violence, but is conditioned by it (164). It is thanks to violence, to the always impure relation to the other, that we have love.

The violence of kinship is manifest in *Beloved* not only through the invocation of blood as a trope for kinship, but also in terms of the literal, material substance that Sethe sheds when she draws the knife across her daughter's throat. That this blood is then incorporated by Denver redoubles the metaphorics of the blood relation. The breast that nourishes Denver is literally covered in the blood of her sister, which suggests that if one sheds blood in order to share it, then "consanguinity" is always haunted by violence. Indeed, the fantasy of consanguinity, or having the same blood, is conditioned by a phantasmatic shedding and incorporation of the other's blood. In her interior monologue, Denver states: "BELOVED is my sister. I swallowed her blood right along with my mother's milk" (205). What is most striking about Denver's language is how the incorporation of Beloved's blood is said to affirm the bond between sisters. Would Beloved be Denver's sister if it were not for this incorporation? If Beloved is Denver's sister *because* Denver swallowed this sister's blood, then Beloved is a sister to the extent that she is incorporated as one. Biology is not enough. The dead sister must be taken in and made *hers*. The literal incorporation of blood affirms a metaphorics of blood precisely by drawing on the latter's figurative power. Thus, this literalization can only and always refer back to its metaphoricity. If incorporating the other were all that was required to claim someone as one's kin, then could we not claim anyone as our kin, regardless of biology? This is precisely the point to be gleaned from Denver's claim. The blood relation must be established apart from biology. The blood relation *is* a blood relation only to the extent that it is registered metaphorically. The literalization of the blood relation occasioned by the yoking of blood to biology obscures the metaphorics of blood. Blood is *never* biology. An *un*incorporated sister — a merely biological sister — is therefore no sister at all. And yet, to incorporate one's sister fully, to make her *mine*, is also finally to negate her.

While the explanations for Beloved's murder that Sethe gives Beloved and Paul D aim at making her actions intelligible, the narrator offers another version that resists intelligibility. It appears in the novel just prior to Sethe's disclosure to Paul D, and is figured as being anterior to the very possibility of explanation:

> Sethe knew that the circle she was making around the room, him, the subject, would remain one. That she could never close in, pin it down for anybody who had to ask. If they didn't get it right off — she could never explain. Because the truth was simple, not a drawn-out record of flowered shifts, tree cages, selfishness, ankle ropes and wells. Simple: she was squatting in the garden and when she saw them coming and recognized schoolteacher's hat, she heard wings. Little hummingbirds stuck their needle beaks right through her headcloth into her hair and beat their wings. And if she thought anything, it was No. No. Nono. Nonono. Simple. She just flew. (163)

This passage is remarkable for how it refuses to explain, to justify, to make intelligible. Sethe simply sees a hat, and hears wings. She does not so much fly as she is flown, propelled by the imagined hummingbirds that lift her up and carry her to perform her deed. Her agency — if we can even say that it finally belongs to her — is figured as independent of conscious thought: "*If* she thought anything, it was No." Although this No would appear to reject schoolteacher's claim on her children, Morrison's language suggests that her *No* is conditioned by a *possible* rather than actual thought. That Sethe might have thought nothing suggests that the agency of her(?) actions does not belong to consciousness, that it resides finally in the imagined hummingbirds that stick their beaks into her headcloth. Insofar as her agency emerges from outside, it cannot then be attributed to some kind of internal, and therefore maternal, instinct. To claim that Sethe's actions exceed consciousness, moreover, is to refuse the assimilation of the body to the mind *(Geist)*. Sethe's "No" would describe a spectral agency that belongs neither to the mind nor the body. Indeed, the anteriority of her "agency" in relation to consciousness reflects the Levinasian doctrine of an ethical responsibility that precedes consciousness, a responsibility that seizes us prior to our acceptance of it — just as the hummingbirds seize Sethe.

The novel thus centers on a primal scene of infanticide that it can never finally explain in rational terms.[28] The impossibility of closing in on this scene, however, does not stop Sethe from trying to explain it. Only by grasping it "right off" and immediately, the narrator suggests, can "anybody who had to ask" come to understand it. Yet, as Derrida reminds us, such an immediate and originary understanding of the other finally effaces that other. Although Paul D is Sethe's immediate interlocutor here, we as readers become Sethe's interlocutors by proxy. We read *Beloved*, in part, so that we too might come to grasp the ethical dimensions of her act: not only why she does it, but whether her actions are justified. Yet Sethe ceases to be other at the very moment that we claim to "get it." Here the language that posits the comprehension of otherness as "getting" or "having" affirms understanding and moral judgment as an activity of coming into possession of the other. For the other to remain irreducible to the same (yet not absolutely other), however, we must get it by allowing for the paradoxical possibility that we can never finally get it entirely.

Notwithstanding our efforts to comprehend and understand them, Sethe's actions finally escape us, they take flight, just like the hummingbirds' wings that propel her to commit her deed. These musical birds recall the motifs of song and flight in Morrison's *Song of Solomon*, where flight (whether the eponymous character's leap from the cliff or Mr. Smith's suicide) promises transcendence to a spiritual world free from slavery and racial conflict. The hummingbirds in *Beloved* perhaps anticipate the hoped-for transcendence that Sethe imagines for the daughter she is soon to murder.

While the motivations behind Beloved's murder remain opaque, Sethe is unequivocal in her belief that Beloved has "come back to me, my daughter, and she is mine" (204). Returning home to see smoke rising from the chimney, Sethe ponders: "The ribbon of smoke was from a fire that warmed a body returned to her — just like it never went away, never needed a headstone" (198). Here Beloved is figured as a bodily *presence* that need not be mourned because it was never lost. Given that Sethe exchanges sex for the "seven letters" engraved on her daughter's headstone, the absence and subsequent return of Beloved's body would appear to be implicated in the corporeal loss that Sethe experiences when she sells her body to the engraver (5). That this memorialization is conditioned by Sethe's act of prostitution, and that Beloved's body is imagined not only as having returned to Sethe, but as having never left, never having needed a headstone, suggests a certain revision of Sethe's scene of prostitution. If we follow Sethe's fantasy to its logical conclusion, the act of prostitution that secured her daughter's epitaph would never have taken place: Sethe would never have sold her body. Sethe imagines that her body returns to her, "just like it never went away." Sethe mourns the loss of her body *in* Beloved, which is then fantasized as never having been lost, and therefore not in need of mourning. While Sethe's corporeal loss is narrated through a scene of sexual violence, the mourning of her body as *hers* also describes the condition of Sethe's relation to others more generally. From the sexual violence that slavery wreaks on her body, to the sacrifice of her body for the lives of her children, to the violent, possessive relation that she affirms with her kin, Sethe's body is always and irreducibly marked as a site of mourning.

If Sethe imagines that Beloved is a body returned to her, a body that was never lost, and therefore never mourned, then Beloved's return remains implicated in the dialectic of negation/preservation. Sethe can therefore imagine that Beloved not only is *her* daughter, but *is* her daughter. The copula signals the one-to-one correspondence of the ghost to the daughter, against the possibility that Beloved is not only Sethe's daughter or Denver's sister, but, as Denver puts it simply: "— more" (266). To read Beloved only as the daughter or the sister is to miss how she fails to embody these terms. While Sethe wants to secure for her daughter a safe place in heaven, that spiritual salvation ultimately fails. As Russ Castronovo has shown, both antislavery and proslavery narratives tend to equate freedom with death, and thus depend on an ideology that effaces the materiality of slave suffering.[29] Beloved's failure to become spirit paradoxically "succeeds," however, by giving the lie to the "bourgeois ideology that required martyred slaves to evaporate in some abstract spiritual kingdom" (Weisenburger, 258). Beloved emerges as what Derrida calls a specter of spirit, that is, a materialization of an abstract spirit that — while eschewing the evacuation of materiality that bourgeois ideology requires — also refuses any return to "the body" as a living presence.[30] Beloved's spectrality recalls that of Sandy in Chesnutt's the *Conjure Woman*, who haunts the slave master by becoming indissociable from the material structure of the plantation home. Just as Sandy's ghost maintains a capacity to feel pain, Beloved is "flesh that weeps, laughs" (88). Reversing Christian doctrine, Baby Suggs "told them that the only grace they could have was the grace they could imagine. That if they could not see it, they would not have it" (88). When Beloved takes flesh, her incarnation contests the evaporation of slaves, which "takes" their flesh, indeed, which steals it away from them. Beloved *takes back* her flesh, but in a manner irreducible to embodiment or corporealization. Although Morrison's novel may feed off Christian, abolitionist ideology, the return of Beloved as an angry, fleshy ghost departs considerably from this tradition that "evaporates" slaves into some spirit world. After all, the fleshly presence of the ghost is precisely what inspires its exorcism:

> As long as the ghost showed out from its ghostly place — shaking stuff, crying, smashing and such — Ella respected it. But if it took flesh and came in her world, well, the shoe was on the other foot. She didn't mind a little communication between the two worlds, but this was an invasion. (257)

What is most threatening about Beloved is her refusal to be contained within her "ghostly place." She not only takes flesh, but she invades the ostensibly self-contained, insular world of Sethe, Ella, and the other women. Beloved does not respect boundaries, whether spatial or temporal. And if Sethe imagines Beloved to be "a body returned to her," that fantasy of corporeal return — in which spirit and body, as dialectically opposed terms, are always interchangeable — is contested by her spectral uncontainability (198).[31]

That Beloved fails to contain the mourning she emblematizes is made clear in the final pages of the novel:

> There is a loneliness that can be rocked. Arms crossed, knees drawn up; holding, holding on, this motion, unlike a ship's, smoothes and contains the rocker. It's an inside kind — wrapped tight like skin. Then there is a loneliness that roams. No rocking can hold it down. It is alive, on its own. A dry and spreading thing that makes the sound of one's feet going seem to come from a far-off place. (274)

The mourning that can be contained, rocked, and wrapped up inside one's skin is contrasted to a mourning that roams, that cannot be rocked or held down, that spreads beyond the borders of the self-contained body. This illimitable mourning corresponds to a plurality of Beloveds, the "sixty Million and more" to whom Morrison dedicates her novel. Morrison's image of a "loneliness that can be rocked" at first recalls the rocking of a child in the arms of its mother. It then moves to the rocking of a ship, and conjures up Beloved's earlier interior monologue where she "channels" the ghost of a slave woman who died during Middle Passage, and whose body was thrown into the sea. The ship that quite literally contains the bodies of slaves leaves traces of a violence that spreads beyond the boundaries of space and time. In this way Beloved's return marks a spectrality that cannot be contained by the body that Sethe memorializes. The emergence of the ghost from the name that Sethe has engraved on her epitaph affirms that Beloved bears a proximity to Sethe's dead daughter that cannot be denied. Yet "Beloved" also signifies a generalizability that exceeds the (one) body of the daughter.

The (Almost) White Face of the Other

To claim Beloved as a sister or a daughter or as a historical or literary property will always be haunted by a certain violence, a desire to make her *ours*. Against this violence of appropriation, Levinas introduces the face of the other as that which escapes the economy of the same. As he notes in an interview with Richard Kearney:

> The approach to the face is the most basic mode of responsibility.... The face is not in front of me *(en face de moi)* but above me; it is the other before death.... To expose myself to the vulnerability of the face is to put my ontological right to existence in question. In ethics, the other's right to exist has primacy over my own, a primacy epitomized in the ethical edict: you shall not kill, you shall not jeopardize the life of the other.[32]

Can we then say that Sethe fails to recognize the primacy of Beloved's right to exist? If we read Sethe's act against this Levinasian injunction, then Sethe would appear not to put her "ontological right to existence in question." That Levinas's notion of the face is intended as a corrective to the violence inherent in the Hegelian dialectic of "mutual recognition" is made clear in a passage from *Totality and Infinity*: "The relation with the Other — absolutely other — that shares no border with the Same — is not exposed to the allergy that afflicts the Same in a totality, and on which the Hegelian dialectic rests" (178). While Levinas wants to claim for the face an exteriority immune to the allergy of otherness, how can this absolute other be said to "share no border with the Same" without finally effacing otherness? How are we to understand this notion of the border *(frontière)* as it operates in Levinas's text? On the one hand, to claim that the other and the same share no border could mean that, like distant countries or continents, they simply do not come into contact. On the other hand, the notion that they share no border might mean that they simply *do not have* a border, which is in fact closer to the French: "... qui n'a pas frontière avec le Même." While the former reading suggests that the border or frontier operates as a marker of division, the latter interpretation would signify that there is no absolute, determinable border that separates the other and the same, that the other is *not* totally other.

The violence that attends the emergence of the face in *Beloved* challenges Levinas's privileging of the face as the marker of exteriority *par excellence*. The three interior monologues at the center of *Beloved* are particularly haunted by faces, from Sethe's face that Beloved claims as her own, to the slave faces of Middle Passage whom she "channels": "I am not separate from her [Sethe]   there is no place where I stop   her face is my own and I want to be there in the place where her face is and to be looking at it too" (210). Beloved's stream of consciousness then substitutes Sethe's face for a "dead man on my [Beloved's] face," one of hundreds of slaves thrown on top of one another by storms that rock the ship. When he dies, the man is taken away from Beloved, who then "miss[es] his pretty white points" (211). Beloved cannot find the "man whose teeth I loved," but soon she sees "the woman... with the face I want   the face that is mine." Beloved imagines biting the iron collar around the slave woman's neck with the "teeth of the dead man who died on [her] face," but soon the woman is cast into the sea along with many other slaves.

Beloved's "unspeakable thoughts" render a virtual sea of faces, all of whom Beloved wants to join, to claim, and possess (199). The opening sentence — "I AM BELOVED and she is mine." — marks the only use of punctuation in the entire monologue. Although the period denotes a conventional mark of finality, closure, and separation, its appearance here is ironic given that it punctuates a sentence that denies separation. The sentence cited above — *I am not separate from her   there is no place where I stop* — also makes ironic use of punctuation, or a lack thereof, given that the omission of a period after *I am not separate from her* both eschews the separation and closure that a period conventionally denotes and adds a space that typographically separates the two clauses. *There is no place where I stop* does not stop with a period, and thus typographically performs the refusal of separation that it describes. Yet the sentence also spaces itself from *her face is my own,* opening onto an unlocatable border where Beloved's face stops and Sethe's begins. And this space between Beloved and Sethe names the necessary separation, the indeterminable border between same and other, that the ethical relation requires. *There is no place where I stop* can mean that Beloved is merged with Sethe, but it also suggests that there simply is no *place* where she stops, that where she stops is not precisely a place, in the sense of a determinable location. Where Beloved's face ends and Sethe's begins does not belong to place.

While Beloved's interior monologue both asserts and denies the possibility of fully incorporating the other, Joanne Caputo's recent online publication of *Diversity of Love,* which chronicles the history of Margaret Garner and her child murder, stakes claim to Beloved in a manner that fully disallows her alterity. Caputo asserts that she has established a new genre of scholarship called "historical spiritual nonfiction," which, in addition to more traditional historical research, "includes information Caputo received directly from the deceased Garner and eight (8) other spirits with whom she has been communicating since 1997."[33] What is more, Caputo claims that she is the child whom

Garner murdered in 1856, now reincarnated. Although such a claim is certainly dubious, it is not altogether clear that Caputo's claim is finally opposed to the many other claims that have been made on this story of child murder. The headline of Caputo's press release — "Writer Claims Murdered Slave Child Past" — could describe any one who has written about Margaret Garner or her various reincarnations, and has therefore made certain claims about her or even on her: from Morrison, to Weisenburger, to Winfrey, to the present study.[34] While Caputo is perhaps unique in the literality of her claim, it only signals a fantasy of possession pushed to its absolute limit. Like Beloved, Caputo is "looking for the join," the place where the face of the other is hers (213). *Caputo is Beloved and she is hers.*

Caputo's appropriation of Mary Garner's face ("even though I am white") thus effaces the indeterminable border that separates the other from the same. The fantasy of reincarnation names the ultimate act of appropriation insofar as it returns the other to the self. Yet, it is less Caputo's whiteness than the claim of reincarnation that is most suspect here. For the "historical" Beloved was described in the Cincinnati *Gazette* as "almost white," a "little girl of rare beauty."[35] The *Gazette* also surmised that her mother Margaret was a "mulatto, showing from one-fourth to one-third white blood," and that her only other living daughter, Cilley, was "much lighter in colour than" her mother, "light enough to show a red tinge in its cheeks." The specter of miscegenation haunted Margaret Garner's fugitive slave trial from the beginning, but only at the close of the proceedings was it fully articulated by the abolitionist and feminist Lucy Stone. After the court had adjourned to await the judge's verdict, Stone addressed the audience as to the evils of slavery and the "depths of a mother's love," before finally acknowledging what everyone present already knew too well but refused to admit:[36]

> The faded faces of the negro children tell too plainly to what degradation the female slaves submit. Rather than give her little daughter to that life, she killed it. If in her deep maternal love she felt the impulse to send her child back to God, to save it from coming woe, who shall say she had no right to do so? That desire has its root in the deepest and holiest feelings of our nature — implanted in black and white alike by our common father. (565)

While the audience was undoubtedly scandalized by this public admission of miscegenation, as well as the explicit connection made between mixed-race children and the open secret of sexual relations between slave masters and their female slaves, the *double entendre* of "our common father" certainly brings the point home. Stone's language ostensibly means to explain the origins of maternal love in a God who instills in both black and white the desire to protect one's children. Yet, the subtext of Stone's language also reveals (perhaps unintentionally) the slave master as this "common father" who plants his seed in "black and white alike." The pun thus aligns the slave master with the Christian father/spirit, and implicitly sexualizes these "deepest and holiest feelings of our nature." Posing God as white, the conflation of father/master figures this God as a miscegenator by analogy: a spirit who becomes a specter through the mixing of his seed with black blood. As I will show in chapter 3, the imagined contamination of miscegenation curtails the master's aim of transcendent continuity, a project tacitly modeled on the Christian father/spirit's incarnation in a finite son whose death/resurrection conditions the father's immortality.

Of course, it was never proven that Mary Garner was fathered by Margaret's master, Archibald Gaines. And nowhere in Morrison's *Beloved* is it suggested that Sethe's daughter was fathered by Schoolteacher. Yet Morrison's text is certainly not silent on the issue of miscegenation. We know that Baby Sugg's "eight children had six fathers" (23). Nan tells Sethe after the death of her mother that Nan and Sethe's mother, who knew each other from the sea, "were taken up many times by the crew. 'She threw them all away but you.... You she gave the name of the black man. She put her arms around him. The others she did not put her arms around. Never. Never'" (62). Ella gives birth to "a hairy white thing, fathered by 'the lowest yet,'" and, refusing to nurse it, lets it die of starvation (259). But Sethe "had the amazing luck of six whole years of marriage to that 'somebody' son who had fathered every one of her children" (23). What is most striking about the treatment of miscegenation by the text is that it actively excludes both Sethe and Beloved from what it otherwise presents as a rather widespread practice. Given that Sethe was the only child born to her mother who was *not* fathered by a white man, and that she would in turn have had the "amazing luck" of giving birth to four children who were all fathered by the same black man, the text's exclusion of miscegenation from Sethe's blood line appears to constitute more or less an active effacement.

Halle's parentage, however, does remain somewhat unclear. We know that he is the last of Baby Sugg's eight children, and that at least some of her children were fathered by white men. Finding herself pregnant by "the man who promised not to and did," Baby "could not love [the child] and the rest she would not" (23). Yet absent any textual proof that either Sethe or Halle carry any white blood, Beloved's race would not appear to be in question. Given Morrison's public statements that she limited her research on Margaret Garner to the barest details of her child murder, it is difficult to determine if she was even aware of Mary Garner's "almost white" skin at the time that she wrote *Beloved*.[37] The *effect*, however, of referencing Sethe's "amazing luck" is to redouble the novel's idealization of love. The text acknowledges the ubiquity of miscegenation only to exempt Sethe and her offspring from it. Considering the numerous other atrocities that Sethe suffers at the hands of slave masters, her exemption from bearing mixed-race children seems almost too good to be true. Indeed, Sethe is raped when she is already pregnant with Denver but still nursing Beloved. In one of the novel's most disturbing lines, Sethe understates the violence perpetrated against her, telling Paul D that they "took [her] milk" (17). Beyond excluding the possibility that Sethe could have conceived a child as a result of the rape, the effect of this passage is also to pose sexual violence and rape as a foil to the sanctity of motherhood. The theft of milk stands synecdochically for a certain violence perpetrated against motherhood, thus burdening the rape with the weight of *all* violence, indeed, of all that ostensibly conflicts with Sethe's "instinct" to bring milk to her child. Thus, the sacralization of maternity is intensified not only by excluding miscegenation but by opposing this scene of aberrant violence to that most cherished of scenes: a mother breastfeeding her child.

As Weisenburger argues, rarely did abolitionist literature depart from portraying infanticide "as scenes in 'the romance of America'" that articulated "a set of absolute equivalencies: Death = Liberty = Divine" (256). Weisenburger offers Elizabeth Barrett Browning's "The Runaway Slave at Pilgrim's Point" as a notable exception. Here a slave mother murders her child because he is "far too white...too white for me....I covered him up with a kerchief there; / I covered his face in close and tight: / And he moaned and struggled, as well might be, / For the white child wanted his liberty — | / Ha, ha! he wanted the master right."[38] Far from performing the abstraction of slaves into some imagined "spiritual kingdom," Browning mocks the "angels white" who "freed the white child's spirit so" (252). Indeed, the poem emphasizes the corporeality of the dead child: "I carried the body to and fro, . . . I carried the little body on." Finally the slave mother buries the child in the "black earth," leaving "nothing white," a "dark child in the dark!" (253). She blackens the face of her white child with dirt, "and thus we two were reconciled," for "a child and mother do wrong to look at one another, when one is black and one is fair" (253, 251).

Yet *Beloved* departs from the death-liberty-divine equation — inadvertently perhaps — precisely through its exclusion of miscegenation as a possibility that would complicate Sethe's act of infanticide. That whiteness remains to haunt the text is suggested by Beloved's first appearance *not* in but *as* "a white dress," kneeling next to a praying Sethe, "its sleeve around her . . . waist," as if the whiteness that the text excludes from Beloved's skin color returns in the color of her dress (29). Given the conventional, Gothic representation of ghosts as white apparitions, Beloved's appearance as a white dress would seem rather unremarkable. Yet *Beloved* is a text in which color is so laden with meaning that the emergence of a black ghost in a white dress calls for unusual scrutiny. Speaking specifically of *Beloved*, Morrison remarks that she "stripped" the text "of color" so that the reader might "feel" its "hunger" and "delight."[39] Yet this treatment of color is not merely stylistic; it is profoundly political. When Baby Suggs "ponder[s] color," the significance of her meditation extends well beyond the lavender of her quilts (4). That Morrison is acutely aware of the ways in which color comes to signify racially is made clear by her reading of Edgar Allan Poe's *The Narrative of Arthur Gordon Pym,* in which she identifies the novel's closure in "impenetrable whiteness" as symptomatic of how whiteness operates "as both antidote for and meditation on the shadow that is companion to this whiteness."[40] In *Beloved,* however, blackness is no longer the mere shadow of whiteness. Indeed, when Beloved finally materializes to Sethe, Denver, and Paul D, she no longer wears a white but a black dress. This substitution of whiteness with blackness aligns the latter with Beloved's incarnation. By shedding whiteness, blackness steps out from the shadows and becomes flesh.

Race is figured here as clothing, as an outer shell or covering that fails to contain the body. This is not to suggest, however, that race enjoys an unlimited transferability, that one might take it on or off like clothes. Yet race, like clothes, is characterized by a certain failure to contain the body fully. This uncontainability is affirmed by the text's repeated reference to "men without skin," or white men (210–13).

Whiteness names the condition of being "without skin," both in the sense of being unmarked by one's race and lacking the material shell that houses a body. Whiteness is always everywhere and nowhere. Calling our attention to this uncontainability, *Beloved* marks the unmarkedness of whiteness. This marking is thus to be distinguished from the marking of whiteness that scholars in the field of "whiteness studies" often advocate. For the latter implies a disaffiliation from whiteness that seeks to reverse its claim to universality. Yet whiteness achieves its power not solely through its appeal to universality, but through its perpetual oscillation between universality and particularity.[41] Hence, the effort to particularize whiteness fails to address how it must always incarnate itself even as it denies its particularity. Whiteness is always both marked and unmarked. As Richard Dyer has argued, whiteness paradoxically asserts and denies its corporeality through its incessant movement between body and spirit.[42] Whereas whiteness shifts between universality and particularity, however, blackness is deprived of any claim to universality.

From within the terms of normative whiteness, then, blacks can be said to *have* skin because they are inescapably marked by it. By marking the unmarkedness of whiteness, however, *Beloved* troubles the conflict between exterior and interior essence by which normative racial determination is made. If, as Ariela Gross notes, race was determined in the nineteenth-century South by a shifting discourse of essence that moved between a "rhetoric of transparency" on the one hand, and a "rhetoric of veiled and hidden essences" on the other, this oscillation was conditioned by an understanding of blackness as either marked on one's skin or else contained, veiled or hidden beneath it.[43] To have skin is to have a body that is marked and contained by that skin. Despite the tendency within contemporary scholarship, particularly in American cultural studies, to equate the body with a certain reanimation of the socially dead, *Beloved* suggests that whiteness profits from a claim to simultaneous universality and particularity that imprisons racial others within their skin, an enslavement of the socially dead that should caution against the too-often asserted equation of corporeality with social and political agency.[44]

To trace race in *Beloved* is thus to encounter something like the inverse of what Morrison identifies in *Absalom, Absalom!* in which Faulkner "spends the entire book tracing race, and you can't find it. No one can see it, even the character who is black can't see it" (*Art,*

101). If, as readers of Faulkner, we are "forced to hunt for a drop of black blood that means everything and nothing," Morrison's exclusion of white blood from Beloved's lineage sends us on a search to identify its presence, to trace those textual moments in which it appears only to disappear (101). Excluding the specter of miscegenation from the scene of Sethe's infanticide, however, the text does so in the spirit of pure, motherly love. In an odd reversal, whiteness itself becomes a contaminating threat to the purity of this love. The novel thus dramatizes an incessant conflict between the spirit of abolitionism and the specter of miscegenation that is never finally resolved.

If miscegenation is what the novel must foreclose in order to purify Sethe's act of infanticide, this is *not* to suggest that this purification amounts to what some might be tempted to call "reverse racism." The novel certainly does not invoke whiteness as a threat to the future of the black race, as in some odd corollary to Shreve's fantasy in *Absalom, Absalom!* of having "sprung from the loins of African Kings" (a formulation that, we should note, fully erases the maternal role in reproduction). Although it turns out that some white American presidents have indeed fathered children with their black female slaves, it is not so much the threat of miscegenation per se as its erasure from the scene of infanticide that is at issue here. To admit miscegenation into the frame of slave infanticide would be to allow for a much more ambivalent master/slave dialectic, a relation in which the distinction between one's kin and one's property becomes all the more difficult to determine. In addition to betraying the master's position as both owner and biological father, the specter of miscegenation troubles the actions of a mother who — in a single stroke — saves a child from a life of slavery, claims that child as her own, and destroys its "too white" face. Yet if Margaret Garner "saved" her daughter wielding the same handsaw with which she destroyed the master's progeny, her excessive violence, her too-thick love, allegorizes the irreducible violence that haunts any and every kinship relation.

Dis(re)membering History

The critical silence on *Beloved*'s elision of miscegenation thus reflects a proprietorial violence analogous to that which we have been tracing in the novel itself. Reducing Sethe's actions to an idealized portrait of maternal love, critics have come into possession of the infanticidal mother only at the risk of effacing her altogether. As Lucy Stone's statement at the Garner trial demonstrates, however, the acknowledgment of miscegenation in no way guarantees the demystification of motherly love. For Stone brought the issue of miscegenation to light in the very service of the abolitionist paradigm. Similar to contemporary critics, she rendered Garner's actions intelligible only at the price of reducing them to maternal instinct. But what if the entrance of miscegenation on the critical stage could multiply rather than reduce the scenes of interpretation? Or, to use the novel's own metaphor, what if the emergence of miscegenation allowed us to widen rather than narrow the circle of interpretation that Sethe tells us can never finally be closed? That we can never "close in" or "pin it down" would mean that we must resign ourselves as readers to not fully understanding Sethe's act. To shatter the silence on miscegenation, then, is not to claim that we have finally "got it." How might we abandon our will to possession and allow the text to remain *other*, to remain, that is, a specter? And how might this specter resist both the Levinasian injunction to absolute otherness and the temptation to claim the text as ours? As Weisenburger underscores, Margaret Garner was always a "symbolic property" toward which opponents and proponents of slavery were drawn to contest her meaning (134). Yet this seeming failure to affirm a pure, nonviolent relation to the other also names a certain success. It "succeeds" where it fails to incorporate the other whom it must necessarily cannibalize. Its "success" will have been measured by these twin failures: the failure of pure ethics and the failure of pure violence.

In the gap opened up by these two failures lies what Levinas calls the "sensible experience as obsession *by* the other person" (*Autrement*, 123, my emphasis). In French (as in English), one can be obsessed either *by* or *with* something or someone. Yet Levinas's choice of the former preposition emphasizes an inhabiting of the other in the same that eschews the vocabulary by which one is said to be obsessed *with* the other. Here the obsession (in French one might also say *hantise* or "haunting") comes *from* the other, and is anterior to my will or agency: "The paradox of this responsibility consists in the fact that I am obligated without this obligation having begun in me, as if an order had slid itself into my conscience by stealth" (*Autrement*, 28). This sense of being obsessed *by* the other, together with the idiomatic notion of *hantise* as obsession, suggests a certain nonpossessive *possession* by the other. Although Levinas does not adopt a spectral vocabulary, we might rewrite the "sensible experience" of the other in the same precisely in terms of this nonpossession by the other. As Derrida remarks with regard to Levinas: "*Host* or *guest, Gastgeber* or *Gast*, the host would not only be a hostage. It would at least have...the figure of the spirit or phantom *(Geist, ghost)*."[45] For Derrida, "the master of the house...is already a *received* host, the *guest*, in his own home" (81). Ethics begins with this notion that "I" am always a guest in my own home, a ghost in my own body. The nonpossessive possession by the other is conditioned by a certain corporeal dispossession, a loss of "my" body as mine.

In a 1988 interview with Marsha Darling, Morrison addressed the question of ethics with regard to *Beloved:*

> The gap between Africa and Afro-America and the gap between the living and the dead and the gap between the past and the present does not exist. It's bridged for us by our assuming responsibility for people no one's ever assumed responsibility for. They are those that died en route. Nobody knows their names, and nobody thinks about them.[46]

Although Morrison characterizes responsibility in conventional terms as something that we actively assume, for Levinas, responsibility assumes us; it emerges from a "passivity more passive than all passivity" (*Autrement*, 85). Understood in these terms, the gap between the living and the dead is bridged by a responsibility that seizes hold of us, that possesses us prior to our assumption of it. *Beloved, we are hers.*

The question of historical responsibility in *Beloved* finds itself divided between the will to "rememory" the dead on the one hand, and to "disremember" them on the other. As Morrison notes in the interview with Darling, "there is a necessity for remembering the horror, but of course there's a necessity for remembering it in a manner in which it can be digested, in a manner in which the memory is not destructive" (247). In *Beloved*, however, digestion emerges as itself a mode of destruction, a way of dis(re)membering the other. In one of the few passages in which the narrator gives us a glimpse into the thoughts of the ghost, Beloved, upon losing a back tooth, thinks:

> This is it. Next would be her arm, her hand, her toe. Pieces of her would drop maybe one at a time, maybe all at once. Or on one of those mornings before Denver woke and after Sethe left she would fly apart. It is difficult keeping her head on her neck, her legs attached to her hips when she is by herself. Among the things

she could not remember was when she first knew that she could wake up any day and find herself in pieces. She had two dreams: exploding, and being swallowed. (133)

The reference to "keeping her head on her neck" recalls the brutal murder of Beloved, when the depth of the knife wound forces Sethe to support her daughter's head so that it does not fall off. The disremberment that the community of black women enact through their final exorcism of Beloved mimes Sethe's dismemberment of her daughter, as if in exorcising her they dismember her all over again. In this sense, remembering history "in a manner in which it can be digested" — in the sense of not allowing our confrontation with rememories to destroy us — allows that historical responsibility is conditioned by the very violence that it seeks to address, or perhaps, redress. If, as Derrida argues, to eat or not to eat is *not* the ethical question, but rather, how to *eat well*, then we might ask: Is the exorcism of Beloved an example of eating well? Judging from Morrison's language in the closing pages of the novel, this community of black women eats rather too well. There is nothing left of Beloved, no waste or remains: "By and by all trace is gone, and what is forgotten is not only the footprints but the water too and what is down there. The rest is weather" (275). Perhaps it is not a question of eating well, of historical digestion, but rather, of indigestion, of allowing some trace to remain unincorporable and unmournable. Beloved, however, remains both too buried within and too far outside their rememories:

> They never knew where or why she crouched, or whose was the underwater face she needed like that. Where the memory of the smile under her chin might have been and was not, a latch latched and a lichen attached its apple-green bloom to the metal. What made her think her fingernails could open locks the rain rained on? (275)

Is Beloved trying to get in or get out? Does she remain trapped by rusted locks in something like Paul D's tobacco tin, entombed under the sea with the rest of the "underwater face[s]" of Middle Passage (275), or has her exorcism cast her out, leaving her to scratch at the doors, begging to be readmitted to their rememories?

As Pascale-Anne Brault and Michael Naas remark in their introduction to a collection of Derrida's essays on mourning: "In mourning, we must recognize that the friend is now both only 'in us' and already beyond us, in us but totally other."[47] Although we most often think of mourning in terms of the loss of an other who, by virtue of death, is now totally other and removed, Brault and Naas observe that the loss of the other carries with it the paradox that the dead other is now closer to us than ever before, existing only in us. Might this over-proximity explain part of the dread that attends mourning the other who no longer exists outside us, and who therefore lodges inside us like a guest who has overstayed its welcome? As Derrida puts it in *Specters of Marx*, "one occupies oneself with ghosts only to exorcise them, to show them the door" (223). And this welcome is precisely what Sethe's community rescinds at the end of the novel. "So, in the end they forgot her too. Remembering seemed unwise" (274). The novel concludes with the ambiguous exhortation: "This is not a story to pass on" (275). The story is thus at once not to be neglected or put aside, not to be transmitted or repeated to others, and not to be allowed to die. In other words, Beloved is not to be negated, preserved, or superceded in the name of some Hegelian dialectic, but rather, to persist precisely as a specter who resists assimilation, who remains long after the chewing laughter has swallowed her all away.

3

The Haunted House of Kinship

> Haunting is always the haunting of a house.
> And it is not just that some houses are haunted.
> A house is only a house inasmuch as it is haunted.
>
> —Mark Wigley, *The Architecture of Deconstruction*

> Any house is a far too complicated, clumsy, fussy,
> mechanical counterfeit of the human body.
>
> —Frank Lloyd Wright, "The Cardboard House," 1931

Emily Dickinson's "One need not be a chamber to be haunted" begins by posing the phenomenon of haunting as the excess of any structure of containment.[1] While Dickinson's language does not deny the possibility that haunting might be interiorized, its interiorization is deemed inessential and perhaps even secondary to the haunting itself. Chambers, houses, and other such enclosures mark the conventional spaces in which the haunting that is peculiar to the Gothic tends to get contained. In the dynamic of haunting that Dickinson suggests here, however, haunting is imagined as "surpassing Material Place — " (333). Haunting is uncontainable and generalizable.

Yet in the lines that follow, Dickinson moves away from this assertion of haunting's uncontainability toward another set of enclosures — the corridors of the brain — which suggests that her opening gesture performs something less radical than it might first appear. Insofar as these corridors are understood to exceed "Material Place — "

they figure the brain as something like an interior psyche or mind rather than a material organ. The movement beyond material place thus retains the trope of containment despite having denied the brain its materiality. How are we to understand these immaterial corridors of the mind? What insures their continued coherence once their materiality has been denied? Indeed, what nonmaterial walls hold this interiority in place? If such psychic interiority surpasses material place, it does so only by retaining a sense of enclosure that affirms the materiality that it displaces. What is meant by a place without materiality, or for that matter, a materiality without place? What happens to our sense of place once the materiality of place has been put into question?

While Mark Wigley reminds us that the term "'haunting' is etymologically bound to that of 'house,'" this linguistic yoking of haunting to containment may demonstrate that all houses are haunted, but it does not follow that all "haunting is always the haunting of a house," indeed, that haunting is always housed.[2] According to the *Oxford English Dictionary*, the derivation of the verb form haunt is of uncertain origin: "It is not clear whether the earliest sense in French and English was to practice habitually (an action, etc.) or to frequent habitually (a place)." If the latter formulation ties haunting to place, the former exceeds any structure of containment. To claim that haunting is irreducible to house is to understand haunting as anterior rather than *in*terior to those structures that are conventionally thought to contain it. The haunting is the originary possibility of the house. The haunting comes first.

Such questions of materiality, place, and containment are central to any consideration of American slavery and its aftermath in Reconstruction. It is the figure of the house, after all, that Lincoln invoked in his famous 1858 acceptance speech on the occasion of his Republican senatorial nomination. Insisting that "this government cannot endure, permanently, half slave and half free," Lincoln borrowed a phrase from Matthew 12: "'A house divided against itself cannot stand.'"[3] Although Lincoln intended this metaphor to connote the impossibility of sustaining a nation divided along the question of slavery, this division of North and South, as Eric Sundquist observes, "concealed a further division between white and black, one that was paradoxically evident in their literal, physical union and one that, far from being dissolved by a reunion of the warring sections and an abolition of slavery, could only be made more prominently explosive."[4] Given that abolition portended a crisis around the question of racial amalgamation, any return to unity would only lead to further division, if no longer between North and South, then between black and white. Lincoln's metaphor assumes both that the nation *as* house might be returned to an imagined unity, and that the nation is *not* always divided in itself, that the nation as a house, or as a body, to follow Frank Lloyd Wright, somehow precedes and contains a more generalizable haunting, against the possibility that haunting conditions the emergence of the nation as house/body. Indeed, the adjectival transformation of the verb "divided" performed by the title of Lincoln's famous speech — "The 'House Divided' Address" — employs a syntactical inversion that positions the house *prior* to the adjective that modifies or divides it, and thus rhetorically attempts to endow a certain primacy to that structure.

For Sundquist, Lincoln's metaphor conjures up not only the possibility of the nation's dissolution, but also a more covert anxiety that the spread of slavery made possible by the Dred Scott decision (1857) and the Kansas Nebraska Act (1854) would in turn lead to the spread of miscegenation.[5] Notwithstanding this suppressed dread of miscegenation in his speech, Lincoln and other Republicans were persistently charged by the Democrats during the election year of 1864 with championing interracial amalgamation. The frequent rhetorical quip chiding Lincoln for his "miscegenation proclamation" attests to how closely Southern Democrats aligned black freedom with the supposed threat of racial amalgamation.[6] In Reconstruction America, moreover, the problem of containment was registered hierarchically in the continued exploitation of black labor in the form of forced labor contracts (buttressed by the repeated decrying of "black laziness"); spatially in the emergence of the Jim Crow laws that worked to control black movement; and corporeally in the fascination and violence that greeted the movement over the color line that miscegenation made possible. Although the conventional figure (both Platonic and Christian) of the body-as-container denies the inhabiting of one body in another, the threat of miscegenation would seem to lie in its confirmation of a chiasmatic relation between and within white and black bodies *prior* to any racial admixture. If, as I will attempt to show, all bodies are related in a chiasmatic way, then all bodies are in some sense miscegenated bodies. Indeed, it remains unclear whether we can still retain the trope of containment that the signifier "body" always seems to imply once its integrity has been called into question. The white body, like the body of the nation, is always divided in itself by the other(s) it excludes.

The conception of the body as container is precisely what Mark Twain's *Pudd'nhead Wilson* both challenges and reasserts in its allegorical invention of a thirty-one-parts-white child, Valet de Chambre, aptly called "Chambers" for short.[7] Chambers's mother, Roxy, stealthily exchanges him for the slave master's child, Thomas, in order that her child might escape the bonds of slavery. This substitution thus goes some degree toward interrogating the notion of the body as a self-contained whole. To the extent that Chambers can pass for white, the notion that his body contains an irreducible blackness is contested. Moreover, Twain's juxtaposition of the Chambers/Thomas pair with the *sometimes* conglomerate Italian twins, Luigi and Angelo, further questions the corporeal integrity of the former pair. For what is perhaps most striking about Twain's treatment of the twins in *Pudd'nhead* is his "forgetting" to separate them. Retaining the Italian couple from *Those Extraordinary Twins*, the shorter novella that gave birth ("Cesarean-like," he tells us) to *Pudd'nhead*, Twain cannot seem to decide if the twins in the latter text are conjoined (as they are in the original story) or not. Although the twins are introduced in *Pudd'nhead* as separate, Angelo describes him and his brother as their parents' "only child" (90).

Twain exploits this problem of separability to great comic effect in *Those Extraordinary Twins*. The narrator tells us that Angelo sometimes "wished that he and his brother might become segregated from each other and be separate individuals, like other men" (253). Always the ironist, Twain cleverly refers to the politics of "separate but equal" by linking segregation to the problem of bodily integrity. The threat to white racial purity that miscegenation augured was always behind the desire for segregation. Moreover, Angelo's desire to be "separate" from but "equal" to Luigi further grafts the conjoined twins onto the Chambers/Thomas pair. It expresses a desire to possess an uncontaminated body, a body that is unhaunted by the body of the other. When Luigi reveals to Aunt Betsy and Patsy that he is in fact six months older than his brother even though they were born at the same time, he proclaims: "We are no more twins than you are" (260). We might read Luigi's language as he likely intends it, that is, that neither he and Angelo nor Betsy and Patsy are twins. But there is also the suggestion here that Luigi's revelation is all in jest, and that "we are no more twins than you are" means that not only are Luigi and Angelo conjoined twins, but that we are all conglomerate, miscegenated bodies, spectral beings that haunt one another from within.

The implication of such a reading is that the haunting of one body by another is not confined to miscegenated bodies, properly speaking. One need not be Chambers to be haunted. That Dickinson traces a move from the chamber to the haunted self, before finally arriving at "The Body" — a corporeality that is figured as warding off a "superior specter" within — further underscores the conventional conflation of body and house. Chambers's name in particular sounds an ironic note insofar as the "fiction of law" requires that the one-thirty-second part of him that is black count for the whole (64). This synecdochic logic by which Chambers's spectral blackness is transposed into a racial signification that is nowhere discernible understands his body as the receptacle of an invisible blackness that in turn belies the visible whiteness of his body. When Twain allegorizes such a disavowal by noting that, in reference to Roxy, "the one sixteenth of her which was black out-voted the other fifteen parts and made her a negro," he ironically endows a certain agency of suffrage to this invisible blackness, a right that is nonetheless denied to Roxy in the political sphere. By underscoring how this spectral blackness is given complete power over her being, Twain affirms the persistence of what Saidiya Hartman refers to as a "metaphysics of blood that transformed race into a sanguineous substance."[8] For blackness to "out-vote" whiteness requires a synecdochic substitution of blackness for whiteness notwithstanding the invisibility of the former.[9]

That Chambers remains contained by his blackness despite Roxy's substitution of him for Thomas is confirmed when Roxy reveals to the false Thomas that he is in fact her own son and therefore black. Setting the scene of Roxy's revelation in the haunted house behind Judge Driscoll's home, Twain invokes the trope of containment along the lines of Wright's description of the house as a "counterfeit of the human body." Referring to his refusal to fight Luigi, Roxy remarks: "It's de nigger in you, dat's what it is. Thirty-one parts 'o you is white, en only one part nigger, and dat po' little one part is yo' *soul*" (157). Roxy's designation of Chambers's one-part nigger as his soul positions the dilemma figured by his miscegenated body squarely within the Platonic and Christian traditions, in which the body is understood to be a "prison" of the soul. Yet the synecdochic logic by which the part comes to stand for the whole has an almost Foucauldian resonance insofar as Chambers's "nigger" soul emerges as the prison of Chambers's body.[10] Just as Foucault's inversion of the body/soul dichotomy stops short of displacing the trope of containment that conditions it, the formulation of Chambers's "nigger" soul figures that soul as imprisoning his body within the walls of an invisible blackness. Such immaterial soul-like walls recall those that Dickinson imagines as holding in place an interiority that nonetheless exceeds the materiality of place. As we asked of Dickinson's retention of interiority, we might also ask of this conception of blackness as not only soul-like, but more strangely, as entombing Chambers within its imaginary walls. How can Chambers's blackness be construed as constituting both his innermost part and that which materializes and congeals the borders of his body? If Chambers's soul-like blackness is figured as being both inside and outside his body, what finally holds this body together as a bounded being?

Echoing the Platonic resonance of debates around both miscegenation and segregation, Morton Keller remarks that the United States Supreme Court decision in 1896 which gave the go-ahead to "separate but equal" confined blacks to the "Plessy prison."[11] Like Twain's fictional Roxy and Chambers, Homer Plessy's "mixture of colored blood was not discernible in him," as he was "in the proportion of seven eighths Caucasian and one eighth African blood" (537). This landmark case centering on the question of separate but equal accommodations involved what — since the completion of the transcontinental railroad in 1869 — had become a dominant mode of transportation, one that greatly advanced the mobility of all Americans. The effort to restrain the movement of black Americans by distinguishing between white and black spaces thus ought to be read alongside the promise of unimpeded mobility that locomotion implied. The train from which Plessy was excluded becomes the *vehicle* for a certain movement across racial borders. Quoting Blackstone in his dissent from the majority opinion, Justice Harlan affirmed that "personal liberty... consists in the power of locomotion... without imprisonment or restraint."[12] Given that the segregation of whites and blacks always involved an effort to prevent blacks from inhabiting "white" spaces, the doctrine of "separate but equal" might be better characterized as designating blacks "contained" and therefore *not* equal.

Most striking about the anxiety aroused by the proximity of white and black bodies is how it admits of a certain chiasmatic relation between these differently raced bodies, an intersection of ostensibly separate bodies that is nonetheless denied by the proscription against miscegenation. While Hartman, for instance, is on board with the conventional view that *Plessy* evinced "fears of engulfment and contamination" that further demonstrate how the "integrity of bodily boundaries and racial self-certainty was at the heart of this anxiety," such fears of interracial proximity imagine a phantasmatic inhabiting of black bodies in white bodies that is in considerable tension with the very "real" contamination that miscegenation is thought to portend (206). If the white imagination can fantasize about an erasure of bodily boundaries in which the white body is penetrated by a spectral blackness, then the anticipated danger that miscegenation would seem to pose is rendered moot. For "encounters between scandalously proximate bodies" — whether on a train, a steam boat or on the street — are already imagined as acts of miscegenation (206). According to the racist logic by which interracial proximity threatens to contaminate white bodies, the miscegenation that the segregation of whites and blacks is designed to prevent will have always already taken place.

While Hartman, along with Sundquist, identifies the *possibility* of miscegenation as more traumatic for the racist imaginary than the *actuality* of miscegenation, such an argument relies on a division between "unreal" and "real" acts of interracial reproduction, between the threat of miscegenation and something like "miscegenation itself." But what is "miscegenation" if not precisely the sign of an impossible possibility, the sign of something that can both never *really* take place, and yet has always already taken place? That is to say that the problem of miscegenation, pace Sundquist and Hartman, lies less in the threat of contamination than in its disavowal. This is not to suggest that black bodies pose some real, material threat to white racial purity, only that the pollution that interracial mixing is thought to portend denies a chiasmatic relation between all bodies. As I argued in chapter 1 with regard to the master/slave dialectic, the master does not so much deny *his* body when he conscripts the slave to perform those actions that the master would otherwise do. Rather, the master denies the *fiction* of bodily possession that enables his disavowal. Although the liberal doctrine of possessive individualism has often been invoked to redress the wrongs of slavery, the enslavement of the other is conditioned by the dream of self-possession. For only on account of the conceit that the master('s) body is *his* does that body become available for its denial, and the slave('s) body therefore becomes available for its expropriation.

Similarly, I would suggest, the proscription on miscegenation "forgets" that *my* body is never properly my own, and is therefore never in an uncontaminated relation to the body of the other.

Insofar as the racist imagination understands the white body as fully proper to itself, however, it does so by construing whiteness as an inalienable property. This inalienability, as Cheryl Harris notes, would at first seem to preclude whiteness from the domain of property given the traditional liberal view of property that affirms its transferability.[13] In a paradoxical sense, what marks the determination of property *as* property is the possibility of its becoming im-proper, detached from its owner. Yet Harris goes on to show that alienability is not the exclusive determinant of what counts as property, and that when it comes to the property value in whiteness, "its inalienability may be more indicative of its perceived value, rather than its disqualification as property" (1734). The historical construction of whiteness as property protects an investment in whiteness in terms of reputation and status. Thus in *Plessy v. Fergusson*, Albion Tourgée, one of Plessy's attorneys, argued that the Louisiana law deprived him of his property as a white man:

> How much would it be *worth* to a young man entering upon the practice of law, to be regarded as a *white* man rather than a colored one? ... Is it possible to conclude that *the reputation of being white* is not property? Indeed is it not the most valuable sort of property, being the master-key that unlocks the golden door of opportunity?[14]

While the court denied Tourgée's claim, they nonetheless admitted that — even if the law protected a property investment in whiteness — Plessy, as a black male, had no claim to such property:

> It is claimed by the plaintiff in error that, in any mixed community, the reputation of belonging to the dominant race, in this instance the white race, is property, in the same sense that a right of action, or of inheritance, is property. Conceding this to be so, for the purposes of this case, we are unable to see how this statute deprives him of, or in any way affects his right to, such property. If he be a white man and assigned to a colored coach, he may have his action for damages against the company for being deprived of his so called property. Upon the other hand, if he be a colored man and be so assigned, he has been deprived of no property, since he is not lawfully entitled to the reputation of being a white man. (549)

Although the majority opinion flatly rejects the notion that whiteness constitutes property in any legal sense, the language that closes this excerpt from the decision oddly resuscitates the very claim that it has denied, asserting that Plessy "is not lawfully entitled to the reputation of being a white man." Given that the court had already rejected Plessy's due process claim because his race "did not properly arise on the record," and therefore was not relevant to the question of the constitutionality of separate accommodations, their consideration of the damage done to Plessy's property in the form of reputation depended on the "issue of race classification that the Court had previously declined to address" (*Plessy*, 549; Harris, 1749). The court's tautology seems to go something like this: whiteness is not property, and even if it were, Plessy (whose race is not an issue here) would have no claim to such property because he is black!

The law thus works to preempt the estrangement of whiteness such that the latter achieves its status as property despite, or perhaps because of, its inalienability. Whiteness always returns to itself. Although the law figures it on one level as inalienable, blackness returns to itself as a proper identity *only* in a contaminated form. Yet the anxiety of contamination also imagines this proper blackness as fully improper, as an uncontainable threat to white bodies that in turn belies the inalienability of whiteness. If whiteness achieves its property status because of its inalienability, then the property value of whiteness — in fantasizing its penetration by a threatening blackness — allegorizes its own dissolution. The crucial point here is not that whiteness is figured in terms of the proper while blackness is imagined as improper. For the anxiety of racial mixing inadvertently gives the lie to the inalienability of whiteness, and more generally, to the fantasy of possessing an indivisible body.

What we are calling the disavowal of contamination thus seems to surface whenever reference is made to *the* body or *my* body. To claim that this body is mine is to deny its relation to the other/body, to insist on the presence of my body *prior* to its coming into relation with other bodies. What the white imagination both recognizes and refuses in its anxiety around racial purity is precisely this possibility of the body's not being mine, a corporeal impropriety that is always tied to the body's mortality. Yet the racialization of this impropriety denies this loss of corporeal integrity and presence by figuring such contamination *only* in relation to the threat of a differently raced body. The *racialization of contamination* thus seeks to affirm the white body as a living presence by making the black body stand in for the threat of death that haunts any life.

As I noted in the Introduction, the Civil War witnessed the rise of modern mourning rituals — most notably the practice of embalming — that evinced a certain denial of mortality. That the father of our "house divided," Abraham Lincoln, was the first American president to be embalmed connects the racial divisions that became even more abyssal after emancipation to the modern interdiction of death. The preservation of Lincoln's body correlated with the Christian rhetoric that circulated in response to the president's assassination on Good Friday. As a *New York Times* journalist put it: "It was eminently fitting that such a deed should be done on the very day when the Christian Church celebrates the crucifixion, the martyrdom of her Divine Head.... The memory of him will be the more precious for the sacred memories with which it is entwined."[15] Combined with the president's corporeal preservation, the comparison with Jesus fell squarely within the spirit/body dialectic that figures so profoundly in Western conceptions of normative kinship. As Gary Laderman observes, "the family that appropriated [Lincoln's] body was...the national family, which had lost its 'father' (as well as its sons) as a result of war."[16] Laderman goes on to argue that the preservation and display of Lincoln's body allowed the fallen president to serve also as a "surrogate son to those parents who had lost their offspring and knew the ultimate fate of their sacrificed children — mass, anonymous burial in profane southern soil" (162). In a separate discussion, Laderman notes that the sight of decaying and unburied bodies on Civil War battlefields evoked racial anxieties that exacerbated this sense of desecration. Describing the gruesome aftermath of the battle at Antietam, *Harper's Weekly* observed that "the faces of those who had fallen in battle were, after more than a day's exposure, so black that no one would ever suspect that they had been white. All looked like negroes, and as they lay in piles where they had fallen, one upon another, they filled the by-standers with a sense of horror."[17] As with the bodies of dead Union soldiers, Lincoln's embalmed corpse began to show signs of decay throughout its long journey from Washington to Springfield. A *New York Times* journalist described Lincoln's pallor as "leaden, almost brown...the eyes deep sunk and close held upon the socket....[Decomposition] has already undone much of the cunning workmanship, and it is doubtful if it will be deemed wise to tempt dissolution much further."[18] While the limitation of African Americans to the role of grave diggers during the early part of the Civil War extended their social death to a more intimate contact with material death, the invocation of race in the context of corporeal decay worked to disavow and project white mortality onto blacks. The fear that white bodies might turn black links the spirit/body dialectic and its disavowal of death to late nineteenth-century anxieties around miscegenation and racial indeterminacy — as if the practice of embalming not only promised eternal preservation but protected white bodies from the impending doom of racial amalgamation.

In this sense, the fear of interracial mixing emerges as a displacement of a more profound set of anxieties that circle around the nonpresence of the white body. Here we are talking not only about the possible alienation of an "inalienable" whiteness but also of the death that the desire for racial purity seeks to deny. If we consider that the patriarchal model of kinship, exemplified by the Christian tradition, requires the incarnation of the spirit/father in a son whose death preserves the father's immortality, racial amalgamation threatens to derail the reflexivity of the father's self-relation. The model of the Divine family — while performing a temporary detour through the materiality of the mother's body — must finally suppress the materiality of the mother/child relation through its transubstantiation into Spirit. The specter of miscegenation thus threatens to materialize (and thus *de*-immortalize) the father/spirit.

It is precisely this dialectic of spirit and body that John Irwin identifies in his "speculative reading of Faulkner."[19] For Irwin, the Christian dialectic of father and son offers not so much a material genealogy in which the father's immortality is secured through the reproduction of new physical life, but rather, a spiritual one whereby the promise of an afterlife is made good as long as one accepts the sacrifice of Jesus: "The priests who renew that sacrifice in the Mass are, like Jesus, celibate, partly as a sign that they have to do not with the generation of new physical life, a physical life that must always be in bondage to death, but with the generation of a new spiritual life — they are ghostly fathers" (131). Following from Ernest Jones's theory of "the fantasy of the reversal of generations," Irwin argues that Faulkner's fiction is deeply invested in an antagonistic "revenge" fantasy in which the son murders, negates, and finally becomes the father as the condition of the latter's immortality. Yet if, as Jacques Derrida insists, "the first spiritualization also, and already, produces some specter," such a specter would emerge as a contamination of spirit, as the remainder that resists assimilation and totalization.[20] In this sense, the "spirit" of kinship is always haunted by the possibility of its spectralization, insofar as contamination inheres in the father's self-relation from the start. The specter does not emerge from an external (racial) other, but rather is inscribed in the relation between the father and his own death, the death whose amortization the insistence on racial purity intends yet fails to perform.

The Fall of the House of Sutpen

That the divided nation is always also a haunted nation is suggested by Toni Morrison in her *Playing in the Dark*: "For a people who made much of their 'newness' — their potential, freedom, and innocence — it is striking how dour, how troubled, how frightened and haunted our early and founding literature truly is."[21] Here Morrison echoes earlier Americanist critics, such as Leslie Fiedler and Harry Levin. Whereas Levin argued in *The Power of Blackness* (1958) that our literature is haunted by the shadow of blackness, an often (though not exclusively) racialized figure that is the dialectical underside of American newness and life, Fiedler, in his classic study *Love and Death in the American Novel* (1960), diagnosed American literature as "bewilderingly and embarrassingly, a gothic fiction, nonrealistic and negative, sadist and melodramatic — a literature of darkness and the grotesque in a land of light and affirmation."[22] Despite its pathologizing tendencies, this identification of America with haunting at least gestures toward a demythologized vision of American life and culture. Notwithstanding Lincoln's assumption of integrity, the nation is founded on its divisibility rather than its indivisibility, its production and exclusion of a blackness that is thought to contaminate the nation/body. Yet this phantasmatic production of contaminating blackness obscures how the nation/body is divided in itself from the beginning. That is, the point is not simply that the body of the nation remains haunted by the racial others it excludes — as if the nation/body preceded its phantomization — but rather, that its spectrality is *anterior* to this very exclusion. The disavowal of the spectrality through which the figures of nation, body, house, and family emerge conditions the abjection and exclusion of blackness.[23]

Although the negative valence of the term "contamination" animates antimiscegenation sentiment, I continue to use the word here in part to retrieve it from its pejorative connotations. Moreover, I want to insist that miscegenation — understood as contamination, and therefore as a *différance* that delays and defers any return to self-presence or self-containment — is the condition of *any* life, indeed, of any-body. The prohibition on miscegenation thus vainly attempts to exclude the difference that enables all generation. Walter Benn Michaels argues something similar in *Our America,* when he states that the "technology of reproduction is also the technology of contamination."[24] That is to say that heterosexuality is inherently a "form of miscegenation" (48). Michaels traces the emergence of incest and homosexuality (particularly in nativist, modernist texts) as twin means to prevent the mixing of blood between different families. If "what is outside the family is also outside the race," heterosexual reproduction is always a precarious affair with regard to the nativist anxiety toward difference (8). The imperative of exogamous, heterosexual reproduction threatens the imperative of racial endogamy. Yet Michaels's formulation — although a compelling diagnosis of how the conflation of family/race works in the nativist texts that he examines — is not precisely the same as the claim that I advance here: that *différance* is the possibility of all generation. For Michaels's argument that *intra*racial reproduction is miscegenous still retains the notion of two self-present bodies who contaminate one another through sexual reproduction. This assumption implies that contamination requires sexual contact, and that "I" become contaminated only on the condition of such exposure. Michaels's argument, that is, remains tied to the biologism on which the miscegenation taboo rests. For the proscription on miscegenation literalizes contamination as a material, corporeal "fact." In this view, miscegenation is "what happens" when two bodies "reproduce" rather than the always-already happening that conditions their relation as such. In short, to understand reproduction in terms of *différance* means that my relation to others (and to myself *as* other) is contaminated from the start.[25] Miscegenation names the disavowed specter that haunts the apparent self-presence of "my body." To be *against* interracial sex is thus not only to be against death, but to find that one's refusal to be *near* death, indeed, to be against it in this other sense of the term, must begin by foreclosing alterity. *Not* to be near death is in some sense not to be at all.

In Faulkner's *Absalom, Absalom!,* this disavowal of finitude occasions Thomas Sutpen's pursuit of his grand "design." Sutpen works to build a house only to have it "come down like it was built out of smoke, making no sound, creating no rush of displaced air and not even leaving debris."[26] By the "house of Sutpen," we mean not only the material structure that he tears out of the Louisiana swamp, but also the house as lineage or race. The linguistic chain that links house, haunt, family, and race means that there is no unhaunted kinship, no undivided house of Sutpen. The Sutpen race cannot finally exclude the racial otherness that it imagines as dividing it against itself.

Indeed, after Quentin and Shreve appear to have finished their discursive reconstruction of the old south, it is the specter of miscegenation that remains, that exceeds the walls of their narrative frame:

> So it took Charles Bon and his mother to get rid of old Tom, and Charles Bon and the octoroon to get rid of Judith, and Charles Bon and Clytie to get rid of Henry; and Charles Bon's mother and Charles Bon's grandmother got rid of Charles Bon. So it takes two niggers to get rid of one Sutpen, dont it?... Which is all right, it's fine; it clears the whole ledger, you can tear all the pages out and burn them, except for one thing. And do you know what that is?... You've got one nigger left. One nigger Sutpen left. Of course you can't catch him and you dont even always see him and you never will be able to use him. But you've got him there still. You still hear him at night sometimes. Dont you? (302)

Juxtaposed with the patronym "Sutpen," the epithet "nigger" foregrounds the ruination of the slave master's grand "design." All that remains of the Sutpen lineage is the father's mulatto great grandson, an absent presence of mixed white and black blood that nevertheless demands to be heard: "They could hear him; he didn't seem to ever get any further away but they couldn't get any nearer and maybe in time they could not even locate the direction of the howling anymore" (301). Everywhere present yet nowhere visible, Jim Bond defies any fix on his direction, place, or location. His proximity is chiasmatically related to the obscure distance from which his unintelligible howling hovers over the ruins of the former plantation.

While historically the problem of racial mixing engendered by sexual relations between slave masters and their female slaves was "solved" through the codification of the mother's status in any mixed-race offspring, *Absalom* asks what would happen if a child refused the matrilineal prescription and demanded paternal recognition.[27] Although Charles Bon's mother is not a slave, Sutpen's repudiation of her and her child echoes the historical reduction of the mixed-race child to the status of the mother. Notwithstanding Sutpen's rejection of racial alterity, Bond's haunting thwarts the patriarchal design of immortality. For nothing less than this difference between immortality and *revenance* is implied by the distinction between spirit and specter — that is, between Thomas Sutpen and Jim Bond. Although Sutpen repudiates his mulatto wife and child because they cannot be "adjunctive to the forwarding" of his "design," that design ultimately fails to contain these specters within its restricted economy (211).

The inspiration for Sutpen's design, as we later discover, originates in what might be characterized as the novel's "primal scene": the poor, young Thomas Sutpen is sent to the "big house" with a message from his father who works on the plantation, only to find himself standing before a black servant who informs him that he may only enter through the back door. Humiliated by what must seem to him to constitute a perversion of the natural order of racial hierarchy, Sutpen leaves his family and sets out to have his own "land and niggers and a fine house to combat them with" (192).

Sutpen's encounter with the "monkey nigger" at the door engenders a certain self-dissolution that he immediately projects onto the black servant. He considers what it might be like to strike at this black face, but concludes that

> they (the niggers) were not it, not what you wanted to hit... when you hit them you would just be hitting a child's toy balloon with a face painted on it, a face slick and distended and about to burst into laughing and so you did not dare strike it because it would merely burst and you would rather let it walk on out of your sight than to have stood there in the loud laughing. (186)

This complicated image of the balloon face, like Jim Bond's howling, moves in several directions at once, and thus defies any effort at interpretive containment. Indeed, it is the very image of something about to burst from its structure of containment. It recalls the shattering laughter that, according to Bataille, exceeds dialectical oppositions.[28] That is, the explosive laughter suggests a certain deconstruction of the master/slave dialectic. As Derrida puts it in a reading of Bataille, the *Aufhebung* is "laughable in that it signifies the activity of a discourse exhausting itself to reappropriate every negativity."[29] Yet this image also figures a denial of black sentience that means to remain fully within the violence of a restricted economy of dialectics. The incongruity of laughter with pain figured by the balloon face rehearses the familiar spectacle of the coffle in which — fueled by the assumption that the "'poor negro' is naturally a cheerful, laughing animal" — the pain of slavery was so often suppressed through forced theatricalization and song.[30]

But if the laughing face rehearses the dismissal of black sentience, it also bears the traces of the very pain and violence that it disavows. For the balloon face resembles what a black face might look like with a rope around its neck, hanging from a tree. This possibility is confirmed when the passage goes on to yoke this image to lynching, to the murder of "no actual nigger, living creature, living flesh to feel pain and writhe and cry out" (187). This refusal to recognize black sentience is made difficult, however, by the figuration of this "loud and terrible laughing" as escaping the bonds of containment. Indeed, Thomas must refrain from bursting the balloon, lest the threatening laughter escape through the walls of its "paper-thin distension" (189, 187). This distended materiality, swelling outward to the point of its dissolution, returns us to the paradoxical image of Chambers's soul-like blackness that is imagined as securing the borders of his body, notwithstanding its immateriality. Read next to the image of the balloon face, it is blackness that would appear to have the last laugh, to explode beyond the limits of its premature entombment in something like a body. Perhaps it is this same laughter that converges with Jim Bond's howling, a howling laughter of sorts whose ubiquity leads Shreve to declare:

> In time the Jim Bonds are going to conquer the western hemisphere. Of course it wont be in our time and of course as they spread toward the poles they will bleach out again like the rabbits and birds do, so they wont show up so sharp against the snow. But it will still be Jim Bond; and so in a few thousand years I who regard you will also have sprung from the loins of African kings. (302)

An odd temporal disjunction: *I who regard you now will have been of mixed blood*. The proximity of the future anterior to the present form "I who regard you (now)" plunges this future past into Shreve's present. His present is already his future past, which means that the racial amalgamation that he imagines as taking place in some future past will have already divided his present/presence. Although Shreve insists that the Jim Bonds of the world will not conquer the West in "our time," something of this Pan-Western miscegenation already seems to inhabit Shreve's present. That it *is* and "will still be Jim Bond" whose race will have haunted this bleached-out whiteness figures this whiteness as having already been infected by blackness.

Faulkner's denouement of *Absalom* in a bleached-out yet still miscegenated whiteness both rehearses and displaces what Toni Morrison identifies as a familiar strategy of narrative closure: a resolution into an "impenetrable whiteness" exemplified by the ending of Poe's *The Narrative of Arthur Gordon Pym*. Such figures of whiteness, according to Morrison, "surface in American literature whenever an Africanist presence is engaged" (33). They "function as both antidote for and meditation on the shadow that is companion to this whiteness — a dark and abiding presence that moves the hearts and texts of American literature with fear and longing" (33). While Poe's "shrouded human" whose skin is of "the perfect whiteness of snow" imagines that whiteness as pure and indivisible, the whiteness that closes *Absalom* can no longer lay claim to such unfathomability (32). For the snow-like whiteness that concludes Faulkner's text remains inseparable from, and therefore cut across by, the shadowy blackness that occasions its appearance as pristine and unadulterated.

If *Absalom* betrays the property of whiteness as fully penetrable and alienable, it does so by calling into question the boundaries that separate *my* body from the body of the other. Faulkner's text is pervaded by a sense of ghostly inhabiting of one body in another. This inhabiting is most striking in the love triangle that develops between Henry, Judith, and Bon. The triangle evinces a tripartite transgression of the prohibitions on miscegenation, incest, and same-sex desire that in turn deconstructs the integrity of their bodies. This despite the figuration of Judith as the container of Henry's and Bon's hom(m)osexual desire:

> It was not Judith who was the object of Bon's love or of Henry's solicitude. She was just the blank shape, the empty vessel in which each of them strove to preserve, not the illusion of himself nor his illusion of the other but what each conceived the other to believe him to be — the man and the youth, seducer and seduced. (95)

While this familiar image of woman-as-receptacle would seem to fall squarely within a homosocial tradition in which the bonds between men are preserved by making the container/woman into an alibi for an unavowable same-sex desire, the function of Judith as a vessel is perhaps less secure than it would at first appear.[31] Earlier the text describes Judith and Henry as constituting a "single personality with two bodies both of which had been seduced almost simultaneously by a man whom at the same time Judith had never even seen" (73). Although this passage suggests that Bon seduced the conglomerate pair of Judith and Henry, soon the text asserts with equal conviction that "it must have been Henry who seduced Judith, not Bon...as though by means of that telepathy with which as children they seemed at times to anticipate one another's actions as two birds leave a limb at the same instant" (79). Stopping short of ascribing any agency of seduction to Judith, the text does make it difficult to maintain the trope of containment that it announces. If both Bon and Henry can be figured as the seducers of Judith, and if the latter's seduction is understood to take place through a form of unmediated telepathy, Judith cannot be so easily contained within the homosocial matrix; indeed, the boundary that separates the bodies of Henry, Bon, and Judith becomes crossed by a certain kindred possession. The figuration of Judith as a vessel is undermined by a sense of mutual inhabiting, of an erasure of those corporeal boundaries that would hold her in place as the receptacle for Henry's and Bon's desires.

Indeed, although Judith is not present when Henry seduces Bon, Judith is said to be seduced by the latter nonetheless. Her seduction extends to Bon the telepathic relation that already obtains between her and Henry. The three are one, yet always more than one. They metamorphose into one another such that the relation of each body to itself is always haunted by its appropriation in and through the other. But because there can be no ultimate corporeal synthesis of their "three" bodies into "one," they remain in excess of one another. We thus cannot finally decide for whom each individual's desire is intended, for the very integrity of their desires is shown to be divided in itself, "untroubled by flesh" (77). While we might read Henry's desire as extending across the body of his sister to its "real" aim in Bon, it is equally true to say that Bon is merely the "vessel" through which an unavowed incestuous desire might find expression. As the text explains, only by transforming into Bon can Henry shatter his sister's virginity:

> Perhaps this is the pure and perfect incest: the brother realizing that the sister's virginity must be destroyed in order to have existed at all, taking that virginity in the person of the brother-in-

law, the man whom he would be if he could become, metamorphose into the lover, the husband; by whom he would de despoiled, choose for despoiler, if he could become, metamorphose into the sister, the mistress, the bride. (77)

Henry's desire emerges as an amalgamation of incestuous, homosexual, and interracial desires. Given this mix of social prohibitions and their transgressions, we might understand "Henry's desire" as a kind of miscegenated desire, a desire, or rather, a set of desires that cannot properly be said to belong to Henry. The impropriety of these desires not only makes it impossible to assign their ownership to any one body, but it also prompts us to ask after the relative integrity of both the proscriptions and the transgressions that govern them. If Henry loves Bon, as the text so often reminds us, how is that love to be characterized? Is it incestuous? homosexual? interracial? The multiple and conflicting desires that haunt the pages of *Absalom* are without a body; they are spectral desires whose impropriety marks bodies as absent to themselves, mourning their own loss in and through their appropriation by the other.

Quentin's "Rosy Orifice"

If the father achieves immortality by reproducing his negated body in the body of the child — negated, that is, because the possibility of the father's absence and death underwrites his self-reproduction — that negated body is finally what returns to the father, *preserved* if only in its transcendent, spiritual form. The father's transubstantiation into spirit requires the very body that it negates. Not only does such a dialectic perform a phantasmatic retention of the father's living body above and beyond his death, but it also has the consequence of violently negating the mother as well as the biological kin upon which the structure of the normative family is based. To the extent that it disavows difference, and therefore death, normative reproduction reduces itself to a certain narcissistic project of self-relation and self-recognition.

This disavowal of death *as* sexual reproduction raises the question of whether there might be alternative versions of reproduction that do not reduce to this equation. Might there be nonnormative modes of reproduction, and even nonreproductive forms of kinship, that do not require such self-reflection? Does sexual reproduction presuppose this denial of death? Given that the term "kinship" denotes a relation to the same *kind*, a kinship based on alterity might seem hopelessly unimaginable. Kinship could therefore never be imagined in terms of a pure relation to alterity, for no matter how it might be envisioned to affirm the alterity of the other, kinship would never finally escape the economy of the same. For any kinship relation (whether biological or nonbiological) that aims to surmount the gap between self and other manifests a certain "metaphysics of presence." To understand one's "self-presence" in terms of what Derrida calls an "originary mourning," on the other hand, would be to open up a relation to the other that no longer requires that other as the "proof" and "guarantee" of one's presence.[32] Kinship would announce an ethical relation to the other that affirms the other's fundamental alterity, an otherness of the other that exceeds — while not fully escaping — the economy of the same.

If the kinship between Henry, Bon, and Judith appears to constitute something of an anomaly or an aberration, that is because its heightened sense of mutual incorporation illuminates the originary mourning that haunts any relation between self and other. This allegory of kinship as mourning, however, is in considerable tension with Bon's quest for paternal recognition, which seeks to affirm the self-presence that the father's repudiation has negated: "Maybe...he [Bon] would walk into the house and see the man who made him and then he would know; there would be that flash, that instant of indisputable recognition between them and he would know for sure and forever" (255). Sutpen's denial of his mixed-race son — while conforming to the demands of normative kinship that require the sublation of one's kin as the guarantee of paternal immortality — is all the more necessary given the contaminating threat that Bon poses to his father's immortal transcendence. The material residue that miscegenation leaves on the father's spirit only intensifies Sutpen's paternal violence. If there is any comedy to be found in Sutpen's "design," however, we might look to its anxious and repeated effort to ward off the specter of miscegenation that has always already arrived. Disguised in the cloak of racial contamination, Sutpen's finitude haunts his quest for immortality from the start. For Bon to demand paternal recognition is to show Sutpen's dream of worldly transcendence for what it is: merely a dream.

Bon's quest for paternal recognition thus reaches beyond the economy of presence by uncovering the disavowal of death that subtends Sutpen's quest for an inheritance devoid of racial *différance*. As Bon remarks to Henry, "it's the miscegenation, not the incest, which you can't bear" (285). Bon then goes on to refuse his fraternal relation to Henry, asserting: "No I'm not [your brother]. I'm the nigger that's going to sleep with your sister. Unless you stop me" (286). This denial of fraternity positions Bon as an external threat to the Sutpen family notwithstanding his "blood" tie. Denying his incestuous desire for Judith, Bon lends a certain priority to the racial exogamy that threatens to dismantle Sutpen's design. For Sutpen to refuse his daughter to Bon on the grounds of incest would be to admit to the miscegenation. To avow the miscegenation would be to admit defeat in the face of death, to acknowledge that the only inheritance Sutpen can leave is spectral rather than spiritual.

Although Sutpen ultimately fails to achieve immortal transcendence, that is not to suggest that nothing remains of him beyond his death, only that the legacy that he leaves behind is something both more and less than a "paternal line," with all the restrictions and exclusions of difference that such linearity implies. Sutpen gets his heir, but that monstrous progeny is the product of an unwanted paternity, one that opens up the economy of paternal presence to a plurality of spectral inheritances unanticipated by the confines of his design. To the extent that something of Sutpen remains beyond the defeat of his quest for immortality, one might take issue with the narrator's assessment that the failure of his design consequently "efface[s] his name and lineage from the earth" (6). For it is less the destruction of the Sutpen name and lineage than its spectralization that we witness in *Absalom*. Falling from spiritual transcendence to a sort of spectral *revenance*, Sutpen engenders through his failure a plurality of ghosts. As Derrida reminds us in *Specters of Marx*, there is always more than one specter, more than one possible inheritance.

One of these many Sutpen ghosts emerges at the beginning of the text in Rosa Coldfield's "summons, out of another world almost" to Quentin. Described as haunting Rosa's voice "where a more fortunate one would have had a house," the ghost of the very man for whom the containment of others was a lifetime project ironically lacks any material place that would house his own haunting (4). It is this uncontainability that makes his *revenance* available to a host of inhabitings, not the least of which are the ghosts that come to inhabit Quentin: "His very body was an empty hall echoing with sonorous defeated names; he was not a being, an entity, he was a commonwealth. He was a barracks filled with stubborn backlooking ghosts" (7). Although here Faulkner's language figures Quentin's body as fully containing these ghosts, the innumerable plurality of these specters would seem almost impossible to contain, to overflow the borders of his body. Indeed, the *one* Quentin is described as "two separate Quentins now talking to one another in the long silence of notpeople in notlanguage" (4). The image of Quentin's body as housing a commonwealth of ghosts is further complicated by the narrator's assertion that Quentin "was still too young to deserve yet to be a ghost but nevertheless... [was] one for all that, since he was born and bred in the deep South" (4). Quentin is both a container of ghosts and a ghost that cannot be contained. In this sense, Quentin's condition names the hauntological state of all ghosts who have yet to become ghosts. That is to say, the condition of all so-called "mortals."

If Quentin represents (more than) one of the many specters generated by Sutpen's fallen spirit, this plurality opens itself up to still more "garrulous outraged baffled ghosts" (4). The Quentin-Shreve dialectic that frames the latter half of Faulkner's text uncovers other possible inheritances, specters that transmogrify into forms unanticipated by their historical predecessors. While Shreve's and Quentin's discursive exchange might seem to be haunted only by the specters of miscegenation, it begins to change shape by virtue of their appropriation of this history. In "reconstructing" their history of the Sutpen family, Quentin and Shreve shift the narrative away from the homosocial, "erotic triangle" of Henry, Bon, and Judith toward the more clearly homoerotic relationship that obtains between Henry and Bon. This shift is conditioned by the homoerotic character of Quentin's and Shreve's relationship. As Irwin observes, "the latent homoerotic content in the story of Bon and Henry may well be simply a projection of Quentin's own state made in the act of narration" (78). Projecting themselves onto the Henry-Bon pair, Quentin and Shreve become "not two... but four, the two who breathed not individuals now yet something both more and less than twins" (236). Later in the text, this inhabiting is "compounded still further, since... both of them [are] Henry Sutpen and both of them [are] Bon, compounded each of both yet either neither" (280). Chiasmatic in their relation to one another — always inhabiting the other yet always exceeding the other — the four are never either fully the same or fully different.

To claim that miscegenation reproduces itself in the specter of homosexuality is not to suggest that this transformation follows any progressive "dialectic of spirit." As in Hegel's dialectic, which unfolds according to a logic whereby each new stage turns out to have conditioned what preceded it, what we observe in *Absalom* is a homoerotic kinship between Quentin and Shreve that is always already articulating the terms by which miscegenation is made legible.[33] Yet, Faulkner's text eschews any sublation of miscegenation into a new, higher level of meaning, now materialized in the specter of same-sex desire. Indeed, homosexuality emerges as both bastard offspring and genitor of a paternal will that works to transmit its seed in an inaberrant form. As both parent and child to miscegenation, same-sex desire can neither be granted priority over, nor can it be understood as the deformed progeny of, the racial endogamy that would appear, on the surface at least, to be the novel's chief preoccupation.

While miscegenation is the explicit subject of Quentin's and Shreve's dialogue, a submerged eroticism surfaces throughout their discursive exchange, described by the narrator as "some happy marriage of speaking and hearing" (253). Their dialogue, moreover, is interrupted at multiple points by a narrative voice preoccupied with Shreve's nakedness. Quentin "glanc[ed]...for a moment at Shreve leaning forward into the lamp, his naked torso pink-gleaming and baby-smooth, cherubic, almost hairless" (247). Here the narrator operates as a proxy for Quentin's gaze. This preoccupation with Shreve's naked torso returns later in the text in a passage that would seem to confirm the homoerotic character of their relationship: "So it is zero outside, Quentin thought; soon he [Shreve] will raise the window and do deep-breathing in it, clench-fisted and naked to the waist, in the warm and rosy orifice above the iron quad" (176). Later this "rosy orifice" is described as a crypt, a transposition that figures this rectum as indeed a grave: "The room was...tomblike: a quality stale and static and moribund beyond any mere vivid and living cold. Yet they remained in it, though not thirty feet away was bed and warmth" (275).[34] Eventually they do get in bed, together no less. Lying next to Shreve, Quentin

> feel[s]...the warming blood driving through his veins, his arms and legs. And now, although he was warm and though while he had sat in the cold room he merely shook faintly and steadily, now he began to jerk all over, violently and uncontrollably until he could even hear the bed, until even Shreve felt it and turned, raising himself...onto his elbow to look at Quentin. (288)

When Shreve asks Quentin if he is cold, the latter replies that he is not, but that he cannot help trembling nonetheless, as if shaking in some sort of involuntary orgasm. Not by accident does blood figure in this erotic scene, given the novel's persistent meditation on blood, "the immortal brief recent intransient blood" (237). Although the transmission of blood is understood throughout the text to guarantee one's immortality, the blood that flows through Quentin is imagined as nonreproductive, incapable of sustaining life. Quentin's blood can never be immortal because he is figured as already dead, producing the symptoms of a body freezing to death despite the burning warmth that floods through him.

If the "rosy orifice" where Shreve's and Quentin's desires find a home lacks the immortal, intransient blood with which to reproduce themselves, their discourse does give birth to the figure of Jim Bond, that howling specter of Sutpen's design. His remaindering is the product of their discourse, a dialectic in ruins that cannot finally account for every expenditure, that cannot finally "clear the whole ledger" (302). The miscegenated offspring of Thomas Sutpen coalesces with the result of Quentin's and Shreve's discursive intercourse, producing a specter of their desire that is less the proof of their immortal transcendence than the possibility of a model of reproduction that eschews the logic of presence. As Sundquist details in his reading of *Absalom!* Faulkner employs the metaphor of marriage in order "to force into crisis and overcome the tragic divisions his novel is built upon" (107). For Sundquist, the problematic of failed union – together with the possibility of its final overcoming – circulates as the novel's central metaphor. Indeed, something like the Hegelian *Aufhebung* surfaces when Shreve announces to Quentin: "'And now...we're going to talk about love'" (253). The narrator goes on to assert that – prior to this turn toward love – "all that had gone on before [was] just so much that had to be *overpassed*.... That was why it did not matter to either which one did the talking, since it was not the talking alone which did it, performed and accomplished the overpasssing, but some happy *marriage* of speaking and hearing" (253, my emphasis). Here their intercourse is figured as enacting the negation, preservation, and supercession of what precedes it. "Discarding the false and conserving what seems...true," Shreve and Quentin are said to produce their legacy by sublating all that comes before (253).

Despite the apparent privileging of dialectical resolution that this passage evinces, the specters that they produce, and for which they cannot fully account, deconstruct the teleology that overpassing implies. Their aural copulation resists the logic of presence that inheres in the vocabulary of the *copula*, of that which links a subject to its predicate, as in Hegel's formulation that the "relationship [between husband and wife]...has its actual existence not in itself but in the child — an 'other,' whose coming into existence *is* the relationship" (273, my emphasis). Their failure to reproduce can be read as "successful" precisely because they refuse the logic of self-reflection and self-duplication. It is a nonreproductive reproduction that recognizes from the start its failure to repeat the self without remainder, without, that is, producing some specter.

On Not Overpassing *Loving*

Faulkner's text gives us a pair of young, Harvard students who imagine from within their homoerotic exchange in 1909 how the reproduction of a mixed-race son nearly eighty years before led to the demise of the Sutpen line. Just as this spectral, disjointed time allows Quentin and Shreve to reconstruct the rise and fall of Sutpen vis-à-vis their own fantasies and desires, it also allows us to plunge into the future anterior of Shreve's miscegenated America, and ask how the interimplication of miscegenation and homosexuality emerges in late-twentieth and early twenty-first century debates around family and kinship. For something not altogether unlike this co(in)habiting of same-sex desire and miscegenation activates more recent political and legal debates around the question of gay marriage. Contemporary debate abounds with analogies that compare the former proscription on miscegenation with the current ban on same-sex marriage. One might doubt the relevance of this somewhat easy equation between two very different historical prohibitions and their material consequences if it were not for the currency that this analogy enjoys in the legal sphere, as evidenced by both case law and legal theory. In critical legal scholarship, the historical relationship between the bans on interracial marriage and gay marriage is frequently glossed as "the miscegenation analogy." As David Coolidge notes, recent years have seen such a proliferation of scholarly legal articles making the analogy that its legitimacy is often taken as self-evident.[35] In his dissent from the majority opinion in *Bowers v. Hardwick*, Justice Blackmun wrote that "the parallel between *Loving* [*v. Virginia*, the 1967 case that ended the ban on interracial marriage] and this case is almost uncanny."[36] Joining Blackmun in his dissent, Justice Stevens also remarked on the parallel between interracial marriage and sodomy: "Neither history nor tradition could save a law prohibiting miscegenation from constitutional attack" (216). He then remarks in a footnote citing *Loving*: "Miscegenation was once treated as a crime similar to sodomy" (216). Indeed, the threat of miscegenation has long been compared to other nonnormative sexual relations, as is suggested by an editorial that appeared in the *New York World* on March 24, 1864. According to the *World*, advocating miscegenation would lead to "incest, or any other abomination which the progressists have not yet dubbed with a euphemistic name."[37] In *Scott v. Georgia* (1869), the State Supreme Court upheld the conviction of Charlotte Scott, an "'unmarried woman of color,'" for having sexual intercourse with Leopold Daniels, an "'unmarried white man.'"[38] Given that the opinion cited the production of miscegenated offspring as "sickly and effeminate" and compared the necessity of prohibiting sex between the races with proscribing sex "between persons of the Levitical degrees," the court's language offers what might be the first legal-historical invocation of the "miscegenation analogy" (324). It suggests, albeit preliminarily, that the analogy is not merely a tool of recent political activism, but rather, articulates how miscegenation and homosexuality are understood to threaten the project of heterosexual self-reproduction.

More recently, the analogy was introduced in *Baehr v. Lewin*, the Hawaii same-sex marriage suit that ultimately failed in its effort to achieve legal recognition of gay and lesbian marriages; *Baker v. Vermont*, in which the Supreme Court of Vermont required the state legislature to grant equal benefits to same-sex partners (which resulted in the creation of a "parallel institution" to marriage called "civil unions"); and finally *Goodridge v. Department of Health*, in which the Supreme Court of Massachusetts became the first state to legalize gay marriage.[39] As Justice Marshall argued in the majority opinion: "Recognizing the right of an individual to marry a person of the same-sex will not diminish the validity or dignity of opposite-sex marriage, any more than recognizing the right of an individual to marry a person of a different race devalues the marriage of a person who marries someone of her own race" (337).

While not denying the legal and historical commonalities between *Goodridge* and *Loving*, I would like to interrogate how the "kinship" between interracial marriage and same-sex marriage that these cases seem to evoke might be conceived otherwise than through the vocabulary of analogy.[40] Justice Blackmun's use of the term "uncanny" to describe this difficult relation underscores the problem at hand. The uncanny, as Freud reminds us, names what is both familiar and unfamiliar, both the same and different. The uncanny involves a return to itself, or to *the* self, that remains haunted by the difference that it works to suppress.[41] The "miscegenation analogy" risks making interracial marriage in some sense *about* same-sex marriage. It returns the problematic of same-sex marriage to itself at the expense of supplanting difference. At its worst, the miscegenation analogy fashions gays and lesbians as the "proper" heirs of a dying or already dead ghost of miscegenation.

Certainly miscegenation is *not* a dead issue — one which, it might be thought, the Supreme Court finally put to rest in 1967. In an address at the Boston University Law School in 1997, Randall Kennedy noted that recent polls "suggest that as much as twenty percent of the white population continues to believe that interracial marriage should be illegal."[42] So while I trace how the specter of miscegenation haunts gay marriage, this is not to claim that gay marriage has come to supplant miscegenation altogether as a political issue. If suggesting that we might consider the proximity between these seemingly unrelated narratives appears to trace an improper historical trajectory, that is precisely the point. To be faithful to these inheritances requires that we undertake what Derrida calls an "unfaithful faithfulness," one that refuses to reduce our historical responsibility to the proper, to what always returns to itself by way of excluding all that might contaminate it.[43] Although the specter of miscegenation *qua* miscegenation is certainly alive and well in its "proper" form, to insist on containing it within an appropriate historical inheritance would be to require the return of miscegenation to itself, to deny its catachrestic transformation into ghosts that — while bearing the residue of their historical predecessors — take on new and unforeseen forms. Indeed, would it not evoke the most comic irony to suggest that we might prohibit in advance the contamination of miscegenation, to preempt, that is, the contamination of contamination? Although the Levinasian ethical injunction to affirm absolute difference suggests that the reduction of miscegenation to "the same" of gay marriage can only negate the historical struggles of racial minorities, if violence and ethics are not opposed (as I argued in my reading of *Beloved* in chapter 2), if the relation to the other, that is, can only be articulated in relation to the violence of the same — then miscegenation and gay marriage are not so much "kindred spirits" (i.e., analogous or the same) as they are "kindred specters" — both "more and less than" twin ghosts of the spirit of heterosexual normativity.

While the dissents of Justices Blackmun and Stevens from *Bowers* lend a certain legitimacy to the argument that we might make the claim for gay marriage by taking the *Loving* decision as legal precedent, it would be a mistake to make gays and lesbians into the proper heirs of *Loving*, to "overpass" *Loving*, as it were, in order to secure a gay political agenda. Not only does the miscegenation analogy often obscure how interracial sex remains a source of great anxiety and contestation, it also says nothing of the punitive consequences that resulted from the violation of miscegenation laws prior to their abolition in 1967. These consequences were certainly *different in kind* from those that gays and lesbians have experienced and continue to experience as a result of their exclusion from the institution of marriage. Richard Loving and Mildred Jeter, like many interracial couples before them, risked imprisonment for attempting to evade the law of Virginia by marrying one another in Washington, D.C., and returning to live in their home state. The recent nonrecognition laws that have emerged with respect to gay marriage, unlike the miscegenation laws, would not criminalize gays and lesbians who marry in one state and move back to their home state. Such marriages would simply be held null and void.[44]

While interracial couples were criminalized for violating miscegenation laws, states that prohibited interracial marriage, as Andrew Koppelman observes, did not universally refuse to recognize the validity of such marriages performed in a state where they were legal. If, for instance, one member of an interracial union died and left property in a state where interracial marriage was illegal, or left an inheritance to children who resided in another such state, the marriage was routinely upheld. Interracial marriages were also often recognized when a married couple moved to a state that prohibited such marriages — if, that is, they demonstrated a genuine intent to domicile there and could not be shown to be attempting to evade the law. The same policy of recognition was applied as well in a few cases in which a couple married in a state prior to its adoption of a statutory prohibition on miscegenation. Arguing for the recognition of gay marriages performed in one state by another where it is illegal, Koppelman remarks that "the blanket rule of non-recognition ... is nearly unheard of in the United States."⁴⁵ Whether or not the non-recognition laws lack legal precedent, the different consequences that resulted from the prohibition on interracial marriage as opposed to gay marriage cannot be denied.

To eschew the politics of analogy, however, is not to disavow any historical relation between miscegenation and same-sex marriage. Something like this disavowal emerges in David Orgon Coolidge's "Playing the Loving Card: Same-Sex Marriage and the Politics of Analogy." After listing the numerous differences between *Loving v. Virginia* and *Baehr v. Lewin,* Coolidge declares the miscegenation analogy to be a political rather than legal argument.⁴⁶ While Coolidge is right that there is "no straightforward relationship between" the two, not only is his too-neat separation of the political from the legal difficult to entertain, but his rejection of the analogy leads to a denial of any historical relationship between miscegenation and same-sex marriage. If they are not the same, this logic appears to go, then they must be fundamentally different, so different in fact that we ought not to see any relationship between them. Coolidge's only solution is to reverse the terms of the analogy in order to support the argument against gay marriage. Whereas the Virginia court in *Loving* was "prepared to deconstruct and redefine marriage in order to achieve racist goals," the Supreme Court of Hawaii, Coolidge wryly muses, is "prepared to deconstruct and redefine marriage in order to advance its vision of social transformation" (9). Although Coolidge's construction of this "counter analogy" is meant to parody the politics of analogy and point to its inevitable failure, his strategy fails to go beyond the political rhetoric that he denounces.

Consider that an analogy, after all, names a comparison of unlike things. An analogy is *not* a homology. Whereas the *Oxford English Dictionary* defines the latter as a "sameness of relation," analogy connotes more modestly "a resemblance of things with regard to *some* circumstances or effects" (my emphasis). Yet the politics of analogy — however attuned to the dangers of reducing difference to sameness — nevertheless protect us from the more risky prospect of having to confront what we might call the politics of mourning. As long as we remain at the level of comparing historical injuries, we need not make what Anne Cheng has argued is a necessary move from listing our historical grievances to examining our historical grief.⁴⁷ In *The Melancholy of Race,* Cheng deftly argues that racial mourning too often gets assimilated to the legal exigency of proving damage, where the only harm that registers is that which is material and calculable. Pointing to the decision in *Brown v. Board of Education* (1954) as a notable exception, Cheng stresses the importance of "allowing racial grief to have its say even if it cannot definitively speak the language of material grievance" (4). Citing evidence from the famous "doll tests" — in which black children who were given the choice of playing with black or white dolls generally chose the latter — Justice Warren, in his written opinion on *Brown*, did not limit the scope of the majority's argument to historical debates that circled around the Fourteenth Amendment, but instead turned to intangible factors — namely, the "feeling of inferiority" that segregation causes, and that "may affect [the] hearts and minds [of black children] in a way unlikely ever to be undone."[48] If the *Brown* opinion offers a rare instance in which the law recognized the unfinished business of mourning, it also suggests that the consolidation of mourning around material grievance has the consequence of containing its effects within circumscribed temporal, political, and identitarian boundaries.

In the meetings of the House Judiciary Committee on the Defense of Marriage Act, Republican Representative from South Carolina Bob Inglis exploded in response to the miscegenation analogy, declaring: "It offends me tremendously to have homosexuals compare themselves to the historic struggle for civil rights among black people.... Black people were economically disenfranchised and cut off from this society, whereas homosexuals... have a higher standard of living than heterosexuals."[49] Similarly, when senator Stan Koki of Hawaii insists that the *Baehr* case is "not an issue of civil rights" because "blacks have suffered economic hardship" whereas gays and lesbians have not, he reminds us that the recognition of a material grievance as it pertains to one minority group can too easily justify disallowing the grief of other groups from having its say.[50] Given that miscegenation is no longer legally prohibited, how does the insistence that the issues of interracial marriage and gay marriage occupy separate political spheres become less about separating the grievances of racial minorities from those of gays and lesbians than making miscegenation in some sense *about* the preservation of heterosexuality? Does not the rejection of any historical relationship between miscegenation and gay marriage both conjure and exorcise the specter of miscegenation not so much to preserve the territory of racial grief from political appropriation, but rather, to defend the institution of heterosexual marriage? Although it is important to recognize the anxiety that interracial sex and marriage continue to produce in post-*Loving* America, it seems equally crucial to note that some of the most virulent opposition to the miscegenation analogy comes from the right of the political spectrum in the name of "traditional" marriage. The historical exclusion of gays and lesbians from the institution of marriage can be discounted, this argument goes, both because the effects of this exclusion fail to transpose grief into a legally recognized grievance, and because whatever grief gays and lesbians might experience, it exists in an altogether different historical register from racial mourning.

It is not clear, however, that miscegenation and same-sex marriage constitute two distinct spheres of historical grief, separate and unequal in their respective labors of mourning. A politics of mourning could ask not only how the reparation of historical injuries fails to terminate historical grief, but how it may be finally impossible to separate the mourning that Cheng argues is intrinsic to race from the mourning that haunts the politics of gender and sexuality as well. If the specter of miscegenation has come to inhabit the debate around gay and lesbian kinship, then how, conversely, do the ghosts of same-sex desire shape how we understand the politics of miscegenation? I want to suggest that the specters of homosexuality always haunt the politics of miscegenation insofar as the prohibitions on both forms of conduct are invested in the reproduction of heterosexuality. As we have seen, the fiction of reproduction lies in its effort to replicate the self as compensation for one's inevitable death. Yet, because this project is always doomed to fail, because one cannot achieve immortality through sexual reproduction, normative heterosexuality must name itself as its own heir, must produce itself as its own offspring. Heterosexual reproduction, in other words, immortalizes itself as reparation for its failure to duplicate the self. If reproduction fails to secure one's immortality, reproduction might preserve itself as the immortal spirit of its own impossibility.

As with miscegenation, same-sex desire emerges as the fallen specter of this immortal spirit, a ghost that is made to bear the material residue of heterosexuality's own failure. The old cliché that "homosexuals cannot reproduce so they must recruit" thus does not so much speak to the impossibility of homosexual reproduction as it denies the failure of heterosexual reproduction. That heterosexuals also fail to reproduce is affirmed by the compensatory anxiety of the reproduction of reproduction. When Coolidge argues in "Playing the Loving Card" that the miscegenation laws "were prepared to deconstruct and redefine marriage in order to achieve racist goals," it is unclear how we are to understand miscegenation law as constituting an anomaly of heterosexual kinship (237). If the reproduction of reproduction names a disavowal of death intrinsic to normative heterosexuality, then the call for racial integrity is less an aberration of heterosexual reproduction than a *racialization* of the disavowal of mortality by which normative heterosexuality proceeds.

One Hundred Years of Miscegenation

The juxtaposition of the terms "homosexuality" and "miscegenation" — far from announcing an absurdly catachrestic association between two fundamentally different historical problematics — takes its cue from the historicity of the terms themselves, both of which were invented in the latter half of the nineteenth century: miscegenation in 1864, homosexuality in 1892 ("heterosexuality" was to come later in 1900). Much blood has been spilled over how to address homosexuality's recent entry into Western discourse, particularly around the question of whether its linguistic belatedness means that homosexuality per se did not exist prior to the end of the nineteenth century.[51] Given the considerable debate that this question provoked during the waxing years of queer studies, I do not wish to rehearse its terms here. By alerting us to the relative novelty of the term "miscegenation," however, I mean to suggest only that the discursive life that it has enjoyed well beyond its circulation as a form of anti-Lincoln mudslinging urges us to consider its emergence within a larger historical context, one in which the coeval invention of terms like "heterosexuality," homosexuality," and "miscegenation" says much about their interimplication in modern conceptions of corporeality. Insofar as the terms appeared at a historical moment that saw a proliferation of discourses concerned with categorization, normalization, pathologization, and above all containment, they emerged between the twin poles of what Foucault calls "societies of blood" and "societies of sex."[52] If societies organized around a sovereign power operate through a "symbolics of blood" in which blood as a signifier both affirms lineages (to have or to be of the same blood) and designates that which one must be willing to risk in the name of defending the sovereign, the collapse of aristocracies and the rise of modern democracies means not only that political power can no longer be secured through blood, but also that "wars are no longer fought in the name of a sovereign that must be defended; they are fought in the name of the existence of all" (180). The transition from blood to sex thus takes the living body as an object of normalization: "The disciplines of the body and the regulations of population constitute the two poles around which the organization of power over life is deployed" (183). He continues: "Life is no longer an inaccessible foundation that only emerges from time to time in the accident of death and its fatality" (187). The analytics of sex is exercised over the life of the body in the modern West, for which the triumph over famine and disease means that death no longer seems so imminent: "Sex becomes a central target for a power that is organized around the maintenance of life rather than the threat of death" (193). That the analytics of sex takes the living body as the site of its policing and regulation suggests that the transition from blood to sex marks the emergence of a peculiarly modern conception of the body, of an ordered, self-contained, *living* body, a body that is present to itself. The emergence of the body is thus tied to what Phillipe Ariès has identified as an interdiction and disappearance of death that is symptomatic of modernity.[53] In this sense, the emergence of the terms *miscegenation* and *homosexuality* is marked not only by the development of mechanisms of sexuality that needed a vocabulary to regulate and order bodies, but also by a certain disavowal of finitude, a refusal of death that requires a hermetically sealed body, a body that no longer bleeds.

To locate miscegenation and homosexuality at the threshold of the historical transformation from blood to sex, however, is not to align miscegenation with blood and homosexuality with sex. As Foucault remarks: "The preoccupation of blood and the law has haunted the management of sexuality for close to two centuries" (196). Blood and sex do not conquer one another "without overlapping, interactions or echoes" (196). Recognizing the contamination of "the same" by different blood, the proscription against miscegenation inadvertently admits of a certain nonhermetic conception of the body. Yet the miscegenation prohibition also denies this chiasmatic relation between bodies to the extent that it *racializes* the misc-sanguinity that conditions any blood relation; strictly speaking, no two people have the same blood. Indeed, anxieties around racial purity evince a desire for an impregnable body even as the sharing of supposedly same (yet different) blood radically undermines that hermetic conception.

If "sex gives access both to the life of the body and the life of the species," the coining of the term miscegenation (literally "mixed species") at a historical moment when increased antipathy toward interracial sex and escalating violence were just on the horizon reminds us that miscegenation is just as much about sex as it is about blood. Foucault remarks famously in *The History of Sexuality Vol. 1* that the modern West transformed sexual practices between same-sex partners that were once merely considered aberrant and consolidated them around the "species" of the homosexual.[54] The invention of the homosexual as species ought not to be read apart from the rise of popular pseudoscientific explanations of racial difference that sought to prevent the mixing of human blood belonging to ostensibly different species. Both miscegenation and homosexuality were conditioned by this policing, regulation, and management of bodily life. Both emerge, that is, with the rise of what Giorgio Agamben, following Foucault, understands as modern "biopolitics."[55] Extending Foucault's claim that modernity puts man's "existence as a living being into question," Agamben maintains that modern biopolitics works to exclude certain forms of life from the zone of the living (188). This politicization of life thus coincides with the modern interdiction of death, I would argue, which immortalizes some lives by reducing others to the status of what Agamben calls "bare life," an abject life that is "included in the political order in being exposed to an unconditional capacity to be killed" (85). While Agamben's prime example is the concentration camp, he also maintains that the biopolitical sphere ultimately extends to all life, and therefore decides more generally which lives are to be excluded from the domain of the living.

The association of male homosexuality with death, of course, has a contemporary resonance in the wake of the AIDS crisis. Moreover, the emergence of AIDS has dealt a devastating blow to the modern Western conceit that plagues, and by extension death, are things of the past. In his "Strange Blood: Hemophobia and the Unexplored Boundaries of Queer Nation," Michael Davidson identifies an inheritance of late nineteenth-century anxieties around blood and racial purity in contemporary AIDS rhetoric, discourses in which hemophiliacs and homosexuals have found themselves engaged in an unlikely and highly charged kinship:

> Blood disorders raise concerns about the porousness of boundaries, the vulnerability of the bodily envelope, the infection of bodily fluids — concerns that parallel phobias about sexual deviance and racial mixing. Hemophobia, in other words, represents the merging of two discourses — one of blood, the other of sexuality — in which anxieties about bodily boundaries in one are articulated through anxieties about gender binaries in the other.[56]

Drawing from Foucault's distinction between "societies of blood" and "societies of sex," Davidson remarks that the latter are "based on maintaining the health of the larger social body.... The policing of the body, the categorizing of its functions, ardors and excesses, becomes the central concern of health and medicine" (45). In this sense, bleeders are threatening precisely because their bodies fail to conform to the modern conception of the body as container. The screening of homosexuals from blood donation in the advent of the AIDS crisis, like the division of black blood from white blood in the nineteenth century, figures both homosexual and miscegenated bodies as in some sense "bleeders." Indeed, their coeval emergence as signifiers of uncontainability paradoxically figures these bodies as bleeding into one another, allowing the miscegenated body in some sense to stand in for the homosexual body.

To Bon's conclusion in *Absalom!* that "it's the miscegenation, not the incest, which you [Henry] can't bear," we might then ask if it is not also precisely an unnamed same-sex desire that the novel cannot support. How might the text employ miscegenation, *not* exclusively, but in part, as a means to name what it cannot name? This is not to suggest that miscegenation merely screens homosexuality — in both senses of concealing *and* revealing it — only to note that the novel's apparent silence on the latter is inversely related to its obsessive speaking of the former. If miscegenation gives voice to Quentin's and Shreve's "marriage of speaking and hearing," it does so by remaining in excess of homosexuality as its "proper" referent.

The Bon(d) of Kinship

As I argued above, Quentin's and Shreve's homosexual miscegenation is conditioned by a discourse on love whose dialectical "overpassing" fails. Although this dialectic recalls both Christian and Hegelian formulations of reproduction, it is Plato's conception of love, particularly in the *Symposium*, that most closely resembles the homoerotic quality of their dialogue.[57] Whereas in Plato's dialogue each "character" gives a eulogy on love only to have Socrates refute them in the interest of affirming some synthesis of all opposing views — an "overpassing to love" in its final and true form — Shreve and Quentin fail to give us any final word on the subject. Despite its pretensions to synthesis, as well as its embedded narrative structure (both of which directly recall Plato's dialogue), their dialogue undoes its own dialectical structure.

In addition to Socrates' speech, the *Symposium* contains the famous speech of Aristophanes, who claims that all humans are halves of an originally whole being that Zeus cut in half as punishment for challenging the gods. According to Aristophanes, love names the pursuit of wholeness in our lost other half. While humans cut off from an androgynous being are attracted to the opposite sex, humans separated from a single gendered being long to be reunited with the same sex. When Socrates goes on to take up the question of love, he preserves Aristophanes dialectical logic while reformulating it. Love, for Socrates, is the desire for something that one does not possess. Notwithstanding Aristophanes' claim of an originary wholeness, Socrates offers Diotima's argument that the object of love is not only goodness, but the "permanent possession of goodness for oneself" (48). Insofar as the object of love is the possession of permanent goodness, the aim of love, Diotima concludes, is immortality. Such immortality can only be achieved, Socrates goes on to suggest, through reproduction, "because reproduction is as close as a mortal can get to being immortal and not dying" (49).

The "goodness" that Faulkner's text makes into an object of love appears under the proper name *Bon*, "Charles Good," as Quentin reminds us (213). Yet this "Bon" that Quentin and Shreve generate constitutes both something more and less than the reproduction of the permanent possession of goodness for themselves. The immortality of this good is spectralized by virtue of Bon's irreducible difference. As the remainder that resists containment within the frame of their dialectic, this "bon," or good, might also be heard in terms of its Americanized pronunciation, "bone," that is, as what remains after all flesh and blood has decayed. Or one might imagine, alternatively, that this "bone" would contain the marrow, or what the *Oxford English Dictionary* defines as "the inmost or essential part," the "goodness." Bon's inmost part, however, is cast in terms of the one drop of black blood that contaminates the whole, and is therefore understood as anything but "good." Bon's name thus bears the weight of these paradoxical meanings insofar as he is figured as both the container of some irreducible essence and the remainder that resists containment.

Shreve's and Quentin's reproduction of Bon, moreover, recalls Diotima's distinction between physical and mental pregnancy:

> When men are *physically* pregnant... they're more likely to be attracted to women; their love manifests in trying to gain immortality, renown, and what they take to be happiness by producing children. Those who are *mentally* pregnant, however... people whose minds are far more pregnant than their bodies; they're filled with the offspring you might expect a mind to bear and produce. What offspring? Virtue, and especially wisdom. (52, emphasis in original)

Here playing off the meaning of the word philosophy (the love of wisdom), Diotima goes on to claim that heterosexual love is in some sense inferior to the love between men, whose creations are truly immortal:

> This kind of relationship involves a far stronger bond and far more constant affection than is experienced by people who are united by ordinary children, because the offspring of this relationship are particularly attractive and are closer to immortality than ordinary children. We'd all prefer to have children of this sort rather than the human kind... since the children themselves are immortal. (52)

Although we might be tempted to follow Diotima's logic here and conclude that Shreve's and Quentin's creation of Bon is superior to heterosexual reproduction because his presence in and as discourse, as speech *(logos)*, preserves their immortality, the transformation of Charles Bon into his spectral grandson, Jim Bond, reminds us that reproduction between two men is no more a guarantee of immortality than heterosexual reproduction. What Jim Bond's ghostliness offers — and what the Americanization of his name performs — is a Bond between Shreve and Quentin that is "far stronger" not because his immortality preserves their continued presence, but rather, because the *bon* (or good) that he promises to be is forever deferred by their bond, left to remain as the ghostly reminder of their "failed" reproduction. In other words, their bond begets a Bon who begets a Bond: this last Bond undoing the bond and the bon that precede it, and thereby transforming their failure into a certain "success." Leaving us only with Bond and his unintelligible howling, moreover, Faulkner's text reminds us that the bondsmen of slavery continue to haunt the bonds of kinship. Jim Bond's name thus allegorizes how kinship and slavery are implicated in one another — that is, the extent to which both kinship and slavery involve a dialectical logic whose pretensions to synthesis are always haunted by the otherness they exclude.

4

The Kinship of Strangers; or, Beyond Affiliation

From San Francisco Mayor Gavin Newsom's decision to issue marriage licenses to same-sex couples, to the legalization of gay marriage by the Massachusetts legislature, to President George Bush's call for a constitutional amendment defining marriage as a relationship between one man and one woman — recent years have witnessed unprecedented political tension around the subject of kinship. While gay activists and conservative politicians have been battling it out over gay marriage, scholars such as Judith Butler, Elizabeth Freeman, and Michael Warner have been urging us to envision queer forms of affiliation beyond the purview of the state.[1] State recognition does not come without state regulation, they remind us, and given the law's sorry record on disciplining queer sexualities, gays and lesbians ought to think twice about securing their legitimacy at the state's hands. As Warner argues, moreover, "queer sexuality" encompasses a wide range of identities and practices beyond those that belong to or are performed by gays and lesbians. Marriage is "designed to reward both those inside it and to discipline those outside it: adulterers, prostitutes, divorcees, the promiscuous, single people, unwed parents, those below the age of consent — in short, all those who become, for the purposes of the marriage law, queer" (89). The position of "queer" is thus infinitely transposable, readily inhabited by anyone unable or unwilling to accede to the norm. Marriage relies on the structural possibility of queerness against which it poses its claims of legitimacy.

To resist marriage, then, is to reject the "invidiousness" of an institution that "sanctifies some couples at the expense of others" (82). Remarking on Illinois Republican Henry Hyde's claim that gay marriage would demean heterosexual marriage, Warner notes how Hyde's enraged moralism obscures the unethical subtext of his argument: "He [Hyde] doesn't just want his marriage to be holy; he wants it to be holy at the expense of someone else's" (82). Although this affirmation of certain relationships against the negation of others may appear to be a gesture *only* of straight marriage, Warner astutely observes that such "selective legitimacy" is a "necessary implication of the institution" (82). While gays and lesbians might imagine that the legalization of gay marriage would remedy the exclusive character of the institution, Warner reminds us that the division between "inside" and "outside" is not only a function of discrimination against gays and lesbians; rather, marriage is conditioned by a dialectic of legitimacy (social life) and illegitimacy (social death) that no liberal ideology of inclusion can undo.

The first section of this chapter considers how both the exclusion of gays and lesbians from the institution of marriage and the demand for their inclusion are implicated in a dialectical model that disavows dying. As I have argued throughout this study, the belief in one's self-presence always betrays a melancholic refusal of death. In the words of Freud, "at bottom no one believes in his own death.... Every one of us is convinced of his own immortality."[2] One never simply believes in one's presence in the present. One believes in one's presence for now and for always. As Heidegger observes in *Being and Time*, moreover, the belief in one's eternal presence is predicated on the conviction that death always happens to *them*: "One says that death certainly comes, but not right away."[3] This "not right away" denies mortality as something with which we are not *presently* involved and thus only applies to others. In the preceding chapter, we witnessed this ontological segregation in Thomas Sutpen's projection of his mortality onto racial and sexual others. While the contemporary activist demand for gay marriage poses legal recognition as the final remedy for the social death of queers, this desire to be made present, I argue, fails to recognize how the supposition of self-presence produces the abjection of gays and lesbians in the first place. That this demand for legal recognition has come to supplant AIDS as a political cause, moreover, further underscores how the preoccupation with gay marriage serves to disavow mortality and mourning.

The second half of this chapter asks how queer theory remains ensconced in an analogous refusal of mourning despite its efforts to imagine forms of belonging beyond the family. For whether promoted by activists who seek legal recognition for their relationships or expanded beyond the normative, heterosexual family, the concept of kinship remains firmly tied to the dialectical model. Notwithstanding its resistance to traditional marriage, queer theory has failed to interrogate the fundamental assumption that kinship — whether biological or nonbiological, straight or queer — constitutes a relation of positive affect and immediacy. The concept of kinship, in other words, presupposes that the distance between self and other might ultimately be bridged. When Warner, for instance, advocates that we disaffiliate queer forms of belonging from the state, he suggests that a queer ethics ought to recognize numerous extralegal modes of kinship. Yet, he does not take into account how these forms of affiliation can become just as idealized as state-sanctioned marriage. Insofar as queer affiliation mimes the conventional belief that kinship can supercede alterity, it remains implicated in a violent reduction of the other to the same. A truly *ethical* queer kinship, on the other hand, would avow rather than deny the originary alterity and absence of "our" kin.

The Death of AIDS and the Birth of Marriage

While the desire for legal recognition implicates gay activism in melancholia, it seems equally important to understand how this melancholia takes it cue, in part, from the exclusion of gays and lesbians from the institution of marriage. Recent legal debates have tended to focus on the opposition of gender and desire that subtends heterosexual marriage. Indeed, in the well-known case in Hawaii, the court determined that the ban on gay marriage amounts to sex discrimination insofar as the law requires that the parties who enter into a contract be of opposite genders.[4] That heterosexual marriage requires the opposition of gender and desire suggests that the ban on gay marriage is implicated in what Judith Butler has aptly termed "heterosexual melancholia."[5] For Butler, the prohibition on homosexuality begins with the bar against desiring one's same-sex parent. This proscription then puts into play a certain melancholic attachment with the gender that has been foreclosed as a possible love object. Gender identity is thus formed in part through a repudiation of the gender that one does not desire. This melancholia emerges in the hyperbolic performance of gender in which "the straight man *becomes*... the man he 'never' loved and 'never' grieved; the straight woman *becomes* the woman she 'never' loved and 'never' grieved" (147, her emphasis). Maintaining that sexual object-choice is produced through a hyperbolization of gender into the categories of "male" and "female," Butler provides an analysis of gender that takes into account the interimplication of sexuality and gender. If male heterosexuality would appear to sustain itself through a hyperbolic performance of masculinity, that is because normative heterosexuality tends to panic when gender performance too closely mimes sexual object-choice. If a heterosexual male acts *like* a woman, how can he still desire her? Or as Butler puts it: "He wants the woman he would never be. He wouldn't be caught dead being her" (137). Death is the price that men must pay for confusing their desire with their gender.

When the Hawaii State Supreme court ruled that denying marriage licenses to gay couples discriminates on the basis of gender, it clearly linked homophobia to the normative opposition of gender and desire. On the face of it, the argument is quite radical in its refusal to sustain the codification of the gender/desire opposition. The court's action suggests that discrimination based on sexual orientation is something like a "straw man" (or woman) for sex-based discrimination.[6] As the court explained: "By its plain language, the Hawaii Constitution prohibits state-sanctioned discrimination against any person in the exercise of his or her civil rights on the basis of sex" (562). Because the Hawaii Constitution provides stronger provisions against sex-based discrimination than does the U.S. Constitution, the court decided that the Hawaii marriage law was unconstitutional. In remanding the case to the lower court, the Hawaii Supreme Court held that the law must be reviewed under "strict scrutiny." That is, because Hawaii law considers gender to be a "suspect classification" (i.e., an immutable characteristic entitled to equal protection by law), the state had to demonstrate a compelling interest in not allowing same-sex couples to marry. With the burden of proof on the state, and limiting that proof primarily to claims that households headed by same-sex couples impeded the healthy development of children, the circuit court ruled on remand that the state cannot deny a couple a marriage license simply because the parties are of the same gender. With this decision, Hawaii appeared poised to become the first state to legalize gay marriage. That is, until November 1998 when the voters circumvented the court's decision by passing a constitutional amendment that defined marriage as a union between a man and a woman.[7]

Although the Supreme Court's holding in *Baehr* that gender is a "suspect" classification would at first appear to subvert the desire/gender opposition, this same court's rejection of a fundamental privacy right for same-sex marriage undermines the radical implications of that subversion. Following from precedent set forth by the U.S. Supreme Court, the *Baehr* majority opinion stated:

> We do not believe that a right to same-sex marriage is so rooted in the traditions and collective conscience of our people that failure to recognize it would violate the fundamental principles of liberty and justice that lie at the base of all our civil and political institutions. Nor do we believe that a right to same-sex marriage is implicit in the concept of ordered liberty, such that neither liberty nor justice would exist if it were sacrificed. (556)

Yet, as Steven Homer deftly observes, the court found that there is no fundamental right to same-sex marriage *only* on the basis of the federal privacy doctrine that takes marriage as inextricable from procreation.[8] While the court goes so far as to suggest that "it is immaterial whether the plaintiffs ... are homosexuals" (in other words, two straight men or women could theoretically marry one another on the basis of the Hawaii constitution's prohibition on gender discrimination), this formulation proposes a disentangling of gender from sexuality that the court is unprepared to sustain (558). Given that the assimilation of marriage to the exigencies of reproduction requires that marriage be defined as a contract between people of opposite genders, the rejection of the privacy argument reinscribes the desire/gender opposition that the determination of gender as a suspect classification would contest. In short, the *Baehr* court ultimately endorsed discrimination based on gender, and by extension, heterosexual melancholia.

Insofar as it conflates marriage with procreation, moreover, the state is implicated in a familiar melancholia of presence that maintains itself through the incorporation of a nonreproductive and "dead" homosexuality. As I showed in chapter 3, normative heterosexuality works to reproduce itself across time in order to compensate for its failure to achieve immortality through sexual reproduction. But is there not also something like *homosexual* melancholia? And is it not precisely this other melancholia that surfaces in the demand for gay marriage? To the extent that the demand for gay marriage rests on the desire for recognition, the state becomes something like the phantom "other" in which gays and lesbians might imagine themselves as finally present, no longer socially dead. Yet, while our culture makes the socially dead stand in for the death that haunts any life, the ontology of gays and lesbians would be made no more secure by the reparation of their social death. This is not because there is some necessary, pathological connection between homosexuality and death, despite the claims of many homophobes. Rather, there is a necessary and irreducible relation between being and death *more generally* that heterosexist culture must deny and project onto the figure of the queer. Given that the social death of gays and lesbians is conditioned by a strict distinction between being and nonbeing, presence and absence, how does the desire for legal recognition preserve the ontological presupposition that first produces the socially dead? This is not to suggest that all gays and lesbians who want to marry understand marriage as synonymous with reproduction, and therefore, with the dream of immortal presence. Yet even those forms of gay kinship that eschew reproduction cannot finally avoid implication in the fantasy of self-presence insofar as the continued existence of their kinship is thought to require the recognition of the state as Other. In this sense, both the de-ontologization of queer kinship and the demand for its re-ontologization owe their origins to a shared — though not necessarily commensurate — disavowal of dying.

Given the emergence of this demand in the wake of numerous calls for a "post-AIDS" gay culture — pronouncements that triumphantly declare the end of AIDS — we might well ask how the melancholia of presence persists in and as the demand for the legalization of gay marriage. The desire to be included in the domain of marriage thus not only excludes gays and lesbians who do not subscribe to the ideology of legalized marriage, but also works to marginalize AIDS and those living with it. And this marginalization of AIDS is itself a melancholic gesture that seeks to supplant the specter of death and dying with the ostensibly future-oriented institutions of marriage and reproduction. Indeed, we might ask how AIDS itself becomes a cathected site of mourning in the wake of its presumptive death. The emergence of the gay marriage issue on the heels of a "dying" AIDS crisis suggests that marriage promises a certain ontologization of those we have lost. Moreover, it reflects an acute anxiety that — if the rumor of the death of AIDS turns out *not* to be an exaggeration — then gay men could find themselves bereft of a life-and-death crisis around which to organize their kinship relations.

We need perhaps look no further than one of Andrew Sullivan's many passionate pleas for gay marriage to glean some sense of how the presumptive "end" of a serious and sustained engagement with the AIDS crisis conditions the call for gay marriage. Responding to the charge that the stigmatization and increased criminalization of gay sex, especially in public, marks the emergence of a "Sex Panic" in American cultural politics, Sullivan writes:

> It is a victim panic, a terror that with the abatement of AIDS we might have to face the future and that the future may contain opportunities that gay men and women have never previously envisaged, let alone grasped. It is a panic that the easy identity of victimhood might be slipping from our grasp and that maturity may be calling us to more difficult and challenging terrain. It is not hard to see what that terrain is. It is marriage.[9]

Setting aside for the moment how anyone, let alone an HIV-positive gay man, could suggest that the "terrain" of marriage is "more difficult and challenging" than an epidemic that has claimed millions of lives over a period of twenty-five years, we cannot but note the sober urgency with which Sullivan solicits us to accede to the "maturity" of marriage. Although Sullivan would have us believe that the move from AIDS to marriage is made possible by the so-called "abatement of AIDS" — by which he means the emergence of new drug therapies for HIV-positive people that have been widely successful in extending their life expectancy — this progressive narrative from "death" (AIDS) to "life" (marriage) obscures how these seemingly separate terrains might overlap. Sullivan's characterization of marriage as more difficult and challenging for gays and lesbians than the AIDS crisis betrays a certain transposition of the anxiety of AIDS into the context of marriage, as if the difficulty associated with marriage works to displace Sullivan's own sense of panic and terror in the face of a medical crisis that is not yet over. Marriage can appear to be "difficult" and "challenging" to Sullivan only because he has supplanted the truly difficult terrain of AIDS with the safety of marriage, and at the risk of trivializing the persistence of the epidemic.

Although Sullivan advocates marriage because he believes that the end of AIDS calls for more sustained and "mature" kinship relations among gay men in particular, it is unclear whether such modes of belonging are as concerned with the living as he would have us believe.

Indeed, Sullivan's manifesto for gay marriage opens with an anecdote about a recent trip to San Francisco that coincided with Halloween, "the night when the boundaries between the dead and the living are supposed to slip, merge, and blur into something more subversive than normality." Lodging in a room that once belonged to a friend's dead lover, Sullivan is clearly impatient with the seemingly interminable grief of his friend, who dares hold on to his lover's possessions and appears to bear "someone with him, some echo that refuse[s] to die away." While Sullivan implicitly diagnoses his friend's condition as melancholic, his abrupt shift to the subject of marriage betrays Sullivan's own disavowal of mourning. As Steven Homer observes, "those friends who have died of AIDS are irretrievably gone. Gone, and marriage won't bring them back." Read against Homer's remark, Sullivan's urgent call to those gay men left behind, to those who not only "escaped infection, or were immune to the virus, but those who contracted the illness, contemplated their own deaths and still survived," emerges less as a summons to the living than a summons to the dead, indeed, a conjuration of sorts that means to make present all of those lives that have been lost.[10] If only gay men could have married instead of had sex with multiple partners, Sullivan implies, then AIDS would have been avoided altogether.

While Douglas Crimp identifies Sullivan's melancholia in terms of an "identification with the homophobe's repudiation of him," we might also trace this melancholia in terms of how it refuses Sullivan's own ghostliness.[11] Although Sullivan observes that his diagnosis is "no different in kind than the diagnosis every mortal being lives with," this recognition of a common hauntological condition is in tension with his repeated assertion of self-presence, often at the expense of those "others" with whom he shares the same diagnosis ("Plagues," 12). In a critique of Sullivan, Phillip Brian Harper notes that Sullivan begins by recognizing how the majority of those infected with HIV — that is, nonwhites both here and in other countries — will not have access to the drugs, only to disavow the significance of their continued suffering and deaths, writing: "But it is also true — and in a way that most people in the middle of this plague privately recognize — that something profound has occurred in these last few months."[12] A diagnosis of HIV infection "no longer signifies death. It merely signifies illness" ("Plagues," 54). Given Sullivan's unlimited capacities for denial, we might suppose that, for him, death no longer signifies death. Indeed, with the death of illness, the death of death cannot be far behind. Yet, it is not only his own death that Sullivan disavows, but the importance of the deaths of those whom he acknowledges will not benefit from the latest medical advances in AIDS treatment. Indeed, the deaths of minorities condition and sustain the denial of his own mortality. If Sullivan can announce that "most people in the middle of this plague... recognize... that something profound has occurred," and write this following his recognition that "most people" means and will continue to mean nonwhites deprived of the best medical care, then AIDS does still signify imminent death for "most [nonwhite] people," despite Sullivan's attempt to supplant this "minority" referent with a presumptive American, white majority. Although whites do not count as the majority of AIDS cases worldwide, they somehow make their way into the "middle of the plague" as a minority whose wealth and political advantage allow Sullivan to dismiss the deaths of nonwhites so easily.

Indeed, Harper goes on to link Sullivan's logic of "I know... but..." to the Freudian concept of fetishism, and by extension, to the fetishization of normative whiteness. This fetishization of whiteness, I would add, is first and foremost a fetishization of white presence. If normative kinship involves a fetishization of the other, a conjuration of the other as an absent presence that anxiously seeks to confirm one's own presence, Sullivan's recognition of a certain kinship with those minorities with whom he shares the same diagnosis evokes the specter of their suffering and dying only as a way of securing his presence through a fetishized construction of whiteness *as* property.[13] Just as Thomas Sutpen's disavowal of miscegenation works to secure his sense of self-presence, Sullivan protects his investment in whiteness by resignifying his diagnosis in terms of illness while leaving poor people of color to bear the burden of his own disavowed death: if AIDS kills minorities, it only makes white people sick. This is not to claim for AIDS a static signification immune to the improvements offered by new drug therapies in the West. Nor is it to suggest that Sullivan's own access to these drugs does not indeed shift what it means for *him* to be HIV positive. Yet to recognize the changing terrain of AIDS says nothing of how so many are excluded from the benefits that Sullivan enjoys, and how his insouciance toward their exclusion relieves him of having to recognize the death that haunts his and any life. After all, having access to good medical care, or being HIV negative, does not make one immune to death.[14]

Since the 1996 International AIDS Conference in Vancouver, which saw the official announcement of the success of protease inhibitors in treating patients infected with HIV, pronouncements that declare the end of AIDS have been ubiquitous, as if by sheer discursive repetition Americans hope to conjure it away for good. In his ironically titled essay, "Not-About-AIDS," David Román traces the emergence and intersection of various AIDS discourses that either talk about AIDS without talking about it, or explicitly (and contradictorily) begin their engagement with AIDS by denying that they are speaking about AIDS. Asking us to consider how "the 'end of AIDS' itself [might] be understood as an AIDS discourse that tells us much about our current relationship to AIDS," Román contests the division between "AIDS" and "post-AIDS" discourse; that is, he resists the separation of the work of mourning that is AIDS from the work of mourning that the announcement of its death betrays.[15]

In his preface to *Love Undetectable,* Sullivan notes that he began to write a book on friendship while in the process of expanding his *New York Times* essay only to discover that "the two subjects [AIDS and friendship] were, after all, inseparable" (ix). His long excursus on the question of friendship that closes the book, "If Love Were All," is a eulogy in part for a close friend who died of AIDS. Sullivan situates his meditation on friendship among some of the most well-known treatises on the subject, including those of Aristotle, Montaigne, and Augustine. What emerges is an often-moving portrait of friendship and Sullivan's pain in coming to terms with its loss. So high does Sullivan elevate friendship above other forms of kinship that we are left wondering how this view sits with his championing of marriage elsewhere:

> For, of all our relationships, friendship is the most common and the most natural. In its universality, it even trumps family. Many of us fail to marry, and many more have no children; others never know their mother and father, and plenty have no siblings. But any human being who has ever lived has had a friend. (176)

Sullivan goes on to argue that "the great modern enemy of friendship has turned out to be love...the love to which every life must apparently lead, the love that is consummated in sex and celebrated in every particle of our popular culture, the love that is institutionalized in marriage and instilled as a primary and ultimate good in every Western child" (198). Given Sullivan's preoccupation with gay marriage, it is strange to say the least that he criticizes this modern cult of love. And indeed, toward the end of the chapter, Sullivan abandons any further inquiry into the politics of friendship when he claims that "the most important cultural aim of the modern homosexual movement... should be to bring the homosexual child back into the fold of his or her family" (232).

Sullivan's call to elevate friendship above marriage and romantic love (however inconsistent that appeal may be) resonates with the recent efforts of many queer scholars who have sought to imagine a kinship beyond family. While Sullivan has become a familiar (and often deserved) target of critique for many queer scholars, it seems crucial to acknowledge an unexpected kinship between him and queer critics. In lieu of gay marriage, Warner, for instance, advocates a queer ethics that fosters "unprecedented kinds of commonality, intimacy, and public life" well beyond the state-sanctioned couple (88). Irreducible to the normative force of the law, such modes of affiliation and belonging challenge what Elizabeth Freeman calls "paper kinship" (83). Freeman identifies the trope of the wedding in American culture as a performance of "embodied interconnection" that does not require the institution of marriage as the proof and guarantee of its value (83). Neither Freeman nor Warner claims that such forms of belonging are radically exterior to the state; that is, they offer no utopian hope of a kinship fully beyond the reach of regulation. But their shared emphasis on an uninterrogated notion of belonging and connectedness reproduces what I have isolated throughout this study as the fundamental phantasm on which kinship is based: the belief that relations of kinship can overcome alterity. When Warner observes, for instance, that "even the most fleeting sexual encounter *is,* in its way, intimate," he imagines a constellation of noninstitutionalized practices that nonetheless remain tied to the fantasy of mutual incorporation (115, his emphasis). Freeman's turn to "tactile kinship" (embodied in the age-old tradition of the handclasp) also relies on this assumption. Noting that "kin-producing touches... draw from popular and even Christian notions of corporeal binding that predate the state's control of marriage," Freeman asks us to consider how an "unofficial though public realm of bodily acts, rather than either an official institution of law or a deterritorialized eroticism, might incarnate a different social order" (94, 84).

But how different is this social order? How does severing the bond between the state and kinship nonetheless fail to challenge the very principle of the social bond as a mode of positive affect and immediate connectedness? How is a kinship based on pre-modern, Christian forms of belonging *queer*? Remaking contemporary kinship in the image of pre-modern forms of affiliation does little to challenge the persistence of "spiritual kinship" and its reduction of alterity. As Alan Bray's work on premodern forms of male friendship shows, rituals of wedded brotherhood invoked an "expanded" concept of kinship that (not surprisingly) relied on tropes of family and blood. Writing of the friendship between King James I and George Villiers (the duke of Buckingham), Bray observes that their letters display a "bewildering profusion" of kinship terms: "Their friendship is both the kinship created by ritual and that created by blood; not only 'gossip,' 'husband,' and 'wife' but also the 'boy' that a father might call his child or the 'dad' that then as now was the term a child used to address its father."[16] And yet, whether biological or nonbiological, blood-based or ritualized, kinship remains a phantasm. To foreground the phantasmatic character of *all* intimacy, however, is not to make the rather absurd suggestion that we ought to abandon all forms of interpersonal connection (as if such a project were even possible). Rather, I mean to underscore that intimacies separated from state institutions, or from the biological family, are still forms of kinship, and thus will continue to bear the threat of violence that accompanies any necessarily failed effort to possess the other.

Extending kinship beyond family, then, still does not address the principle of exclusion on which kinship is founded. In her reading of *Antigone*, for instance, Butler maintains that critiquing the conflation of kinship with family need not "lead to a dismissal of kinship altogether."[17] Rather, kinship might be reimagined in terms of "any number of social arrangements that organize the reproduction of material life, that can include the ritualization of birth and death, that provide bonds of intimate alliance both enduring and breakable, and that regulate sexuality through sanction and taboo" (72). Butler understands Antigone's aberration from kinship as an allegory for a queer intervention into the norms that produce some lives as unintelligible and unlivable: "What sustaining web of relations makes our lives possible, those of us who confound kinship in the rearticulation of its terms? What new schemes of intelligibility make our loves legitimate and recognizable, our losses true losses?" (24). But how does enlarging the field of intelligibility unwittingly retain a violent division between kin and non-kin, between the intelligible and the unintelligible? Such kinship beyond family will not and cannot accommodate *every other.* An expanded concept of kinship must still exclude non-kin as the very condition of its intelligibility. As Lee Edelman argues in a critique of Butler, allowing the figure of negativity (i.e., Antigone) to enter into the field of intelligibility does nothing to displace "the structural position of queerness," but simply vacates the role for someone else.[18] While Butler understands the normative family as a form of idealized kinship, this characterization betrays a certain redundancy; kinship *always* depends on an idealized relation to otherness even in its nonfamilial, nonbiological articulations. And this is true despite Butler's effort to submit rigidly deterministic accounts of kinship (especially Lacan's symbolic) to social revision. To wrest kinship away from symbolic law is still not to address how kinship *in whatever form* promises an immediacy between others that can never fully be realized.[19] In this sense, Warner is partially correct when he recognizes that the reduction of queer relations to marriage only promises to produce a new set of exclusions. Yet such exclusions are not *only* a necessary condition of legal institutions, but are a necessary implication of any social relation — no matter how divorced from the state.

A truly radical critique of kinship must begin with the exclusion of the other that emerges anterior to the obliteration of nonnormative forms of kinship. For the negation inherent to the concept of kinship conditions the erasure of queer forms of belonging. Social death thus ought not to be understood simply as a destruction of kinship, but as an instantiation of kinship's most violent possibilities. An ethical kinship, a kinder kinship, requires that we avow this violence in order to diminish it. Only kinship can curb violence because only kinship can first commit it. Thus, when Blanche DuBois says that she has "always depended on the kindness of strangers," the specificity of her alienation also speaks to a more general condition of violence and mourning. Blanche's words strike us as all the more paradoxical if we recall that kindness means kinship. To be kind to a stranger is to treat her as if she were your kin. But this "as if" always suspends itself over the most apparently immediate relations. Given the irreducible alterity of others, we can only and always address as strangers even those whom we consider our closest kin. "Our" kin must remain strangers so that we can "have" kin. For only by allowing them to retain their otherness might we reduce the violence that nevertheless initiates our relation.

Uncanny Kinship

In his *Intimacy in America*, Peter Coviello approaches this question of alterity through the poetry of Walt Whitman, which constructs American national identity through "an unwavering belief in the capacity of strangers to recognize, to desire, and to be intimate with one another."[20] Indeed, throughout *Leaves of Grass*, the poetic voice imagines an immediacy of relation with a vast range of Americans: farmers, slaves, soldiers, prostitutes, artists, politicians, and so on. Coviello extrapolates beyond Whitman, however, to show that this faith in attachment characterizes American culture more generally to the extent that affect substitutes for a lack of common ancestry as well as geographical dislocation. The language of attachment thus allows a "far-flung citizenry" to claim intimacy with those whom they have never met (166). Whitman's fascination with claiming strangers as kin is also noted by Warner, who observes that Whitman persistently "exploits public sphere discourse" and the "necessary anonymity and nonknowledge of writer and reader."[21] In "A Song for Occupations," for instance, the speaker invites the reader to surmount the impersonal and anonymous scene of publication, to transcend the "cold types and cylinder and wet paper between us," to allow for "contact of bodies and souls."[22] For Warner, the speaker manifests a fantasy of unmediated connection that "the anonymous and indefinite audience of the print public sphere" disallows (41). Whereas Coviello understands this affective ideology as a "dream of *fellowship, of some manner of bond that would make kin of strangers,*" and Warner derives the "definitional impossibility of intimacy" from the gap that publication generates between author and reader, this fantasy is nevertheless inherent in *all* kin-making practices insofar as our relation to our "closest" kin is not finally opposed to the bond that we might imagine with any stranger (174, his emphasis, 40). For the "impossibility of intimacy" is not simply an effect of print media, as Warner maintains, but of an originary loss and mourning of the other that both conditions and limits any claim of spatiotemporal immediacy.

This connection between estrangement and loss is evident in Whitman's "To a Stranger," in which the speaker calls out to an ostensibly anonymous other as if their relation somehow antedated the address itself:

> Passing Stranger! you do not know how longingly I look
>   upon you,
> You must be he I was seeking, or she I was seeking, (it comes
>   to me as of a dream,)
> I have somewhere surely lived a life of joy with you,
> All is recall'd as we flit by each other...
> You grew up with me, were a boy with me or a girl with me.[23]

In what sense is this addressee a stranger, given that the speaker claims to recognize him/her from a dream? Or does the dream reference imply that the addressee uncannily embodies the memory of a former friend? While the poem concludes with the lines, "I am to wait, I do not doubt I am to meet you again, / I am to see to it that I do not lose you," what is the affective and epistemological character of their encounter? In what sense can they be said to have met one another? On the one hand, their "meeting" appears to be based purely on a visual recognition that mimics physical intimacy: "You give me the pleasure of your eyes, face, flesh, as we / pass, you take of my beard, breast, hands, in return." On the other hand, the speaker recalls that, because I "ate with you and slept with you, your body has become not yours only nor left my body mine only," implying contact of a sexual nature prior to this scene of encounter. Remaining agnostic with regard to the temporal origin of their relation, the speaker frustrates conventional oppositions of knowledge and anonymity, proximity and distance, presence and absence, pleasure and its loss. Although the "I" seeks to forestall the loss of this "you," it seems as if the latter already bears the traces of loss, of an absent friend whom s/he both recalls and will someday embody. If "A Song for Occupations" imagines a certain transcendence of alterity, then "To a Stranger" foregrounds estrangement and loss as the (im)possibility of intimacy.

Whitman's trope of cruising not only illustrates the loss at the heart of all intimacy but also offers a means to interrogate normative heterosexuality's generally pejorative view of "anonymous" queer sex.

To what extent does this stigmatization disavow the alterity that heterosexuality claims to overcome through its pretensions of dialectical union? Indeed, the construction of queer sexual life as fundamentally estranged functions to deny the distance that normative heterosexuality nonetheless aims to surmount through its phantasmatic fusion of opposites. In this sense, to claim intimacy with another is always to deny alterity and loss. And this is no less the case for those "nonstandard intimacies" that Warner (along with Lauren Berlant) celebrates for their "world-making" possibilities.[24] Seeking to destigmatize various forms of queer "counterintimacy" — from cruising, to frequenting sex clubs, to tricking — Warner and Berlant suggest that such social formations should not be dismissed as "empty release or transgression," but ought "to count as intimate" to the extent that they manifest "a common language of self-cultivation, shared knowledge, and the exchange of inwardness" (561). Yet this expanded definition of intimacy, much like Butler's enlargement of the domain of social intelligibility, fails to interrogate what *remains normative* in such apparently radical social practices: that is, the very fantasy of inwardness, of mutual incorporation without remainder or loss. Rather than claim queer sexualities as *truly* intimate, we ought to ask how the phantasm of immediacy continues to shape queer sociality even in its most apparently nonnormative forms.

If intimacy is always implicated in a disavowal of absence, then affirming "queer" kinship for its "counterintimacies" is far less novel than it would appear. Celebrating the pleasures of anonymous sex, Warner suggests in an interview published in *Lingua Franca* that "the phenomenology of a sex club encounter is an experience of world making. It's an experience of being connected not just to this person but to potentially limitless numbers of people, and that's why it's important that it be with a stranger. Sex with a stranger is like a metonym."[25] Warner voiced this manifesto for "public" sex after the enforcement of new zoning laws in New York, Los Angeles, and other urban areas began to curtail queer access to sexual culture. While his critique of this sexual panic is certainly laudable, one might also note the highly idealized ground on which this defense of anonymous sex is mounted. On the one hand, to claim that queer world making *requires* sex with strangers reifies the kin/stranger opposition. If the alterity of the other is never sublatable, then "sex with a stranger" is a redundancy. On the other hand, to imagine a relation to *all* others, no matter how removed or absent our relation to them might finally be, is to collapse any distinction between "known" and "unknown" partners. We become kin with everyone. But if one claims everyone as one's kin, then kinship becomes evacuated of all meaning: to be intimate with everyone is to be intimate with no one. Indeed, this formulation of unfettered intimacy recalls the Christian doctrine of universal siblinghood that, as Marc Shell observes, cannot sustain itself without excluding others.[26] Warner's queer universalism likewise risks effacing alterity by imagining a proximity that makes kin of all strangers. This formulation of a kinship without borders thus does not acknowledge the exclusionary violence on which kinship is based. For every guy that you decide to blow in some back room, you necessarily reject and exclude many others. No less or more so than their heterosexual counterparts, queer venues for public sexual culture are also sites of intracultural discrimination and exclusion: of racism, hierarchies of attractiveness, and so on.

Queer theory's effort to transplant kinship to a nonnormative terrain is thus coextensive with a long tradition that has sought to displace the biological basis of kinship. The problem with claiming that queer intimacies somehow surpass biology, however, is that they risk becoming just as idealized as the domain of normative kinship they claim to have left behind. To the extent that they preserve the terms of kinship that they ostensibly negate, queer forms of belonging might be better understood as the sublation of family. As Montaigne's *De l'amitié* shows, nonbiological forms of belonging can easily be reappropriated by the dialectical model. Lauding the superiority of friendship over family, Montaigne cites Aristippus who, "when one pressed him for the affection that he must have toward his children for having come from him, he began to spit, saying that we just as surely engendered lice and worms."[27] Montaigne then goes on to cite Plutarch, who remarked on his relation to his brother that he did not make much of their "having come out of the same hole" (313). Montaigne would have us believe that friendship — unlike marriage, which often has other aims than affection and love — "has no business or commerce than with itself" (315). Yet friendship, as Montaigne conceives it, looks suspiciously like the dialectical model of kinship that seeks to assert one's self-presence through the relation to the other:

> For all that we ordinarily call friends and friendships are only acquaintances and intimacies tied by some occasion or convenience, by the means of which our souls intertwine. In the friendship of which I speak, they were combined and intertwined one in the other, in a union so universal that they erased and could no longer find the seam that joined them. If pressed to say why I loved him, I feel that it could only be expressed by responding: "Because it was him; because it was me." (318)

Montaigne thus returns us to the fantasy of dialectical union, and therefore to the dream of self-presence. Eager to level the edifice of biological kinship, Montaigne nonetheless retains an idealized model of friendship. Yet, the explanation that Montaigne gives for his love — "Because it was him; because it was me" — also suggests a tension within the passage between a dialectic that erases the seam that joins him and his friend, and a relation of *différance* that resists identity. The difference between "me" and "him" remains. In this sense, those friendships that Montaigne dismisses as mere "acquaintances" and "intimacies" where souls intertwine yet fail to become one would also describe the *necessarily* failed union between any two friends — living or dead.

Montaigne's reflections on friendship would appear to confirm Derrida's observation in *The Politics of Friendship* that there is finally nothing that rigorously separates friendship from family and kinship. Friendship, as it has been conceived from the Platonic tradition forward, is synonymous with fraternity and therefore with what Derrida calls the "double exclusion of the feminine," by which the possibility of friendship between women and friendship between men and women is almost nowhere on the horizon. The "philosophical paradigm" thus corresponds to the "essential and essentially sublime figure of virile homosexuality."[28] We must be careful, however — more mindful perhaps than Derrida would appear to be here — about yoking friendship to some transhistorical notion of homosexuality. For the homosexual character of friendship across history is not necessarily or essentially congruent with what we understand in the modern West as sexual relations between men. Perhaps what Luce Irigaray has called *hommosexualité* — which could include both homosexual and homosocial relations between *les hommes* (hence the double "m") but would not necessarily reduce one set of relations to the other — might be better suited to describe the philosophical paradigm of friendship.[29] For the assimilation of friendship to homosexuality leads Sullivan to the rather absurd conclusion that heterosexual men have not cultivated male-to-male friendships, to which we can only respond: well, of course they have. Friendship is certainly not the staked-out terrain of gay men. And fraternity bears no essential relationship to sexual relations between men (to the great chagrin, perhaps, of gay frat boys everywhere!). Calling our attention to the fraternalization or hommosexualization of friendship, however, Derrida's analysis should caution us against the temptation to idealize friendship as somehow escaping all of the trappings of biology, blood ties, and affiliation. Although Sullivan argues that "friendship trumps family," the fraternalization of friendship means that it will have been family all along.

Asking what friendship would look like divorced from the trappings of fraternity, kinship, blood relations, and the family, Derrida suggests that a friendship otherwise than kinship is always to come, *à venir*:

> As if there have always been only specters, on two sides of this opposition, on two sides of the present, in the past and in the future. All phenomena of friendship, all things and all beings that one must love belong to spectrality. "One must love" means: specters, one must love specters, one must respect the specter. (320)

To love is to love a specter. Or as Simon Critchley puts it: "One is only a friend of that which is going to die."[30] This observation leads Critchley to contrast what he calls the *necrophilia* of the traditional conception of friendship — which maintains a strict distinction between the living and the dead — with what Derrida refers to variably as spectrality and sur-vivance: "One might say that sur-vivance is the first opening onto alterity insofar as alterity opens in the relation to mortality.... The precondition of friendship is the acknowledgement of mortality" (259). Mourning is the originary possibility of friendship. As Derrida remarks: "It is *thanks to* death that friendship can be declared" (335). Whether one declares one's friendship on the occasion of the other's death, which is the case with Montaigne, Sullivan, and many famous treatises on friendship, or if one declares it to one's living friends, "it comes down to the same thing, it avows death thanks to that which finally arrives, never missing the chance to declare itself" (335).

Thanks to death. *Grace à la mort*, writes Derrida. By the grace of death, we have friendship.[31] That the expression "thanks to..." bears both a positive and negative valence affirms an ambivalent relationship to death, that is, given that death is responsible both for the end of friendships and for their possibility. We should thank death, even welcome it. And this invitation that we extend toward death begins with an invitation to the other, to the other as specter. To speak *to* the other as specter. For the love of specters. This spectrophilia is something other than what Robert Solomon calls "death fetishism," which responds to the disavowal of mortality by insisting that death is "something to be celebrated, something even to be loved."[32] Solomon takes issue with those who reject the Epicurean thesis that death, because beyond experience, "is of no concern to us," and instead make it "the focal point of our existence" (164).[33] Whereas Epicurus derives his position from the experientialist view that death can be neither good nor bad because such judgments imply "sensation, and sensation ends with death," this says nothing of the process of *dying* that stretches between one's birth and one's biological demise (54). Unlike necrophilia, which celebrates death, spectrophilia avows dying as productive of our relations to others.

This spectrophilia is suggested by the image with which Sullivan closes his book. Andrew, his friends, and Pat's family have taken a boat out into the Gulf to scatter Pat's ashes into the sea. They cast the ashes into the wind, like "powdered sugar," and then suddenly one of Pat's brothers takes his shirt off and yells "'I'm going in'" (252). After hesitating a moment, the others follow suit, and jump into the Gulf to bathe themselves in the waters now sprinkled with the remains of Pat. Sullivan writes:

> I remember the shock of warmth as my body fell into the sea, and the strange mist that surrounded me as I opened my eyes in the water, and the pure, sweet breeze that greeted me as I reached the surface, and looked around me again, and breathed, suddenly, for air. (252)

Sullivan's baptism in the waters that hold the remains of his friend suggests that diving into death is what friendship is all about. Coming up for air, Sullivan returns from the watery grave of friendship to live on, not perhaps as before, but forever immersed in the remains that return to him, and to all of us, in the figure of the friend.

That the friend is always already lost is implied by the Aristotelian apostrophe that Derrida places under close surveillance as he traces its permutations in Kant, Montaigne, Nietzsche, and Blanchot:

"Oh my friends, there is no friend!" As Derrida unknots this paradoxical utterance:

> Someone turns in effect toward his friends, "Oh my friends...," but the apostrophe turns on itself, it carries in it a predicative proposition, it envelopes an indicative proposition. Claiming to state a fact, it also announces a general truth in the form of a judgment: "there is no friend".... How to affirm without contradiction that to have friends one does not have any friend? (261)

This "performative contradiction" that hovers between the plural and the singular "resembles at once both a *recall* and a *call*" (262). It calls on the presence of one's friends in the present. It assumes their presence prior to the call. Yet it also calls *to* them, calls or conjures them up; "it makes a sign toward the future," to a friendship beyond fraternity, a friendship yet to come (262). And if there is no (one) friend, perhaps that is because a nonfraternal friendship requires the rupture of the couple/copula, the couple as the residue of fraternity, kinship, family, and reproduction: of "two souls united in one body." As Derrida asks, "how could one soul inhabit more than one body without haunting them?" (216). So that there can be more than one friend, "a friend never has a proper place.... The body of the friend, his own body, would always be able to be the body of the other. It would stay there as a guest, a visitor, a traveler, a passing occupant. Friendship would be the *Unheimlich*" (202). Friendship, in other words, is fundamentally queer. And its queerness is not reducible to "perverse" sexualities, or to expressions of intimacy that defy social norms, but speaks to an originary alterity by virtue of which the *familial* is always also the *unfamilial*. This *other* queer kinship would be anterior *both* to state-sanctioned marriage and to those forms of ostensibly "queer" belonging that fail to displace the dialectic of affiliation: its phantasm of embodied interconnection always finally ending in the other's *disembodiment*. So rather than kill our kin with kindness — by which they evaporate into so many spirits of our narcissistic fantasies — we might, to borrow from Faulkner, listen to them being ghosts. How else to sever *le fil*, the thread, of affiliation?[34] This "false friend" that traces no linguistic roots to *filiation*, but that has me imagining otherwise.... Oh my kin, there are no kin!

Notes

Introduction

1. Jacques Derrida, *Politiques de l'amitié* (Paris: Éditions Galilée, 1994), 335. Unless otherwise noted, all French translations are mine.

2. Simon Critchley, *Ethics, Politics, Subjectivity: Essays on Derrida, Levinas, and Contemporary French Thought* (New York: Verso, 1999), 270.

3. Philippe Ariès, *Essais sur l'histoire de la mort en Occident du Moyen Age à nos jours* (Paris: Éditions du Seuil, 1975), 70.

4. Gary Laderman, *The Sacred Remains: American Attitudes Toward Death, 1799–1883* (New Haven: Yale University Press, 1996), 155. See also Franny Nudelman, *John Brown's Body: Slavery, Violence, and the Culture of War* (Chapel Hill: University of North Carolina Press, 2004).

5. Jessica Mitford, *The American Way of Death* (New York: Simon and Schuster, 1963), 77, her emphasis.

6. While in the interest of avoiding repetition I employ the terms death, dying, mortality, and finitude more or less synonymously, I ask that the reader always bear in mind the temporal elongation that inheres in *dying*.

7. Zygmunt Bauman, *Mortality, Immortality, and Other Life Strategies* (Cambridge: Polity Press, 1992), 17, his emphasis.

8. Sigmund Freud, "Our Attitude toward Death," in *The Standard Edition* (London: Hogarth Press, 1957), 289.

9. Orlando Patterson, *Slavery and Social Death* (Cambridge: Harvard University Press, 1982).

10. Toni Morrison, *Playing in the Dark: Whiteness and the Literary Imagination* (New York: Vintage, 1992), 35.

11. Russ Castronovo, *Necro Citizenship: Death, Eroticism, and the Public Sphere in the Nineteenth-Century United States* (Durham, N.C.: Duke University Press, 2001), 4.

12. Sharon Holland, *Raising the Dead: Readings of Death and (Black) Subjectivity* (Durham, N.C.: Duke University Press, 2000), 103.

13. Given the conceit of novelty that founds, in part, the ideology of American exceptionalism, perhaps we should not be surprised that Americanist

criticism that flies under the flag of "the new" would mirror the larger cultural denial of death. The christening of the "new American studies," as Djelal Kadir observes, sets the stage for its "inevitable succession in iterative novelty." See his "America and Its Studies," *PMLA* 118.1 (January 2003): 18.

14. David Noble, *Death of a Nation: American Culture and the End of Exceptionalism* (Minneapolis: University of Minnesota Press, 2002), xl. For more on the ideology of American exceptionalism, see Daniel Bell, "The End of American Exceptionalism," *Public Interest* 41 (Fall 1975): 193–223; Gene Wise, "'Paradigm Dramas' in American Studies: A Cultural and Institutional History of the Movement," in *Locating American Studies: The Evolution of a Discipline*, ed. Lucy Maddox (Baltimore: Johns Hopkins University Press, 1999); Donald Pease and Robyn Wiegman, eds., *The Futures of American Studies* (Durham, N.C.: Duke University Press, 2002); Michael Kammen, "The Problem of American Exceptionalism: A Reconsideration," *American Quarterly* 45.1 (March 1993): 1–43.

15. Cited in Bell, "The End of American Exceptionalism."

16. Donald Pease, "The Global Homeland State: Bush's Biopolitical Settlement," *boundary 2* 30.3 (Fall 2003), 3.

17. Jacques Derrida, *Spectres de Marx: L'État de la dette, le travail du deuil et la nouvelle internationale* (Paris: Galilée, 1993), 201. Cited in the text as *Specters*.

18. Although *Specters of Marx* does not include an extended discussion of Heidegger, Derrida's notion of spectrality no doubt owes much to Heidegger's analysis of death in *Being and Time*, in which finitude emerges as one's "*ownmost nonrelational, certain, and, as such, indefinite and not to be bypassed possibility of Da-sein*" (239, author's emphasis). Although we can never experience death empirically, its possibility always already belongs to our being. For Heidegger, authentic being-toward-death does not evade or cover over death by projecting it onto others, but rather anticipates it, not by brooding over death, but rather by avowing the indefinite certainty of death as constitutive of existence. See Martin Heidegger, *Being and Time*, trans. Joan Stambaugh (Albany: State University of New York Press, 1996).

19. Judith Butler, *Antigone's Claim: Kinship between Life and Death* (New York: Columbia University Press, 2000), 81.

20. Baukje Prins and Irene Costera Meijer, "How Bodies Come to Matter: An Interview with Judith Butler," *Signs: Journal of Women in Culture and Society* 23.2 (1998): 280.

21. Julia Kristeva, *Powers of Horror: An Essay on Abjection*, trans. Leon S. Roudiez (New York: Columbia University Press, 1941); Judith Butler, *Bodies That Matter: On the Discursive Limits of "Sex"* (New York: Routledge, 1993).

22. For more on the racial epithet of "spook," see my discussion of Chesnutt's "Mars Jeems's Nightmare" in chapter 1.

23. Richard Wright, *Native Son* (New York: Harper Perennial, 1993), 97.

24. Ralph Ellison, *Invisible Man* (New York: Vintage, 1995), 3.

25. Karla Holloway, *Passed On: African-American Mourning Stories* (Durham, N.C.: Duke University Press, 2002), 2.

26. Abdul R. JanMohamed, *The Death-Bound-Subject: Richard Wright's Archaeology of Death* (Durham, N.C.: Duke University Press, 2005), 2.

27. I place "having" in quotations here to highlight the dispossession of the slave's body, a problem further complicated, as I show in chapter 1, by an originary dispossession inherent in all bodies.

28. See also Freud's "Beyond the Pleasure Principle," in *The Standard Edition*, trans. James Strachey (New York: Norton, 1961). Freud writes: "If we are to take it as a truth that knows no exception that everything living dies for *internal* reasons — becomes inorganic again — then we shall be compelled to say that '*the aim of all life is death*' and, looking backwards, that '*inanimate things existed before living ones*'" (32).

29. Sophocles, *Antigone*, trans. David Greene (Chicago: University of Chicago Press, 1991), 168.

30. Fustel De Coulanges, *La Cité Antique: Étude sur le culte, le droit, les institutions de la Grece et de Rome* (Paris: Librairie Hachette et Cie, 1917), 20; see also Thomas Trautmann, *Lewis Morgan and the Invention of Kinship* (Berkeley: University of California Press, 1987).

31. Simon Critchley, "A Commentary upon Derrida's Reading of Hegel in *Glas*," in *Hegel after Derrida*, ed. Stuart Barnett (New York: Routledge, 1998), 211, my emphasis.

32. Emmanuel Levinas, "L'ontologie est-elle fondamentale?" in *Entre Nous: Essais sur le penser-à-l'autre* (Paris: Grasset, 1991), 20.

33. Jacques Derrida, *Donner la mort* (Paris: Éditions Galilée, 1999).

34. Jacques Derrida, *L'Écriture et la différence* (Paris: Éditions du Seuil, 1967).

35. Emmanuel Levinas, *Autrement qu'être ou au-dela de l'essence*, Le Livre de Poche ed. (The Hague: Martinus Nijhoff, 1978), 138.

36. The language of kinship pervades Levinas's work. In *Otherwise Than Being*, for instance, maternity becomes the paradigm for the ethical bearing of the other in the same: "Maternity signifies responsibility for others — to the point of substituting oneself for the sufferings of others, both in terms of the effect of persecution and the act of persecution to which the persecutor sinks. Gestation — bearing *par excellence* — even bears responsibility for the persecuting of the persecutor" (121).

Levinas's introduction of maternity in *Otherwise Than Being* marks a shift away from the idealization of paternity in *Totality and Infinity*, in which the father's love for the son — despite our cultural indoctrination into the cult of Oedipal violence — is held to be the exemplary ethical relation. See his *Totalité et infini: essai sur l'extériorité* (The Hague: Martinus Nijhoff, 1961).

37. Katherine Franke, "Becoming a Citizen: Reconstruction Era Regulation of African-American Marriages," *Yale J. L & Human* 11 (1999): 253. Seconding Franke, Randall Kennedy notes that "nothing more clearly links Reconstruction to the present than the constitutional and statutory law enacted then that remains on the books, powerfully affecting the texture of our current political life." See his "Reconstruction and the Politics of Scholarship," *Yale Law Journal* 98 (1989): 521.

38. Elizabeth Freeman, *The Wedding Complex: Forms of Belonging in Modern American Culture* (Durham, N.C.: Duke University Press, 2002).

39. David Schneider, *A Critique of the Study of Kinship* (Ann Arbor: University of Michigan Press, 1984), 165.

40. Sigmund Freud, "Mourning and Melancholia," in *The Standard Edition* (London: Hogarth Press, 1975), 245.

41. Sigmund Freud, "The Ego and the ID," in *The Standard Edition* (New York: Norton, 1960), 24.

42. Jacques Derrida, "Ja, ou le faux-bond," *Diagraphe* 11 (1977): 100.

43. David Eng and David Kazanjan, Loss: The Politics of Mourning (Berkeley: University of California Press, 2002), 4.

44. Anne Cheng, *The Melancholy of Race: Psychoanalysis, Assimilation, and Hidden Grief* (Oxford: Oxford University Press, 2000), 94.

45. The conflation of interminable mourning with melancholia is a widely performed critical gesture. Judith Butler's "Melancholy Gender/Refused Identification," and in particular, her dialogue with analyst Adam Phillips about the implications of her theory of gender melancholia both for clinicians and theorists, approach the subject of unsuccessful mourning with some skepticism, anxiously characterizing the preoccupation with that failure as an idealization of psychic illness. Remarking how "mourning has provided the foundation for development in most versions of psychoanalysis," Phillips suggests that it is has "acquired the status of a quasi-religious concept" (153). Echoing Phillips, Butler asserts that the "idealization of mourning" endangers psychoanalysis with "becoming afflicted with the very suffering it seeks to know." She continues: "The resolution of grief becomes unthinkable in a situation in which our various losses become the condition for psychoanalysis as a practice of interminable mourning" (162). Butler then goes on to ask if the "work of permanent mourning" is not in some sense "the result of the force of repudiation itself, aggression in the service of a self-berating bind typical of melancholia?" (163). See Judith Butler, *The Psychic Life of Power: Theories of Subjection* (Stanford, Calif.: Stanford University Press, 1997).

46. Jean-Luc Nancy, *Corpus* (Paris: Éditions Métailié, 1992), 29, his emphasis.

47. Jacques Derrida, *Glas* (Paris: Éditions Galilée, 1974), 29. For help with Derrida's sometimes unwieldy text, the reader may consult John Leavey's

"key" to *Glas*. See John Leavey, *GLASsary* (Lincoln: University of Nebraska Press, 1986).

48. G. W. F. Hegel, *Phenomenology of Spirit*, trans. A. V. Miller (Oxford: Oxford University Press, 1977), 273, my emphasis. See also Patricia Mills, "Hegel's Antigone," in *Feminist Interpretations of G.W.F. Hegel*, ed. Patricia Mills (Philadelphia: Penn State University Press, 1996).

49. The link between dialectics and kinship is further underscored by the Hegelian appropriation of the Latin term *Sublatum*, from whence emerges the German *Aufhebung*. In Roman law, "sublation" designated either the recognition of blood kinship or an agreement to adopt a child regardless of consanguinity. As Marc Shell notes, the term stems from the ritual act of lifting or raising up a newborn child from the ground in order to acknowledge him/her as one's kin (hence the movement of the Hegelian *Aufhebung* through which knowledge is "raised up" to a higher level of understanding). See Marc Shell, *Children of the Earth: Literature, Politics, and Nationhood* (Oxford University Press, 1993). Cited in the text as *Children*. Derrida aptly translates the *Aufhebung* into French as *la relève*, which stems from the verb "relever," meaning "to lift up" or "to relieve."

50. Derrida's argument that reproduction disavows death echoes Plato's *Symposium*, in which Socrates likens reproduction to a quest for immortality, to the "permanent possession of goodness for oneself." *Symposium* (Oxford: Oxford University Press, 1994), 48. See also my discussion of Plato in chapter 3. Plato in turn anticipates Freud's argument in *Beyond the Pleasure Principle* that "germ-cells ... work against the death of the living substance and succeed in winning for it what we can only regard as potential immortality, though that may mean no more than a lengthening of the road to death" (34). Assimilating reproduction to the life instinct, Freud recognizes a desire for immortality that moves within the same dialectical logic that we see in both the divine and in Hegel's family. Recognizing the finitude of life, the life instinct seeks to move out from itself, to reproduce itself in a finite other (the child) in whom the life instinct refuses the very death that it at first appears to recognize. The life instinct, then, is nothing more than a disavowal of death, one that both cancels and preserves life in the face of finitude.

51. Edgar Allan Poe, *The Tell-Tale Heart and Other Writings* (New York: Bantam, 1982), 57.

52. Jacques Derrida, *La voix et le phénomène* (Paris: Presses Universitaires de France, 1967), 108.

53. J. L. Austin, *How to Do Things with Words* (Oxford: Clarendon Press, 1962).

54. For an excellent study on the relation between body and spirit in Poe, see Joan Dayan, *Fables of Mind: An Inquiry into Poe's Fiction* (New York: Oxford University Press, 1987).

55. Lewis Henry Morgan, *Systems of Consanguinity and the Affinity of the Human Family* (Lincoln: University of Nebraska Press, 1997), 10.

56. Emile Durkheim, *Contributions to L'Année Sociologique* (New York: Free Press, 1980), 175.

57. Marc Shell, *The End of Kinship* (Baltimore: Johns Hopkins University Press, 1988), 5. Shell uses the phrase "spiritual kinship" in a somewhat different sense than I use it here to describe a "relationship between a nun or a monk and any other person in the world, which establishes a kinship in God and outlaws as 'spiritual incest' sexual intercourse between them" (10).

58. See also Jacqueline Stevens, *Reproducing the State* (Princeton, N.J.: Princeton University Press, 1999). Contemporary American law, as Stevens argues, compensates for this indeterminability of paternity by fabricating a distinction between legal and biological fathers. Given that the legal father always trumps the biological one, "the effect...is to sacralize paternity in comparison with the apparent materiality and determinacy of maternity" (233). Stevens notes that in *Michael H. v. Gerald D.*, 491 US 110 (1989), the U.S. Supreme Court awarded a marital father custody of a biological father's son because, in the language of the court, "California law, like nature itself, makes no provision for dual fatherhood." (Cited in Stevens, 232.)

59. The association of materiality with femininity and maternity, as feminist philosophers from Luce Irigaray to Judith Butler have shown, has a long and troubled history. In Plato's *Timaeus*, the receptacle that is said to receive all bodies is likened to a mother. This matrix thus receives the unchangeable and indestructible paternal forms by itself being formless. For the receptacle cannot be called "earth or air or fire or water, nor any other compounds or components; but we shall not be deceived if we call it a nature invisible and characterless, all-receiving, partaking in some very puzzling way of the intelligible and very hard to apprehend." See *The Timaeus*, trans. Francis Cornford (New York: The Liberal Arts Press, 1959), 51. In her reading of Plato, Irigaray argues that the material receptacle "is nothing, but shares in everything.... She is in excess of any identification of presence." See her *Speculum of the Other Woman*, trans. Gillian Gill (Ithaca, N.Y.: Cornell University Press, 1985), 307. Following Irigaray, Butler maintains in *Bodies That Matter* that femininity emerges within a phallocentric economy as synonymous with the material only to become subject to a violent erasure, one that produces two kinds of matter: a specular matter that secures the form/matter binary in which "the masculine occupies both terms of the opposition," and an excessive matter that "cannot be said to be anything, to participate in ontology at all" (39). The association of femininity and motherhood with the material, then, is but the precondition of its evacuation, of its becoming masculine/father/spirit. While the masculine form bodies forth as a "body which is no body," the feminine, Butler maintains, is con-

structed as "matter which is no body" (49). *Bodies That Matter: On the Discursive Limits of "Sex"* (New York: Routledge, 1993).

60. David Schneider, *American Kinship: A Cultural Account* (Englewood Cliffs, N.J.: Prentice-Hall, 1968).

61. John Finnis, "Law, Morality, and 'Sexual Orientation,'" *Notre Dame Law Review* 69 (1994): 1066. The article is the published version of his affidavit from the Colorado case. See also Martha Nussbaum, "Platonic Love and Colorado Law: The Relevance of Ancient Greek Norms to Modern Sexual Controversies," *Virginia Law Review* 80 (1994): 1515–1651; Andrew Koppelman, "Is Marriage Inherently Heterosexual?" *American Journal of Jurisprudence* 42 (1997): 51–95. The Colorado case sought to overturn Amendment Two, a referendum passed in 1992 that effectively made it illegal to adopt any statute that would protect the rights of gays and lesbians. As the state had based much of its claim on its interest in protecting the family, both sides offered philosophical expert witnesses to debate the relevance of the state's claims, the result of which was an almost absurd scene of classicists sparring over readings and translations of Plato and accusing one another of perjury.

62. Derrida's *différance* attempts to capture the respective temporal and spatial senses of defer and differ that English splits into two verbs, but French expresses solely through the verb *différer*. Just as a linguistic sign, for Derrida, represents the infinitely deferred presence of the referent, I am arguing that the presence of "our" kin is deferred/differed by their irreducible alterity. See his *Marges de la philosophie* (Paris: Éditions de Minuit, 1972).

63. Judith Butler, *Subjects of Desire: Hegelian Reflections in Twentieth-Century France* (New York: Columbia University Press, 1987), 21.

64. Saidiya Hartman, *Scenes of Subjection: Terror, Slavery, and Self-Making in Nineteenth-Century America* (Oxford: Oxford University Press, 1997), 21.

65. Hortense Spillers, "Mama's Baby, Papa's Maybe," *Diacritics* 17.2 (1987): 74, her emphasis.

66. Dylan Penningroth, *The Claims of Kinfolk: African-American Property and Community in the Nineteenth-Century South* (Chapel Hill, N.C.: University of North Carolina Press, 2003).

1. Giving up the *Geist*

1. A shorter version of this chapter was first presented at the "Mass Symposium" at the University of Southern California in April of 1999, with Sam Weber as respondent, and then later at the "Materiality of Fantasy" panel at the Modern Language Association Annual Meeting in Chicago, December 1999. I thank Professor Weber in particular for encouraging me to think beyond the conventional conception of the body as container.

2. Orlando Patterson, *Slavery and Social Death* (Cambridge: Harvard University Press, 1982).

3. Emily Field Van Tassel, "'Only the Law Would Rule between US': Antimiscegenation, the Moral Economy of Dependency, and the Debate over Rights after the Civil War," *Chicago-Kent Law Review* 70 (1995): 873, 875.

4. Peter Kolchin, *American Slavery: 1619–1877* (New York: Hill and Wang, 1993), 111.

5. Judith Butler, *The Psychic Life of Power: Theories in Subjection* (Stanford, Calif.: Stanford University Press, 1997).

6. René Descartes, *Oeuvres Philosophiques, Tome II* (Paris: Éditions Garnier Frères, 1967), 406. Unless otherwise noted, all French translations are mine.

7. John Locke, *Two Treatises of Government* (Cambridge, England: Cambridge University Press, 1963), 305.

8. Toni Morrison, *Playing in the Dark: Whiteness and the Literary Imagination* (New York: Vintage, 1992), 38. Morrison's claim echoes Paul Gilroy's observation of the "intimate association of modernity and slavery." See *The Black Atlantic: Modernity and Double-Consciousness* (Cambridge, Mass.: Harvard University Press, 1993), 53. See also C. B. MacPherson, *The Political Theory of Possessive Individualism: Hobbes to Locke* (Oxford: Clarendon Press, 1962).

9. Jean-Luc Nancy, *Corpus* (Paris: Éditions Métailié, 1992), 29, his emphasis.

10. Karl Marx, *Economic and Philosophic Manuscripts of 1844*, in *The Marx-Engels Reader*, ed. Robert Tucker (New York: Norton, 1978), 77.

11. *Afro-American Almanac: Historical Documents*. Available at http://www.toptags.com/aama/docs/bcodes.htm. See also William Cohen, "Negro Involuntary Servitude in the South, 1865–1940: A Preliminary Analysis," *The Journal of Southern History* 42.1 (1976): 31–60; Ralph Schlomowitz, "'Bound' or 'Free'?: Black Labor in Cotton and Sugarcane Farming, 1865–1880," *The Journal of Southern History* 50.4 (1984): 569–96.

12. Sidney Andrews, "Three Months among the Reconstructionists," *Atlantic Monthly* 17 (1866): 244.

13. Saidiya Hartman, *Scenes of Subjection: Terror, Slavery, and Self-Making in Nineteenth-Century America* (Oxford: Oxford University Press, 1997), 135.

14. Eric Foner, "The Meaning of Freedom in the Age of Emancipation," *The Journal of American History* 81.2 (1994): 460. See also Avery Gordon, *Ghostly Matters: Haunting and the Sociological Imagination* (Minneapolis: University of Minnesota Press, 1997), 170–75. Like Foner and Hartman, Gordon notes that slaves did not achieve "freedom from the pure fact of the Emancipation Proclamation" (172).

15. Wendy Brown, *States of Injury: Power and Freedom in Late Modernity* (Princeton, N.J.: Princeton University Press, 1995).

16. Charles Chesnutt, *The Conjure Woman and Other Conjure Tales* (Durham, N.C.: Duke University Press, 1993).

17. Robert Bone, *Down Home: Origins of the Afro-American Short Story* (New York: Columbia University Press, 1975), 83.

18. Houston Baker defines conjure as a "transatlantic religion of diasporic and Afro-American masses in the New World. Descended from *vodun*, an African religion in which the priestess holds supreme power, conjure's name in Haiti and the Caribbean is *voodoo*." See his *Modernism and the Harlem Renaissance* (Chicago: University of Chicago Press, 1987), 43.

19. Judith Butler, "How Can I Deny That These Hands and This Body Are Mine?" *Qui Parle* 11.1 (Fall/Winter 1997), 11.

20. See Eric Foner, "Rehearsals For Reconstruction," in *Reconstruction: America's Unfinished Revolution 1863–1877* (New York: Harper and Row, 1988).

21. Pascale-Anne Brault and Michael Naas eds., *The Work of Mourning: Jacques Derrida* (Chicago: University of Chicago Press, 2001), 143.

22. Jacques Derrida, *La voix et le phénomène* (Paris: Presses Universitaires de France, 1967), 108.

23. Guy de Maupassant, *Contes et nouvelles* (Paris: Éditions Albin Michel), 98.

24. Anne Cheng, *The Melancholy of Race: Psychoanalysis, Assimilation, and Hidden Grief* (Oxford: Oxford University Press, 2000), 98.

25. The phrase "restricted economy" comes from Georges Bataille, who characterizes Hegelian dialectics as recovering (from) all of its losses — including that loss and absence which is death. Contrasting such an economy with a "general one," Bataille argues that human life is founded on a surplus that can never be fully exhausted or contained within the Hegelian synthesis. See Georges Bataille, *La part maudite* (Paris: Les Éditions de Minuit, 1967).

26. Although conjure sometimes achieves powerful effects in Chesnutt's stories (as in "The Marked Tree," wherein conjure brings about the destruction of an entire plantation family), Eric Sundquist remarks that conjure historically "posed no direct threat to the plantation regime and seldom changed the balance of power in the slaves' favor." See his *To Wake the Nations* (Cambridge, Mass.: Harvard University Press, 1993), 368.

27. Jacques Derrida, *L'Écriture et la différence* (Paris: Éditions du Seuil, 1967), 377.

28. Herman Melville, *Billy Budd, Sailor and Other Stories* (New York: Bantam, 1984), 206.

29. The *Oxford English Dictionary* cites Lou Shelly's *Hepcats Jive Talk Dictionary* (1945) as the first racially coded recording of "spook." See also *Wicked*

Words: A Treasury of Curses, Insults, Put-Downs, and Other Formerly Unprintable Terms from Anglo-Saxon Times to the Present (New York: Crown, 1989).

30. Dickson Bruce remarks that "Chesnutt was never committed to a distinctive black identity. His alienation from black North Carolinians was striking. He certainly felt his own superiority to most black people around him. As a teenager, in fact, he actually thought of passing over the color line to live as white.... Chesnutt wanted, above all, to be part of the American elite — an elite that happened to be white rather than black." See his "The Color Line and the Meaning of Race," in *Black American Writing from the Nadir* (Baton Rouge: Louisiana State University Press, 1989), 172. See also Chesnutt's essay, "What Is a White Man" (1889), reprinted in *Interracialism: Black-White Intermarriage in American History, Literature, and Law*, ed. Werner Sollors (Oxford: Oxford University Press, 2000).

31. Teresa Goddu, *Gothic America: Narrative, History, and Nation* (New York: Columbia University Press, 1997), 132.

32. Jacques Derrida, *Spectres de Marx: L'État de la dette, le travail du deuil et la nouvelle internationale* (Paris: Galilée, 1993), 202, his emphasis. Cited in the text as *Specters*.

33. It is precisely this danger of reproducing the thingliness of the slave that haunted Booker T. Washington's so-called "accommodationist" politics. Insisting on the "dignity" of manual labor, Washington's materialism has typically been read as constituting a simple acquiescence to the ideologies of slavery that exploited the black body. While Nicholas Bromell argues that, for Washington, "the typical African American should not aspire to perform mental labor, or to become learned," Washington does not wholly exclude mental and intellectual work among blacks (208). In his famous Atlanta Exposition Address, for instance, Washington observes that "there is as much dignity in tilling a field as in writing a poem," thus rhetorically equating manual and mental labor rather than privileging one over the other (70). And yet, this apparent mind/body integration gets eclipsed by the subsequent trope of the hands, which yokes blacks firmly to manual labor: "In all things that are purely social we can be as separate as the fingers, yet one as the hand in all things essential to mutual progress" (129). Not by accident do the hands of labor return in this affirmation of the Jim Crow ideology of "separate but equal." Washington's metaphor thus imagines that equality can emerge despite the social separation of whites and blacks. See *Washington's Up From Slavery* (Oxford: Oxford Univer-sity Press, 1995); Nicholas Bromwell, *By the Sweat of the Brow: Literature and Labor in Antebellum America* (Chicago: University of Chicago Press, 1993).

34. Karl Marx, *Capital*, in *Marx-Engels Reader*, ed. Robert Tucker (New York: Norton, 1978), 115. Cited in the text as *Capital*.

35. Much could be said with regard to Marx's assertion that the use-value is "not a thing of air" in terms of the assumption that air is immate-

rial. The history of Western materialism, as Daniel Tiffany notes, bears witness to a persistent negotiation with the basic tenets of atomism, which proceed from an equation of materiality with *in*visibility, beginning with that which is perceivable only to the intellect: the atom. Thus Marx's claim that "not an atom of matter enters into [the] composition" of the exchange-value, and therefore "it seems impossible to grasp," likewise equates matter with the visible and the tangible (*Capital*, 313). That Marx was in dialogue with the tenets of atomism is confirmed by his doctoral thesis on Epicurus and Democritus. Yet it is clear from his equation of the invisible with the *im*material in *Capital* that Marx's materialism departs from its atomist inheritances in significant ways. See Daniel Tiffany, *Toy Medium: Materialism and Modern Lyric* (Berkeley: University of California, 2000).

36. Karl Marx, *Das Kapital* (Hamburg: Erster Band, 1890), 37.

37. G. W. F. Hegel, *The Philosophy of History* (New York: Dover Publications, 1956), 93.

38. Harriet Beecher Stowe, *Uncle Tom's Cabin or, Life among the Lowly* (New York: Penguin, 1986), 230.

39. Such disdain for the corporeal led Friedrich Nietzsche to characterize Christians as "despisers of the body." He writes: "Body am I entirely, and nothing else; and soul is only a word for something about the body" (34). Nietzsche's dismissal of the Christian soul, however, does not seek to reduce the body to a thing-in-itself. For it is this very positivist conceit that Nietzsche takes to be the flip side of the Christian negation of the body. If Christianity can only negate the body, then science can only seem to affirm it as an ultimate empirical ground. See his "On the Afterworldy" and "On the Despisers of the Body," in *Thus Spoke Zarathustra*, trans. Walter Kaufmann (New York: Penguin, 1966).

40. Plato, *Phaedo* (Oxford: Oxford University Press, 1993).

41. Sandy's haunting also foregrounds the erasure of the distinction between domestic and market economies that Gillian Brown argues is central to the institution of slavery: "Slavery disregards [the] opposition between the family at home and the exterior workplace. The distinction between work and family is eradicated in the slave, for whom there is no separation between economic and private status" (505). For Brown, this "contagion of the market" emerges in *Uncle Tom's Cabin,* in which Dinah's kitchen "look[s] as if it [has] been arranged by a hurricane blowing through it" (503). While Brown (like Patterson) does not consider how kinship is implicated in appropriation and violence prior to its exposure to the market, Sandy's haunting of the plantation kitchen might be read in terms of this chiasmatic relation between property and kinship. See Gillian Brown, "Getting in the Kitchen with Dinah: Domestic Politics in *Uncle Tom's Cabin,*" *American Quarterly* 36.4 (1984): 503–23. Not by accident, perhaps, does Toni Morrison's *Beloved* describe the "spiteful" 124 Bluestone Road by detailing the

ravages that the baby ghost wages in the family kitchen: tiny handprints appear in a cake; chickpeas and soda crackers are strewn about; the dining table rushes toward Paul D, and so on.

42. Slave resistance in the United States most often involved individual or small-group acts rather than full-scale subversion. Only a handful of such rebellions took place in America, perhaps the most well-known of which is Nat Turner's rebellion in 1831. Less spectacular were the day-to-day resistances of stealing food, spitting in food, lying, work stoppage, etc. For more on large-scale rebellion, see Kenneth Greenberg, ed., *The Confessions of Nat Turner and Related Documents* (New York: Bedford Books, 1996). For more on small-scale resistance see Saidiya Hartman, "Redressing the Pained Body," in *Scenes of Subjection*; Peter Kolchin, *American Slavery*, 161–68.

2. Beloved's Claim

1. Toni Morrison, *Beloved* (New York: Plume, 1987), 200.

2. Hortense Spillers, "Mama's Baby, Papa's Maybe," *Diacritics* 17.2 (1987): 74, her emphasis.

3. David Schneider, *A Critique of the Study of Kinship* (Ann Arbor: University of Michigan Press, 1984), 177.

4. Barbara Bennett Woodhouse, "'Who Owns the Child?': Meyer and Pierce and the Child as Property," *William and Mary Law Review* 33 (1992): 1042. See also Merry Jean Chan, "The Authorial Parent: An Intellectual Property Model of Parental Rights," *New York University Law Review* 78 (2003): 1186–226.

5. Dylan Penningroth, *The Claims of Kinfolk* (Chapel Hill, N.C.: University of North Carolina Press, 2003), 73.

6. Emmanuel Levinas, *Autrement qu'être ou au-dela de l'essence* (The Hague: Martinus Nijhoff, 1978), 31. Cited in the text as *Autrement*. Unless otherwise noted, all French translations are mine.

7. Toni Morrison, "Unspeakable Things Unspoken: The Afro-American Presence in American Literature," *Michigan Quarterly Review* 28 (1989): 32.

8. Emmanuel Levinas, *Totalité et infini: essai sur l'extériorité* (The Hague: Martinus Nijhoff, 1961), 16.

9. Jacques Derrida, *L'Écriture et la différence* (Paris: Éditions du Seuil, 1967), 182. Cited in the text as *L'Écriture*.

10. Jacques Derrida, *Donner la mort* (Paris: Galilée, 1999), 109.

11. See Penelope Deutscher, "Mourning the Other: Cultural Cannibalism, and the Politics of Friendship (Jacques Derrida and Luce Irigaray)," *differences: A Journal of Feminist Cultural Studies* 10.3 (1998): 165.

12. Steven Weisenburger, *Modern Medea: A Family Story of Slavery and Child-Murder from the Old South* (New York: Hill and Wang, 1998), 279.

13. Cited in Weisenburger, 87.

14. Mary A. Livermore, "The Slave Tragedy at Cincinnati," *The National Anti-Slavery Standard,* February 16, 1856.

15. Slavoj Žižek, *The Fragile Absolute or, Why is the Christian Legacy Worth Fighting For* (New York: Verso, 2000), 154, his emphasis. Also writing within a psychoanalytic frame, Jean Wyatt argues that *Beloved* imagines a "maternal symbolic" that contests the paternal substitution of "the word" for the lost maternal body. While she alludes to Sethe's lack of separation from her children as an "oppressive plenitude," and further links the novel's vocabulary of possession to the language of the slave master, Wyatt does not explore how a maternal symbolic might still carry the threat of its own violence (237): "The hope at the end of the novel," Wyatt concludes, "is that Sethe, having recognized herself as subject, will narrate the mother-daughter story and invent a language that can encompass the desperation of the slave mother who killed her daughter" (249). Maternal violence emerges as an anomaly driven *only* by "desperation" within an otherwise nonviolent mother-daughter dyad. If there is any violence to be found in the maternal symbolic, this argument seems to suggest, it would have to be an effect of what Spillers characterizes as the invasion of property relations into the domain of kinship. See Wyatt's "Giving Body to the Word: The Maternal Symbolic in Toni Morrison's *Beloved*," in *Understanding Toni Morisson's Beloved and Sula,* ed. Solomon O. Iyasere and Marla W. Iyasere (Troy, N.Y.: Whitston Publishing Company, 2000). See also Caroline Rody, "Toni Morrison's *Beloved*: History, 'Rememory,' and a 'Clamor for a Kiss,'" in this same volume. Rody contends that the "historical project of the novel is in a profound sense a mother-quest, an African-American feminist 'herstory' that posits a kind of 'mother of history'" (97).

16. Homi Bhabha, *The Location of Culture* (New York: Routledge, 1994), 17.

17. Yung-Hsing Wu, "Doing Things with Ethics: *Beloved, Sula,* and the Reading of Judgment," *Modern Fiction Studies* 49.4 (2003): 794.

18. In recent years, critics have become increasingly interested in problematizing the ethics of Sethe's act. In addition to Wu, see James Phelan, "Sethe's Choice: Beloved and the Ethics of Reading," *Style* 32.2 (1998): 318–332; Mark Reinhardt, "Who Speaks for Margaret Garner? Slavery, Silence, and the Politics of Ventriloquism," *Critical Inquiry* 29 (2002): 81–119.

19. Elizabeth Fox-Genovese, "Unspeakable Things Unspoken: Ghosts and Memories in *Beloved*," in *Modern Critical Interpretations: Beloved,* ed. Harold Bloom (Philadelphia: Chelsea House Publishers, 1999), 101. Cited in the text as *Unspeakable.*

20. See Weisenburger, 259; see also Elizabeth Fox-Genovese, *Within the Plantation Household: Black and White Women of the Old South* (Chapel Hill, N.C.: University of North Carolina Press, 1988), 323–333.

21. "Toni Morrison, In Her New Novel, Defends Women," *The New York*

Times, August 26, 1987. Morrison came across the 1856 article while editing *The Black Book.* See "A Visit to the Slave Mother Who Killed Her Children," *The American Baptist,* February 12, 1856, reprinted in *The Black Book,* ed. Middleton Harris (Random House: New York, 1974).

22. Section 6 of the Fugitive Slave Law of 1850 reads: "And be it further enacted, That when a person held to service or labor in any State or Territory of the United States, has heretofore or shall hereafter escape into another State or Territory of the United States, the person or persons to whom such service or labor may be due... may pursue and reclaim such fugitive person." Section 7 continues: "And be it further enacted, That any person who shall knowingly and willingly obstruct, hinder, or prevent such claimant... from arresting such a fugitive from service or labor... or shall rescue, or attempt to rescue, such fugitive from service or labor, from the custody of such claimant... or shall aid, abet, or assist such person so owing service or labor as aforesaid, directly or indirectly, to escape from such claimant... or shall harbor or conceal such fugitive, so as to prevent the discovery and arrest of such person... shall, for either of said offences, be subject to a fine not exceeding one thousand dollars, and imprisonment not exceeding six months." *The Avalon Project at the Yale Law School.* Available at www.yale.edu/lawweb/avalon/fugitive.htm.

23. Much of Margaret's case hinged on whether a prior visit with her master across the border into Cincinnati necessarily released her from bondage. Because she did not come into the state as a fugitive upon this first visit, the master could not make a claim under the Fugitive Slave Law. The law usually required, however, that the slave claim his or her freedom while on free soil, something which Margaret had failed to do. See Julius Yanuck, "The Garner Fugitive Slave Case," *The Mississippi Valley Historical Review* 40.1 (1953): 47–66; William G. Hawkings, *Lunsford Lane* (New York: Negro Universities Press, 1969), 119–36.

24. For a reading that departs from the trend toward historical recovery, see Teresa Heffernan, "Beloved and the Problem of Mourning," *Studies in the Novel* 30.4 (1998): 58–73.

25. Barbara Christian, "Beloved, She's Ours," *Narrative* 5.1 (1997): 40.

26. Winfrey has stated her identification with Sethe in countless interviews. "I've always thought I could play Sethe, from [the time I read] the first page. I don't know how to explain it: instinct. From the moment I read [the book], I always knew that I was Sethe, and that Danny Glover was Paul D." See "Odd Couples," *Philadelphia City Paper,* October 15–22, 1998. Available at www.citypaper.net/articles/101598/critmas.odd.shtml.

27. In an essay that reads *Beloved* against historical accounts of Margaret Garner, Angelita Reyes argues that Garner's escape from Kentucky challenged the traditional characterization of the "tragic mulatta" as weak and fragile. Despite her careful attention to the politics of miscegenation,

however, Reyes does not pursue how Morrison — by excluding the possibility of miscegenation — misses the opportunity to counter the image of the tragic mulatta through her invention and development of Sethe's character. See Angelita Reyes, "Rereading a Nineteenth-Century Fugitive Slave Incident: From Toni Morrison's *Beloved* to Margaret Garner's Dearly Beloved," *Annals of Scholarship* 7 (1990): 464–86.

28. See Avery Gordon, *Ghostly Matters: Haunting and the Sociological Imagination* (Minneapolis: University of Minnesota Press, 1997). Gordon argues similarly that Sethe is "struggling to articulate a story that exceeds . . . a rationalistic and objective explanation. . . . All those things of which Sethe speaks in a rush of words that claim her relation to the child she murdered and the place she knows she cannot return herself or her children to represent the failure of explanation" (141).

29. Russ Castronovo, *Necro Citizenship: Death, Eroticism, and the Public Sphere in the Nineteenth-Century United States* (Durham, N.C.: Duke University Press, 2001).

30. Jacques Derrida, *Spectres de Marx: L'État de la dette, le travail du deuil et la nouvelle internationale* (Paris: Galilée, 1993).

31. For more on the dialectical relation between spirit and body, see Fernando Vidal, "Brains, Bodies, Selves, and Science: Anthropologies of Identity and the Resurrection of the Body," *Critical Inquiry* 28 (2002): 930–74.

32. Richard Cohen, ed., *Face to Face with Levinas* (Albany: State University of New York Press, 1986), 23.

33. Joanne Caputo, *The Diversity of Love*. Available at www.yellowsprings.com/margaretgarner.

34. Joanne Caputo, "Writer Claims Murdered Slave Child Past," Press Release, January 24, 2002.

35. Reprinted in *The National Anti-Slavery Standard*, February 23, 1856.

36. Levi Coffin, *Reminiscences* (New York: Arno Press, 1968), 565.

37. Whether or not Morrison was aware of Margaret's mixed-race status, we would be mistaken to attribute the significance of this elision *entirely* to Morrison's authorial intentions. Regardless of her intentions, in other words, it is the effect of this exclusion (the idealization of maternal love) that should concern us here. Morrison's recent libretto for Richard Danielpour's opera, *Margaret Garner* (which, like *Beloved*, is only loosely based on the historical personage), is also silent on the possibility that Margaret or her children are the product of interracial sex. While act 1 concludes with the rape of Margaret by her master, Edward Gaines, no children are produced from the rape. This would not, however, exclude the possibility that some or all of Margaret's children could have been fathered by Edward Gaines's brother (from whom Edward inherited Margaret and her children), though this likelihood is never explicitly acknowledged during the opera. See *Margaret Garner: A New American Opera*. Available at http://margaretgarner.org.

38. Elizabeth Barrett Browning, *Poems* (New York: James Miller, 1866), 250, her ellipses.

39. Toni Morrison, "The Art of Fiction No. 134," interview by Elissa Schappell, *The Paris Review* 128 (1993): 115. Cited in the text as *Art*.

40. Toni Morrison, *Playing in the Dark: Whiteness and the Literary Imagination* (New York: Vintage, 1992), 33.

41. As Robyn Wiegman has argued, the particularization of whiteness tends to shift the burden of racial injury to the site of the white body, and thus erases the history of racial violence against nonwhite bodies. See her "Whiteness Studies and the Paradox of Particularity," *Boundary 2* 26.3 (1999): 115–50; Warren Montag, "The Universalization of Whiteness: Racism and Enlightenment," in *Whiteness: A Critical Reader*, ed. Mike Hill (New York: New York University Press, 1997).

42. Richard Dyer, *White* (New York: Routledge, 1997).

43. Ariela Gross, "Litigating Whiteness: Trials of Racial Determination in the Nineteenth-Century South," *Yale Law Journal* 108, 109 (1998): 123. For more on the question of racial determination and the politics of miscegenation more generally, see Martha Hodes, *White Women/Black Men: Illicit Sex in the Nineteenth-Century South* (New Haven, Conn.: Yale University Press, 1997); Martha Hodes, ed., *Sex, Love, Race: Crossing Boundaries in North American History* (New York: New York University Press, 1999); Werner Sollors, ed., *Interracialism: Black-White Intermarriage in American History, Literature, and Law* (Oxford: Oxford University Press, 2000); Werner Sollors, *Neither Black nor White Yet Both: Thematic Explorations of Interracial Literature* (New York: Oxford University Press, 1997); Paul Spickard, *Mixed Blood: Intermarriage and Ethnic Identity in Twentieth-Century America* (Madison: University of Wisconsin Press, 1989).

44. To give but one example of how contemporary critics equate the body with social life, see Cynthia Dobbs, "Toni Morrison's *Beloved*: Bodies Returned, Modernism Revisited," *African American Review* 32.4 (1998): 563–78. Dobbs identifies in Morrison's text a "move toward the body" that is "philosophically, aesthetically, and politically radical" (564).

45. Jacques Derrida, *Adieu à Emmanuel Levinas* (Paris: Galilée, 1997), 192.

46. Danille Taylor-Guthrie, ed., *Conversations with Toni Morrison* (Jackson: University of Mississippi Press, 1994), 247.

47. Pascale-Anne Brault and Michael Naas, eds., *The Work of Mourning: Jacques Derrida* (Chicago: University of Chicago Press, 2001), 11.

3. The Haunted House of Kinship

1. Thomas H. Johnson, ed., *The Complete Poems of Emily Dickinson* (New York: Back Bay Books, 1961).

2. Mark Wigley, *The Architecture of Deconstruction: Derrida's Haunt* (Cambridge, Mass.: MIT Press, 1993), 163.

3. Abraham Lincoln, *"House Divided" Address* (Springfield: Illinois State Historical Society, 1958), 3.

4. Eric Sundquist, *Faulkner: The House Divided* (Baltimore: Johns Hopkins University Press, 1983), 105.

5. *Dred Scott v. Sandford* 60 US 393 (1857); Kansas-Nebraska Act (1854). *The Avalon Project at Yale Law School*. Available from www.yale.edu/lawweb/avalon/kanneb.html. The Dred Scott case addressed whether the temporary residence of a slave in free territory (in this case Illinois) necessarily freed him of the bondage of slavery. The Supreme Court determined that Dred Scott was not a citizen of the United States according to the meaning put forth in the Constitution, and therefore his residence in a free state did not confer on him free status. The Kansas-Nebraska Act was proposed by Stephen A. Douglas, chairman of the Senate Committee on Territories. Following the doctrine of "popular sovereignty," Douglas proposed that the slavery question in the new territories ought to be left to the settlers to decide. Section 19 of the act reads: "When admitted as a State or States, the said territory, or any portion of the same, shall be received into the Union with or without slavery, as their Constitution may prescribe at the time of their admission."

6. The term "miscegenation," literally "mixed species," was introduced during the election year of 1864 in an anonymous pamphlet circulated in an effort to discredit Lincoln and abolitionist Republicans for advocating interracial amalgamation. The pamphlet marked the beginnings of a peculiarly late-nineteenth-century antipathy toward interracial sex and marriage. The writers of the pamphlet portrayed themselves as abolitionists (though they were in fact proslavery Democrats) who held the belief that racial amalgamation was crucial to human progress. They solicited responses from abolitionists who favored miscegenation and received many letters from prominent actors in the movement. The hoax was exposed soon after Lincoln was reelected. See Sidney Kaplan, "The Miscegenation Issue in the Election Year of 1864" (1949), reprinted in *Interracialism: Black-White Intermarriage in American History, Literature, and Law* ed. Werner Sollors (Oxford: Oxford University Press, 2000). See also Werner Sollors, *Neither Black Nor White Yet Both: Thematic Explorations of Interracial Literature* (Oxford: Oxford University Press, 1997); Paul Spickard, *Mixed Blood: Intermarriage and Ethnic Identity in Twentieth-Century America* (Madison: University of Wisconsin Press, 1989); Martha Hodes, *White Women/Black Men: Illicit Sex in the Nineteenth-Century South* (New Haven, Conn.: Yale University Press, 1997). Cited in the text as "White Women." As Hodes underscores, the complicated history of interracial sex belies the late twentieth-century assumption that

it was always viewed as abhorrent. The practice of lynching black men for the supposed rape of white women was rare before the Civil War, reaching its peak between 1882 and 1900. For a review of Hodes that questions how rigid the distinction actually was between antebellum and postbellum attitudes toward miscegenation, see Ariela Gross, "Book Review: *White Women/Black Men: Illicit Sex in the Nineteenth-Century South*," *Law and History Review* (2002): 686–88.

7. Mark Twain, *Pudd'nhead Wilson* (New York: Penguin, 1987).

8. Saidiya Hartman, *Scenes of Subjection: Terror, Slavery, and Self-Making in Nineteenth-Century America* (Oxford: Oxford University Press, 1997), 186. See also Krister Friday, "Miscegenated Time: The Spectral Body, Race, and Temporality in *Light in August*," *The Faulkner Journal* 16.3 (Fall 2000/2001): 41–62.

9. For more on the synecdoche of racial determination, see Lee Edelman, "The Part for the (W)hole: Baldwin, Homophobia, and the Phantasmatics of 'Race,'" in *Homographesis: Essays in Gay Literary and Cultural Theory* (New York: Routledge, 1994).

10. See C. J. Rowe ed., *Plato's Phaedo* (Cambridge, England: Cambridge University Press, 1993); Michel Foucault, *Surveiller et punir: la naissance de la prison* (Paris: Gallimard, 1975).

11. Charles Lofgren, *The Plessy Case: A Legal-Historical Interpretation* (New York: Oxford University Press, 1987).

12. *Plessy v. Ferguson*, 163 US 537 (1896), 557.

13. Cheryl Harris, "Whiteness As Property," *Harvard Law Review* 106 (1993): 1710–91.

14. Cited in Harris, 1749.

15. "Is President Lincoln a Martyr?" *New York Times*, April 26, 1865.

16. See Gary Laderman, *The Sacred Remains: American Attitudes Toward Death 1799–1883* (New Haven, Conn.: Yale University Press, 1996), 162.

17. *Harpers Weekly*, October 11, 1863: 655.

18. *New York Times*, April 25, 1865.

19. John Irwin, *Doubling and Incest/Repetition and Revenge: A Speculative Reading of Faulkner* (Baltimore: Johns Hopkins University Press, 1975).

20. Jacques Derrida, *Spectres de Marx: L'état de la dette, le travail du deuil et la nouvelle internationale* (Paris: Galilée, 1993), 203. Unless otherwise noted, all French translations are mine.

21. Toni Morrison, *Playing in the Dark: Whiteness and the Literary Imagination* (New York: Vintage, 1992), 35.

22. Harry Levin, *The Power of Blackness: Hawthorne, Melville, and Poe* (New York: Alfred Knopf, 1958); Leslie Fiedler, *Love and Death in the American Novel* (New York: Scarborough Books, 1960), 29.

23. The implication here is that what scholars in contemporary race and sexuality studies, following Kristeva, often call the "abject" — under-

stood as designating those minority populations that are cast off, degraded or otherwise repudiated — is not reducible to the spectral. For the latter would designate the condition of all life. See Julia Kristeva, *Powers of Horror: An Essay on Abjection*, trans. Leon S. Roudiez (New York: Columbia University Press, 1941). For an example of contemporary appropriations of Kristeva in the field of queer theory, see Judith Butler, *Bodies That Matter: On the Discursive Limits of "Sex"* (New York: Routledge, 1993).

24. Walter Benn Michaels, *Our America: Nativism, Modernism, and Pluralism* (Durham, N.C.: Duke University Press, 1995), 48.

25. That sexual contact with another is not a requirement for this contamination to have taken place means that *asexual* reproduction and even cloning would be "miscegenous."

26. William Faulkner, *Absalom, Absalom!* (New York: Vintage, 1986), 215.

27. As Peter Bardaglio notes, this "American legal innovation" broke from English common law, which determined that the child's status followed that of the father. See Peter Bardaglio, "'Shameful Matches': The Regulation of Interracial Sex and Marriage in the South before 1900," in *Sex, Love, Race: Crossing Boundaries in North American History*, ed. Martha Hodes (New York: New York University Press, 1999), 114. Sex between black men and white women, moreover, was thought to pose a considerable threat to racial purity, and thus to the preservation of the father/spirit's immortal presence. While Martha Hodes notes that "white men turned a convenient ideological somersault to justify their own access to black women while furiously denouncing sex between black men and white women on the grounds of racial purity," such a contradiction was absolutely necessary if the father's immortal self-presence was to be preserved ("White Women," 199). In the Reconstruction South, white women were often thought to be the sole carriers of racial identity, an ideology that permitted continued sexual relations between white men and black women while forbidding those between black men and white women. As the receptacles of racial purity, the wombs of white women had to be protected from black insemination. Yet the figuration of these white female bodies as containers of pure whiteness masks the ideology that converts their materiality into the white father/spirit. Pondering the insurrectionary possibilities of a new "guerrilla warfare" in which white males might smuggle vials of black sperm into "banks of unborn golden people," Patricia Williams asks wryly: "What happens if it is no longer white male seed that has the prerogative of dropping noiselessly and invisibly into black wombs? ... Instead it will be disembodied black seed that will swell white bellies; the symbolically sacred vessel of the white womb." See Patricia Williams, *The Alchemy of Race and Rights* (Cambridge, Mass.: Harvard University Press, 1991), 188.

28. Georges Bataille, "Hegel, Death, and Sacrifice," trans. Jonathan Strauss, *Yale French Studies* 78 (1990): 9–28.

29. Jacques Derrida, *Écriture et la différence* (Paris: Éditions du Seuil, 1967), 377.

30. Cited in Hartman, 33.

31. See Eve Sedgwick's seminal work on (homo)erotic triangles, *Between Men: English Literature and Male Homosocial Desire* (New York: Columbia University Press, 1985).

32. See Jacques Derrida, *Aporias*, trans. Thomas Dutoit (Stanford, Calif.: Stanford University Press, 1993).

33. G. W. F. Hegel, *Phenomenology of Spirit*, trans. A. V. Miller (Oxford: Oxford University Press, 1977).

34. I allude, of course, to Leo Bersani's argument that the anus is constructed as the site and origin of AIDS, a figure that is imagined as producing death rather than life, and therefore speaks to a pervasive and deeply imbedded cultural anxiety over the "intolerable image of a grown man, legs high in the air, unable to refuse the suicidal ecstasy of being a woman" (212). Leo Bersani, "Is the Rectum a Grave?" in *AIDS: Cultural Analysis/Cultural Activism*, ed. Douglas Crimp (Cambridge, Mass.: MIT Press, 1988). See also Ellis Hanson, "Undead," in *Inside/Out: Lesbian Theories, Gay Theories*, ed. Diana Fuss (New York: Routledge, 1991).

35. According to Coolidge's research, seventy-five law review articles in major legal journals were published between 1990 and 1995 alone. See his "Playing the Loving Card: Same-Sex Marriage and the Politics of Analogy," *Brigham Young University Journal of Public Law* 12 (1998): 201–38.

36. *Bowers v. Hardwick*, 478 US 186 (1986), 211.

37. Cited in Sidney Kaplan, "The Miscegenation Issue in the Election Year of 1864," 242.

38. *Scott v. Georgia*, 39 GA 321 (1869), 321.

39. *Baehr v. Lewin*, 74 HI 530; 85a P.2d 44 (1993). *Baker v. Vermont*, 170 VT 194; 744 VT A.2d 864 (1999). *Goodridge v. Department of Health*, 440 MA 309 (2003).

40. We should note that analogy constitutes one of the most familiar forms of legal argumentation and is the backbone of much civil rights advocacy. The analogies that gay civil rights activists frequently make between sexual orientation and race take their cue from a long history of feminist advocacy that has argued that discrimination on the basis of gender "is like" race discrimination. The politics of analogical reasoning, however, are far more complicated than its opponents tend to admit. Given the legal system's reliance on precedent and a reluctance to grant suspect status to classifications other than race (the failure of the ERA is perhaps exemplary here), civil rights advocates find it difficult to avoid analogical arguments altogether. For more on the role of analogies in civil rights law, see Serena Mayeri, "'A Common Fate of Discrimination': Race-Gender Analogies in Legal and Historical Perspective," *Yale Law Journal* 110 (2001): 1045–87;

Trina Grillo and Stephanie Wildman, "Obscuring the Importance of Race: The Implication of Making Comparisons between Racism and Sexism (or Other-isms)," *Duke Law Journal* 41 (1991). Available at http://web.lexisnexis.com; Janet Halley, "Gay Rights and Identity Imitation: Issues in the Ethics of Representation," in *The Politics of Law: A Progressive Critique*, ed. David Kairys (New York: Basic Books, 1998); Devon Carbado, "Black Rights, Gay Rights, Civil Rights," *UCLA Law Review* 47 (2000): 1468–1519. On the role of legal analogies more generally, see Cass Sunstein, "Commentary: On Analogical Reasoning," *Harvard Law Review* 106 (1993): 741–91.

41. Sigmund Freud, "The 'Uncanny,'" in *The Standard Edition* (London: Hogarth Press, 1975).

42. Randall Kennedy, "How Are We Doing with Loving: Race, Law, and Intermarriage," 77 *Boston University Law Review* (1997): 815–822.

43. Jacques Derrida, "Marx and Sons," in *Ghostly Demarcations: A Symposium on Jacques Derrida's Specters of Marx* (New York: Verso, 1999).

44. Over two-thirds of the states have adopted laws that refuse to recognize gay marriages performed in other states. For instance, the text of the California Defense of Marriage Act reads: "Only marriage between a man and a woman is valid or recognized in the state of California," California Family Code, sec. 308.5 (2001). Such laws are designed to circumvent the "full faith and credit" clause of the U.S. Constitution. Article 4, section 1 reads: "Full faith and credit shall be given in each state to the public acts, records, and judicial proceedings of every other state. And the Congress may by general laws prescribe the manner in which such acts, records, and proceedings shall be proved, and the effect thereof." U.S. Constitution art. 4, sec. 1 (2002).

45. Andrew Koppelman, "Same-Sex Marriage and Public Policy: The Miscegenation Precedents," *Quinnipiac Law Review* 16 (1996): 127. See also James Trosino, "American Wedding: Same-Sex Marriage and the Miscegenation Analogy," 73 *Boston University Law Review* (1993): 93–120.

46. Among the differences in the two cases, Coolidge notes that the Hawaii marriage law "is positive not prohibitory," that is, it does not impose any penalties on same-sex couples who attempt to marry. As Coolidge puts it rather dismissively: "In Hawaii, no one was charged with a felony; the State simply sent them a polite letter and returned their marriage applications" (5). He goes on to note that, in contrast to *Baehr*, no one planned *Loving*, suggesting that the plaintiffs' strategic publicization of the state's rejection of their applications was opportunistic. Yet such legal orchestrations are in no way anomalous. Indeed, *Plessy* was engineered by none other than Albion Tourgée, who later became one of Homer Plessy's attorneys.

47. Anne Cheng, *The Melancholy of Race: Psychoanalysis, Assimilation, and Hidden Grief* (Oxford: Oxford University Press, 2000), 175.

48. *Brown v. Board of Education*, 347 US 483 (1954), 494.

49. Cited in Andrew Sullivan, ed., *Same-Sex Marriage: Pro and Con* (New York: Vintage, 1997), 219.

50. Cited in Coolidge, 4.

51. Animating this debate, of course, is David Halperin's now famous claim: "Before 1892 there was no homosexuality, only sexual inversion." See his *One Hundred Years of Homosexuality and Other Essays on Greek Love* (New York: Routledge, 1990), 15.

52. Michel Foucault, *Histoire de la sexualité: la volonté de savoir* (Paris: Gallimard, 1976).

53. Phillipe Ariès, *Essais sur l'histoire de la mort en Occident du Moyen Age à nos jours* (Paris: Éditions du Seuil, 1975).

54. Given that late-nineteenth-century America marks a peculiarly heightened period of racial strife, it is easy to forget how sexuality plays more than a mere supporting role in the racial politics of the era. As Lisa Duggan has shown in her study of the Alice Mitchell/Freda Ward murder, the affirmation of legitimate sexuality went along with the sanctioning of legitimate violence. That so much public outcry could attend Alice Mitchell's 1892 murder of her female lover in Memphis, while the lynching of three black men three months later in the same city was treated as almost routine, shows how questions of race are always in conversation with sexuality. The racialization of the "lesbian love murder story," Duggan maintains, invokes the twin figures of the lesbian and the black male as dangerous threats to white domesticity. See her *Sapphic Slashers: Sex, Violence, and American Modernity* (Durham, N.C.: Duke University Press, 2000).

55. Giorgio Agamben, *Homo Sacer: Sovereign Power and Bare Life*, trans. Daniel Heller-Roazen (Stanford, Calif.: Stanford University Press, 1998).

56. Michael Davidson, "Strange Blood: Hemophobia and the Unexplored Boundaries of Queer Nation," in *Beyond the Binary: Reconstructing Cultural Identity in a Multicultural Context,* ed. Timothy Powell (New Brunswick, N.J.: Rutgers University Press, 1999), 44. Reminiscent of Bersani's observation of the rectum as grave, Davidson also notes that the cultural characterization of hemophiliacs as "mama's boys" — a label conditioned by the nature of the disorder itself, whereby boys receive a recessive gene from their mothers — is reinforced by their dependency on the blood of others, which places them in a "passive or 'receptor' position with respect to the health delivery systems" (51).

57. Plato, *Symposium* (Oxford: Oxford University Press, 1994).

4. The Kinship of Strangers

1. Judith Butler, "Is Kinship Always Already Heterosexual?" *differences: A Journal of Feminist Cultural Studies* 13.1 (2002): 14–44; Elizabeth Freeman, *The Wedding Complex: Forms of Belonging in Modern American Cul-*

ture (Durham, N.C.: Duke University Press, 2002); Michael Warner, *The Trouble with Normal: Sex, Politics, and the Ethics of Queer Life* (Cambridge, Mass.: Harvard University Press, 1999).

2. Sigmund Freud, "Our Attitude toward Death," in *The Standard Edition* (London: Hogarth Press, 1957), 289.

3. Martin Heidegger, *Being and Time,* trans. Joan Stambaugh (Albany: State University of New York Press, 1996), 238.

4. *Baehr v. Lewin,* 74 HI 530; 852 P.2d 44 (1993). While the majority opinion in *Baker v. Vermont* did not broach the question of sex discrimination, Justice Johnson's dissent, in part, from the majority argues that the rejection of marriage licenses to same-sex couples is "a straightforward case of sex discrimination." See *Baker v. Vermont,* 170 VT 194; 744 A.2d 864 (1999), 252. He also chastised the majority for shirking its duty to remedy this discrimination immediately by leaving it to the legislature to decide how gays and lesbians shall receive the same benefits as heterosexuals, either by including the former in existing marriage laws or inventing a parallel domestic partnership system. After much deliberation, the state legislature opted for the latter, and on April 26, 2000, the governor of Vermont signed into law a bill that legalized so-called "civil unions" for same-sex couples. The civil unions afford gay couples almost all of the same state benefits that married heterosexual couples receive.

5. Judith Butler, *The Psychic Life of Power: Theories in Subjection* (Stanford, Calif.: Stanford University Press, 1997).

6. The case began in December of 1990, when three same-sex couples were denied marriage licenses from Hawaii's Department of Health on the basis that the Hawaii statute (*Hawaii Revised Statutes* 572-1) requires that the two parties be of opposite sex. The three couples then sued the state, arguing that the statute violated their right to privacy, their right to equal protection, and their right to due process of law. Although the lawsuit was dismissed by the Circuit Court on the grounds that the couples had failed to "state a claim of relief" (i.e., regardless of whether the violation was true or false, the law did not have to provide them a right of recovery), the couples brought the case before the Hawaii Supreme Court on appeal. While the Supreme Court rejected the right to privacy argument, a close reading of Hawaii's Equal Protection Clause provided enough doubt to cause the case to be remanded to the Circuit Court. That is, the Supreme Court found that Hawaii's equal protection clause was in fact "more elaborate" than that in the U.S. Constitution (562). Article 1, section 5 of the Hawaii Constitution states that "no person shall ... be denied the equal protection of the laws, nor be denied the enjoyment of the person's civil rights or discriminated against in the exercise thereof because of race, religion, sex or ancestry." *Hawaii Revised Statutes, Constitution,* art. I, sec. 5 (2001).

7. Following the passage of this constitutional amendment by Hawaiian voters, the Supreme Court of Hawaii overturned the circuit court's decision on remand that the denial of same-sex marriage violated the state constitution. See *Baehr v. Mikke*, 92 HI 634 (1999). Note that the defendant named in the case changed to "Mikke" when Lawrence Mikke took over for John Lewin as Director of the Department of Health.

8. Steven Homer, "Against Marriage," *Harvard Civil Rights-Civil Liberties Law Review* 29 (Spring 1993). Available at http://web.lexisnexis.com.

9. Andrew Sullivan, "The Marriage Moment," *The Advocate*, January 20, 1998. Available at http://proquest.umi.com.

10. Andrew Sullivan, "When Plagues End," *New York Times*, November 10, 1996. Cited in the text as "Plagues."

11. Douglas Crimp, *Melancholia and Moralism: Essays on AIDS and Queer Politics* (Cambridge, Mass.: MIT Press, 2002), 8.

12. Phillip Brian Harper, "Gay Male Identities, Personal Privacy, and Relations of Public Exchange: Notes on Directions for Queer Critique," *Social Text* 52–53 (1997): 5–29.

13. Cheryl Harris, "Whiteness As Property," *Harvard Law Review* 106 (1993): 1710–91. See my extended discussion of Harris in chapter 3.

14. In the subsequent publication of his book *Love Undetectable*, Sullivan included a revision of his *New York Times* article that is as problematic as the original. Of particular note are the changes made to the passage that I critique here. Clearly responding to the vehement criticisms of gay activists who were disturbed by his seeming dismissal of those who constitute the majority of HIV infections worldwide, Sullivan asserts: "I do not apologize for the following sentence. It is true — truer now than it was when it was first spoken, and truer now than even six months ago — that something profound has occurred these last two years." If Sullivan is as firm in his opinion as he claims, then we might ask why he proceeds to make three key revisions to his original essay. He removes the phrase "most people in the middle of this plague," and adds the following qualifications: "... a diagnosis of HIV infection in the West"; and "For those who can get medical care...." If he need not apologize for the original essay, then why does he add these qualifications here? Given his revisions, of course, there is no need to apologize for what he writes *here*. That he cannot let those changes speak for themselves, however, belies his rejection of the apologetic mode. In short, the alterations perform the apology that he denies. See his *Love Undetectable: Notes on Friendship, Sex, and Survival* (New York: Vintage, 1998), 7–8.

15. David Román, "Not-About-AIDS," *GLQ* 6:1 (2000): 2.

16. Alan Bray, *The Friend* (Chicago: University of Chicago Press, 2003), 103.

17. Judith Butler, *Antigone's Claim: Kinship between Life and Death* (New York: Columbia University Press, 2000), 74.

18. Lee Edelman, *No Future: Queer Theory and the Death Drive* (Durham, N.C.: Duke University Press, 2004), 102–9.

19. Butler's argument is that the Lacanian effort to distinguish symbolic structures of kinship from biology too often results in a "theological" defensiveness that posits political and social rearticulations of kinship as dangerous and anarchistic (21).

20. Peter Coviello, *Intimacy in America: Dreams of Affiliation in Antebellum Literature* (Minneapolis: University of Minnesota Press, 2005), 127.

21. Michael Warner, "Whitman Drunk," in *Breaking Bounds: Whitman and American Cultural Studies*, ed. Betsy Erkkila and Jay Grossman (New York: Oxford University Press, 1996), 40.

22. Mark Van Doren, ed., *The Portable Walt Whitman* (New York: Penguin, 1977), 97.

23. Walt Whitman, *Leaves of Grass* (New York: Bantam, 1983), 103.

24. Lauren Berlant and Michael Warner, "Sex in Public," *Critical Inquiry* 24:2 (1998): 559, 558.

25. Caleb Crain, "Pleasure Principles: Queer Theorists and Gay Journalists Wrestle over the Politics of Sex," *Lingua Franca* 7.8 (1997): 30. See also Warner's analysis of the social necessity of strangers in "Publics and Counterpublics," *Public Culture* 14.1 (2002): 49–90.

26. Marc Shell, *Children of the Earth: Literature, Politics, and Nationhood* (New York: Oxford, 1993). Shell's central point is that the doctrine that "'all men are brothers'" too easily slides into the formulation that "'only my brothers are men, all others are animals'" (22).

27. Michel de Montaigne, *Essais Livre* vol. 1 (Paris: Imprimerie Nationale Éditions, 1998), 313. Unless otherwise noted, all French translations are mine.

28. Jacques Derrida, *Politiques de l'amitié* (Paris: Éditions Galilée, 1994), 310.

29. See Luce Irigaray, *Speculum of the Other Woman*, trans. Gillian Gill (Ithaca, N.Y.: Cornell University Press, 1985).

30. Simon Critchley, *Ethics, Politics, Subjectivity: Essays on Derrida, Levinas, and Contemporary French Thought* (New York: Verso, 1999), 270.

31. For a contrasting approach to the relation between fraternity and mortality, see Dana Nelson's *National Manhood: Capitalist Citizenship, and the Imagined Fraternity of White Men* (Durham, N.C.: Duke University Press, 1998). Extending the observation that homosocial relations are often secured through the exclusion of racial and sexual others, Nelson asks why white, male fraternity is also articulated in relation to other dead or absent white men, suggesting that this necrophilia might be understood as a symptom of a melancholic desire for an imagined unity and wholeness. Nelson argues, however, that this failed unity might be translated into successful modes of truly democratic human interconnection once it no longer requires the

exclusion of others. By contrast, I have attempted to show throughout this study that the desire for unity and wholeness fails precisely because of the other's irreducible alterity, and by extension, the other's absence and death.

32. Robert Solomon, "Death Fetishism, Morbid Solipsism," in *Death and Philosophy*, ed. Jeff Malpas and Robert Solomon (New York: Routledge, 1998), 162.

33. Epicurus, *Letters, Principal Doctrines, and Vatican Sayings*, trans. Russel Geer (New York: The Library of Liberal Arts, Published by the Bobbs-Merrill Company, Inc., 1964), 54. See also Ivan Soll's discussion of being dead versus dying in his "On the Purported Insignificance of Death: Whistling before the Dark?" in *Death and Philosophy*.

34. The English "affiliation" stems from the French *filiation:* hence, *fils, fille* (son, daughter). In Latin, *filius* and *filia* stem from the verb *fellare*, "to suck" and the Greek *thl*, "nipple." A *filius* is literally "one who sucks at the mother's breast." Despite appearances, *filius* and *filum*, from whence we get the French *fil* (thread), do not appear to be etymologically related. I thank Seth Schein and Ruth Caston for consultation on the Latin.

Index

Abjection, 9–10, 69, 76, 108, 136, 175n23
Abolitionism, 5, 74–76, 83, 87, 89, 92–93, 173n6
Absalom, Absalom! (Faulkner), 17, 38, 91–92, 109–21, 131–34
Agamben, Giorgio, 7–8, 130
Agency, 11, 13, 40, 59, 65, 81, 91, 93, 101, 114
AIDS, 6, 23, 130–31, 136–44, 176n34
Alterity, 1–2, 15–19, 23, 28, 34–35, 38, 42, 47, 71–73, 77, 86, 109–11, 115–16, 137, 145–55
Amalgamation, 98–99, 107, 112, 115, 173n6. *See also* Interracial sex; Miscegenation
American exceptionalism, 7, 157n13
Animality, 74, 76, 79, 181n26
Antigone (Sophocles), 9, 14–15, 146–47
Appropriation, 15, 25, 34–36, 38–43, 47–49, 52, 59, 71–74, 84, 87, 111, 114–15, 118, 126, 167n40
Ariès, Philippe, 1–3, 6, 129
Aristippus, 151
Aristotle, 35, 144
Assimilation, 31–32, 35, 52, 57, 96, 108
Aufhebung, 25, 33, 111, 120, 161n49. *See also* Sublation

Augustine, 32, 144
Austin, J. L., 26
Autonomy, 38–43, 47–49, 65–67

Baehr v. Lewin, 122, 125–26, 139, 177n46, 180n7
Baker v. Vermont, 122, 179n4
Ball, Alan, 1
Bardaglio, Peter, 175n27
Bataille, Georges, 111, 165n25
Bauman, Zygmunt, 4, 8, 13
Beloved (Morrison), 34, 38, 68–96
Berkeley, George, 7
Berlant, Lauren, 150
Bersani, Leo, 176n34
Bhabha, Homi, 74
Blackness, 5, 64, 90–91, 100–105, 108, 112–13
Blackstone, William, 102
Body, 3, 6, 8, 10–15, 23, 26–27, 33–36, 38–67, 81–84, 90–91, 94, 97–120, 129–31, 149, 155, 159n27, 162n59, 163n1, 167n38, 172n41, 172n44. *See also* Corporeality; Embodiment; Materiality
Bone, Robert, 43, 49, 52
Bowers v. Hardwick, 122, 124
Brault, Pascale-Anne, 95–96
Bray, Alan, 146
Bromwell, Nicholas, 166n33
Brown, Gillian, 167n40

183

Brown, Wendy, 42
Browning, Elizabeth Barrett, 89
Brown v. Board of Education, 126
Bush, George, 135
Butler, Judith, 9–12, 18, 33, 38–40, 44, 49–50, 58, 65, 135, 137–38, 146–47, 150, 160n45, 162n59, 181n19

Cannibalism, 68, 73, 93
Caputo, Joanne, 77, 86–87
Castronovo, Russ, 5–6, 12, 83
Cheng, Anne, 22, 48, 125–27
Chesnutt, Charles, 36, 55, 166n30
Christian, Barbara, 78
Christianity, 14–15, 23–24, 27–29, 35, 38, 58, 63, 73, 83, 88, 99, 101, 106–7, 131, 145–46, 151, 167n38
Civil War (American), 3, 70, 106–7, 173n6
Commodification, 40, 52, 58–66
Conjure Woman, The (Chesnutt), 43–67
Consanguinity, 27–28, 79, 161n49
Consciousness, 62–63, 71, 81
Contamination, 8, 17, 34, 62, 88, 99–100, 103–9, 116, 123, 129, 132, 175n25
Coolidge, David Orgon, 121, 125, 128, 176n35, 177n46
Corporeality, 6, 10–12, 28, 33–34, 38–40, 47–51, 58–63, 66, 71, 82–84, 90–91, 94, 99–101, 105–9, 114, 128–30, 145–46. *See also* Body; Embodiment; Materiality
Coviello, Peter,148
Crimp, Douglas, 142
Critchley, Simon, 2, 15, 153

Danielpour, Richard, 171n37
Darling, Marsha, 94
Davidson, Michael, 130–31, 178n56
Defense of Marriage Act, 8, 32, 126, 177n49

Derrida, Jacques, 2, 8, 10, 15–16, 20, 26, 31, 37, 47, 57, 62, 68, 72–73, 81, 83, 94–96, 107–8, 111, 116–17, 123, 152–55, 158n18, 161n49, 161n50, 163n62
Descartes, René, 38, 44
Deutscher, Penelope, 73
Dialectics, 4, 7–8, 10, 12, 14–16, 21–24, 29–38, 43–44, 49–51, 54–55, 59, 63, 65, 69–71, 82, 84–85, 92, 96, 103, 106–8, 111, 115, 118–21, 131–37, 150–55, 161n49, 165n25, 171n31
Dickinson, Emily, 97–98, 101–2
Dickson, Bruce, 166n30
Différance, 32, 39, 65, 109, 116, 152, 163n62
Disavowal, 3–10, 16, 21–26, 29, 31–34, 38–40, 46–50, 58, 77, 79, 101, 103, 105–9, 112, 115–16, 125, 128–29, 136, 140, 142–43, 150, 154, 161n50
Dispossession, 36, 38, 40, 47, 58, 69, 77, 94, 159n27
Dred Scott v. Sandford, 99, 173n5
Duggan, Lisa, 178n54
Durkheim, Émile, 14, 27
Düttman, Alexander García, 23
Dyer, Richard, 91

Edelman, Lee, 147, 174n9
Ellison, Ralph, 11, 66
Emancipation, 5, 19, 41–42, 64, 106. *See also* Freedom; Liberty
Embalming, 1, 3, 106–7
Embodiment, 6, 10–11, 50, 66, 83, 155. *See also* Body; Corporeality; Materiality
Empathy, 65–66
Eng, David, 21–22
Ethics, 15–17, 21, 34, 71–73, 77, 85, 93–94, 124, 137, 145, 169n18
Exchange-value, 40, 52, 59–62

Index

Expropriation, 15, 23, 36, 39–40, 59, 103
Exteriority, 71–73, 85

Face, 15, 73, 84–87
Facts in the Case of M. Valdemar, The (Poe), 25–27
Fiedler, Leslie, 108
Finnis, John, 32, 163n61
Foner, Eric, 42–43
Foucault, Michel, 101–2, 128–31
Fox-Genovese, Elizabeth, 75, 78
Franke, Katherine, 18–19
Freedmen's Bureau, 40
Freedom, 5, 35–36, 39–43, 47, 64, 70–71, 83, 99, 108, 164n14, 170n23. *See also* Emancipation; Liberty
Freeman, Elizabeth, 18–19, 135, 145–46
Freud, Sigmund, 4, 20–23, 48, 123, 136, 143, 159n28, 161n50
Friendship, 2, 15–16, 34, 95, 142–46, 149–55
Fugitive Slave Law, 76, 170n22
Fungibility, 58–59
Fustel de Coulanges, 14–15

Garner, Margaret, 74–78, 86–93, 170n27, 171n37
Geist, 24, 81, 94. *See also* Spirit
Gender, 127, 131–2, 137–9, 176n40
Ghostliness, 8, 10–13, 18, 28, 30–31, 44, 49–50, 55–63, 66–72, 82–84, 90, 94–96, 113, 117–18, 123–24, 127, 133, 142, 155. *See also* Hauntology; Spectrality
Goddu, Teresa, 56–57
Goodridge v. Department of Health, 122–23
Gordon, Avery, 164n14, 171n28
Grief, 20–23, 33, 125–27, 147, 160n45. *See also* Loss; Melancholia; Mourning
Gross, Ariela, 91

Harlan, John Marshall, 102
Harper, Phillip Brian, 142–3
Harris, Cheryl, 104–5
Hartman, Saidiya, 33, 41–42, 47, 58–59, 64–66, 101, 103
Hauntology, 9–12, 25, 118, 142. *See also* Ghostliness; Spectrality
Hegel, G. W. F., 8, 15, 23–25, 33, 49–50, 54, 62–63, 67, 85, 96, 119–21, 161n49, 161n50, 165n25
Heidegger, Martin, 3, 12–13, 136, 158n18
Henry, Patrick, 5
Heterosexuality, 6, 8–10, 18, 32, 109, 122, 124, 126–28, 133, 135, 137–39, 149–53
Hodes, Martha, 173n6, 175n27
Holland, Sharon, 6–7, 12
Holloway, Karla, 12
Holmes, Thomas, 3
Homer, Steven, 139, 142
Hommosexualité, 152–53
Homophobia, 10, 32, 138, 140, 142
Homosexuality, 8–9, 32, 109, 115, 118–22, 126–31, 137–40, 145, 152–53, 178n51. *See also* Same-sex desire
Hyde, Henry, 135–36
Hyle, 58, 62

Immortality, 4, 7–8, 14, 23–25, 34, 62–63, 73, 88, 107, 111, 115–17, 120, 127, 130, 132–33, 161n50, 175n27
Incest, 109, 113–17, 122, 131, 162n57
Incorporation, 20, 57, 65, 67, 69, 73, 79–80, 86, 93–95, 116, 139, 145, 150
Infanticide, 72–81, 89–93
Inglis, Bob, 126
Interracial sex, 17, 99, 103, 107, 109, 115, 121–22, 130, 171n37, 173n6. *See also* Amalgamation; Miscegenation

Intimacy, 145–52, 155
Invisible Man (Ellison), 11, 66
Irigaray, Luce, 152, 162n59
Irwin, John, 107, 118

JanMohamed, Abdul, 12–13, 22
Jolliffe, John 76

Kansas-Nebraska Act, 99, 173n5
Kazanjian, David, 21–22
Kearney, Richard, 84
Kennedy, Randall, 123, 160n37
Koki, Stan, 126
Koppelman, Andrew, 124–25
Kristeva, Julia, 10, 174n23

Labor, 6, 23, 39–43, 46–49, 52, 56, 59–61, 99, 122, 166n33, 170n22. *See also* Work
Lacan, Jacques, 147, 181n19
Laderman, Gary, 3, 106
Levin, Harry, 108
Levinas, Emmanuel, 15–17, 71–74, 81, 84–85, 93–94, 123, 159n36
Liberty, 5, 41–42, 64, 70–71, 89–90, 102, 139. *See also* Emancipation; Freedom
Lincoln, Abraham, 3, 5, 98–99, 106, 108, 128, 173n6
Locke, John, 39
Loss, 1–2, 20–25, 47–49, 69, 77, 82, 94, 96, 105, 115, 144, 147–50, 106n45,165n25. *See also* Grief; Melancholia; Mourning
Love, 15–16, 20–21, 29, 37, 69, 71, 73–79, 87–89, 92–93, 113, 115, 120, 131–33, 137–38, 144–47, 151–54
Loving v. Virginia, 121–25, 128

Marriage, 8, 17–19, 27, 31, 32, 37, 119–28, 131, 135–47, 151, 155, 177n44, 177n46, 179n4, 179n6, 180n7

Marx, Karl, 49, 52, 59–62, 166n34
Master/slave dialectic (Hegel), 33, 44–50, 55, 55–59, 65, 69, 92, 103
Materiality, 6, 24, 29, 45, 50, 58, 60, 98, 162n59, 166n33, 166n34. *See also* Body; Corporeality, Embodiment
Maternity, 68–69, 73–78, 81–89, 92–93, 159n36, 162n58, 162n59, 169n15, 171n37. *See also* Motherhood
Maupassant, Guy de, 47–48
Mayeri, Serena, 176n40
Melancholia, 20–22, 136–42, 160n45, 181n31. *See also* Grief; Loss; Mourning
Melville, Herman, 54
Memory, 94–95, 149
Michaels, Walter Benn, 109
Middle Passage, 84–85, 95
Miscegenation, 8, 18, 78, 87–93, 99–104, 107–13, 116–131, 143, 170n27, 173n6. *See also* Amalgamation; Interracial sex
Miscegenation analogy, 18, 121–27
Mitford, Jessica, 3
Montaigne, Michel de, 144, 151–54
Morgan, Henry Lewis, 14, 27
Morrison, Toni, 5, 39, 71, 75–76, 89–94, 108, 113, 169n4, 171n37
Mortality, 3–8, 12–13, 24–25, 49, 105–7,128, 136, 143, 153–4, 157n6, 161n50, 181n31
Motherhood, 74–76, 79, 89, 162n59. *See also* Maternity
Mourning, 1–7, 12–15, 20–23, 31, 38, 47–49, 69, 82–84, 95–96, 106, 115–16, 125–27, 136, 140–144, 147–149, 153–55, 160n45. *See also* Grief; Loss; Melancholia

Naas, Michael, 95–96
Nancy, Jean-Luc, 23, 35, 39–40

Natal Alienation, 4–5. *See also* Social death
Native Son (Wright), 10–11
Necrophilia, 6, 12, 15, 153–54, 181n31
Necrophobia, 6, 12
Nelson, Dana, 181n31
Newsom, Gavin, 145
Nietzsche, Friedrich, 154, 167n38
Noble, David, 7
Nussbaum, Martha, 32

Ontology, 2, 5, 9–26, 64, 71–72, 85, 136, 140

Particularity, 13, 23, 91, 172n41
Passivity, 71, 94
Paternalism, 37–38
Paternity, 27, 69, 73, 110, 116–19, 159n36, 162n58, 169n15
Patterson, Orlando, 4–5, 10, 17, 33–38, 59, 64, 69
Pease, Donald, 7
Penningroth, Dylan, 34, 70
Performativity, 26, 155
Phillips, Adam, 160n45
Plato, 35, 58, 63, 99, 101–2, 131–32, 152, 161n50, 162n59, 163n61
Plessy v. Fergusson, 64, 102–5, 177n46
Plutarch, 151
Poe, Edgar Allan, 11, 90, 113
Possession, 15, 21–22, 33–40, 49–50, 56, 62, 66–67, 69, 71–72, 77–78, 81, 87, 92–94, 103, 114, 132, 169n15
Possessive individualism, 38–39, 103
Presence, 4, 7–12, 15, 18, 21–26, 29, 32–34, 57, 63–64, 66–67, 71, 74, 82–83, 92, 105–13, 116–17, 120–21, 133, 136, 139–43, 149, 151–52, 155, 163n62, 175n27

Property, 33–34, 38–39, 45–46, 57, 59, 66, 68–70, 74–75, 84, 92–93, 104–5, 113, 124, 143, 167n40, 169n15
Prosthesis, 46, 52–53, 57, 65
Pudd'nhead Wilson (Twain), 100–102
Punctuation, 86

Race, 4, 18, 21, 88–92, 101–7, 109–13, 116, 121–27, 166n30, 171n37, 175n27, 176n40, 178n54
Racism, 10, 14, 22, 47, 92, 151
Rankin, John, 65
Reconstruction, 19, 40–43, 47, 98–99, 160n37, 175n27
Religion, 14, 28, 165n18
Reproduction, 19, 23–25, 28–29, 32, 73, 92, 103, 107, 109, 115, 120–28, 131–33, 139–40, 146, 155, 161n50, 175n25
Resistance, 6, 15, 36, 40–43, 49, 51, 53–59, 65, 78, 137, 168n41
Responsibility, 21, 71, 73, 81, 85, 93–95, 123, 159n36
Restricted economy, 49–53, 57, 66, 111, 165n25
Reyes, Angelita, 170–71n27
Rody, Caroline, 169n15
Román, David, 144
Romer v. Evans, 32

Sameness, 1, 16–17, 53, 65, 71–73, 81, 84–87, 93–94, 115–18, 123–25, 128–30, 137
Same-sex desire, 9, 113, 119, 121–27, 130–31, 135–37, 130–31, 135–39, 177n46, 179n4, 179n6, 180n7. *See also* Homosexuality
Schneider, David, 19, 27–32, 69
Scott v. Georgia, 122
Segregation, 3, 100, 102–3, 126, 136
Sentience, 58, 62, 66, 111–12
September 11 terrorist attacks, 7

Servitude, 41–42, 45–47, 50, 54. See also Slavery
Sexuality. See Heterosexuality; Homosexuality
Shell, Marc, 27–28, 151, 161n49, 162n57, 181n26
SIDS (Sudden Infant Death Syndrome), 75
Singularity, 15, 21, 67, 72, 75
Six Feet Under, 1–2
Slavery, 4–5, 8, 17–19, 33–96, 98–103, 112, 134, 164n8, 166n33, 167n40, 168n41, 173n5, 173n6. See also Servitude
Social death, 5–13, 17–18, 33, 37, 51, 57, 59, 67, 69, 107, 136, 140, 147. See also Natal alienation
Solipsism, 72
Solomon, Robert, 154
Soul, 5–6, 14, 28, 58, 62–63, 74, 101–2, 112, 148, 152, 155, 167n38
Spectrality, 8–13, 23, 28, 32–35, 49, 57, 63, 66–69, 71, 74, 81, 83–84, 93, 100–3, 108, 115, 117, 121, 132–33, 153, 158n18. See also Ghostliness; Hauntology
Spectrophilia, 15, 154
Spillers, Hortense, 33, 69, 169n15
Spirit, 1, 5–8, 23–24, 26, 28–38, 49–51, 57, 61–63, 66–67, 73, 76, 82–94, 106–8, 111, 115–19, 124, 127, 146, 155, 161n54, 162n57, 167n59, 171n27,175n27. See also *Geist*
Spiritualism, 5–6, 61
Spook, 10–12, 55, 66–67, 165n29
Stevens, Jacqueline, 162n58
Stone, Lucy, 87–88, 93
Subjection, 34, 40–42
Sublation, 24, 35, 67, 116, 119, 1551, 161n49. See also *Aufhebung*
Sullivan, Andrew, 141–45, 152, 154, 180n14

Sundquist, Eric, 98–99, 103, 120, 165n26

Tiffany, Daniel, 166n34
Tourgée, Albion, 104, 107, 177n46
Tragic mulatta, 170n27
Trickster figure, 43
Turner, Nat, 168n41

Uncanny, 122–3, 148, 155. See also *Unheimlich*
Uncle Tom's Cabin (Stowe), 57, 62, 167n40
Unheimlich, 155. See also Uncanny
Use-value, 40, 52, 59–62

Violence, 4, 10–19, 22, 34, 37–41, 51, 53–59, 69–79, 82–85, 89, 92–95, 99, 111–19, 124, 137, 146–48, 151, 159n36, 167n40, 169n15, 172n41, 178n54

Warner, Michael, 17, 135–37, 145, 147–48, 150–51
Washington, Booker T., 166n33
Weisenburger, Steven, 74–76, 83, 87, 89, 93
Whiteness, 10, 54, 79, 87, 90–92, 101, 104–13, 143, 172n4
Whitman, Walt, 148–49
Wiegman, Robyn, 172n45
Wigley, Mark, 97–98
Williams, Patricia, 175n27
Winfrey, Oprah, 77, 87, 170n26
Woodhouse, Barbara Bennett, 70
Work, 39, 40, 47, 49, 52, 167n40. See also Labor
Wright, Frank Lloyd, 97, 99
Wu, Yung-Hsing, 75
Wyatt, Jean, 169n15

Žižek, Slavoj, 74

Christopher Peterson is visiting assistant professor of literature at Claremont McKenna College in California.

www.ingramcontent.com/pod-product-compliance
Lightning Source LLC
Chambersburg PA
CBHW021857230426
43671CB00006B/428